BLOOM'S

HOW TO WRITE ABOUT

Maya Angelou

CAROLYN WEDIN

Introduction by Harold Bloom

BLOOM'S
LITERARY CRITICISM
An Infobase Learning Company

Bloom's How to Write about Maya Angelou

Bloom's Literary Criticism
An imprint of Infobase Learning
132 West 31st Street
New York NY 10001

Library of Congress Cataloging-in-Publication Data

Wedin, Carolyn, 1939–
 Bloom's how to write about Maya Angelou / Carolyn Wedin ; introduction by Harold Bloom.
    p. cm. — (Bloom's how to write about literature)
 Includes bibliographical references and index.
 ISBN 978-1-60413-891-7 (hardcover)
 1. Angelou, Maya—Criticism and interpretation. 2. Criticism—Authorship.
 I. Bloom, Harold. II. Title. III. Title: How to write about Maya Angelou.
 PS3551.N464Z97 2011
 818'.5409—dc22

                                                                                    2011019831

Bloom's Literary Criticism books are available at special discounts when purchased in bulk quantities for businesses, associations, institutions, or sales promotions. Please call our Special Sales Department in New York at (212)967-8800 or (800)322-8755.

You can find Bloom's Literary Criticism on the World Wide Web at
http://www.infobaselearning.com

Text design by Annie O'Donnell
Cover design by Ben Peterson
Composition by Kerry Casey
Cover printed by Yurchak Printing, Landisville, PA
Book printed and bound by Yurchak Printing, Landisville, PA
Date printed: November 2011
Printed in the United States of America

10 9 8 7 6 5 4 3 2 1

All links and Web addresses were checked and verified to be correct at the time of publication. Because of the dynamic nature of the Web, some addresses and links may have changed since publication and may no longer be valid.

CONTENTS

SERIES
INTRODUCTION

BLOOM'S How to Write about Literature series is designed to inspire students to write fine essays on great writers and their works. Each volume in the series begins with an introduction by Harold Bloom, meditating on the challenges and rewards of writing about the volume's subject author. The first chapter then provides detailed instructions on how to write a good essay, including how to find a thesis; how to develop an outline; how to write a good introduction, body text, and conclusions; how to cite sources; and more. The second chapter provides a brief overview of the issues involved in writing about the subject author and then a number of suggestions for paper topics, with accompanying strategies for addressing each topic. Succeeding chapters cover the author's major works.

The paper topics suggested in this book are open ended, and the brief strategies provided are designed to give students a push forward on the writing process rather than a road map to success. The aim of the book is to pose questions, not answer them. Many different kinds of papers could result from each topic. As always, the success of each paper will depend completely on the writer's skill and imagination.

HOW TO WRITE ABOUT MAYA ANGELOU: INTRODUCTION

by Harold Bloom

M AYA ANGELOU'S achievement, more even in her ongoing autobiography than in her verse, has a complex relation to at least two
among the principal antecedents of African-American memoirs: the slave
narrative and the church sermon. Since she is a spellbinder of a story-
teller, other elements in African-American tradition, including the blues
and the oral eloquence of street ways, also enter into her work. Though
Angelou is essentially a secular biographer, her extraordinary and persistent sense of self, one that rises both through and above experience,
seems to me to go back to the African-American paradigm of what I have
called the American Religion. What survived of West African spiritual-
ity, after the torments of the Middle Passage from Africa to America,
was the gnosis that early black Baptists in America spoke of as "the little
me within the big me." Though converted to the slaveowners' ostensible
Christianity, they transformed that European faith by a radical "knowing" that the "little me" or most inward self did not stem from the harsh
space and time of the white world but emanated ultimately from their
unfallen cosmos that preceded the Creation-Fall of the whites. Angelou's
pervasive sense that what is oldest and best in her own spirit derives
from a lost, black fullness of being is one of the strongest manifestations
in African-American literature of this ancient gnosis.

I think that this is part of the secret of Angelou's enormous appeal to American readers, whether white or black, because her remarkable literary voice speaks to something in the universal American "little me within the big me." Most Americans, of whatever race or ethnic origin, share the sense that experience, however terrible, can be endured because their deepest self is beyond experience and so cannot be destroyed. Particularly in her best book, *I Know Why the Caged Bird Sings*, Angelou achieves an almost unique tone that blends intimacy and detachment, a tone indeed of assured serenity that transcends the fearful humiliations and outrages that she suffered as a girl. Hundreds of thousands of readers have found in *Caged Bird* an implicit image of the resurrection of their own innermost self, a fragment of divinity that transcended natural birth and so can never die.

Maya Angelou's poetry also has a large public. It is, in every sense, "popular poetry" and makes no formal or cognitive demands on the reader. Of Angelou's sincerity, good will toward all, and personal vitality, there can be no doubt. She is professedly an inspirational writer, of the self-help variety, which perhaps places her beyond criticism.

Her lyric cadences, to my ear, have little resemblance to the blues and seem closer to country music. Angelou's most persuasive defender is the scholar-critic Robert B. Stepto, who carefully distinguishes her use of folk idioms and forms from her weaker work. Stepto essentially asks us to yield to Angelou's self-presentation and thus to import the autobiographical volumes back into the weaker poems.

Angelou seems best at ballads, the most traditional kind of popular poetry, which link her to folk traditions. The function of such work is necessarily social rather than aesthetic, particularly in an era totally dominated by visual media. One has to be grateful for the benignity, humor, and wholeheartedness of Angelou's project, even if her autobiographical prose necessarily centers her achievement. She is a passionately *sincere* poet, whose purpose is to inspire her audience to keep going.

HOW TO WRITE
A GOOD ESSAY

by Laurie A. Sterling and Carolyn Wedin

WHILE THERE are many ways to write about literature, most assignments for high school and college English classes call for analytical papers. In these assignments, you are presenting your interpretation of a text to your reader. Your objective is to interpret the text's meaning in order to enhance your reader's understanding and enjoyment of the work. Without exception, strong papers about the meaning of a literary work are built upon a careful, close reading of the text or texts. Careful, analytical reading should always be the first step in your writing process. This volume provides models of such close, analytical reading, and these should help you develop your own skills as a reader and as a writer.

As the examples throughout this book demonstrate, attentive reading entails thinking about and evaluating the formal (textual) aspects of the author's works: theme, character, form, and language. In addition, when writing about a work, many readers choose to move beyond the text itself to consider the work's cultural context. In these instances, writers might explore the historical circumstances of the time period in which the work was written. Alternatively, they might examine the philosophies and ideas that a work addresses. Even in cases where writers explore a work's cultural context, though, papers must still address the more formal aspects of the work itself. A good interpretative essay that evaluates Shakespeare's use of argument in *Cymbeline* cannot simply give a history of the Gallic wars without firmly grounding this discussion in the play

1

itself and using it to show the validity of both Lucius's and the queen's arguments. In other words, any analytical paper about a text, even one that seeks to evaluate the work's cultural context, must also have a firm handle on the work's themes, characters, and language. You must look for and evaluate these aspects of a work, then, as you read a text and as you prepare to write about it.

WRITING ABOUT THEMES

Literary themes are more than just topics or subjects treated in a work; they are attitudes or points about these topics that often structure other elements in a work. Writing about theme therefore requires that you not just identify a topic that a literary work addresses but also discuss what that work says about that topic. For example, if you were writing about the theme of resolutions in *All's Well That Ends Well,* you must not simply discuss the main resolution of the romance between Helena and Bertram but also minor resolutions of issues along the way, such as the king's illness and Parolles's betrayal of his comrades.

When you prepare to write about thematic concerns in a work of literature, you will probably discover that, like most works of literature, your text touches upon other themes in addition to its central theme. These secondary themes also provide rich ground for paper topics. A thematic paper on *All's Well That Ends Well* might consider forgiveness or trickery in the story. While neither of these could be said to be the central theme of the story, they are clearly related to a main theme of nature versus nurture and could provide plenty of good material for papers.

As you prepare to write about themes in literature, you might find a number of strategies helpful. After you identify a theme or themes in the story, you should begin by evaluating how other elements of the story—such as character, point of view, imagery, and symbolism—help develop the theme. You might ask yourself what your own responses are to the author's treatment of the subject matter. Do not neglect the obvious, either: What expectations does the title set up? How does the title help develop thematic concerns? Clearly, the title "A Rose for Emily" says something about the narrator's attitude toward the title character, Emily Grierson, and all she represents.

WRITING ABOUT CHARACTER

Generally, characters are essential components of fiction and drama. (This is not always the case, though; Ray Bradbury's "August 2026: There Will Come Soft Rains" is technically a story without characters, at least any human characters.) Often, you can discuss character in poetry, as in T. S. Eliot's "The Love Song of J. Alfred Prufrock" or Robert Browning's "My Last Duchess." Characters are, however, essential components in Shakespeare's romances. Many writers find that analyzing character is one of the most interesting and engaging ways to work with a piece of literature and to shape a paper. After all, characters generally are human, and we all know something about being human and living in the world. While it is always important to remember that these figures are not real people but creations of the writer's imagination, it can be fruitful to begin evaluating them as you might evaluate a real person. Often you can start with your own response to a character. Did you like or dislike the character? Did you sympathize with the character? Why or why not?

Keep in mind, though, that emotional responses like these are just starting places. To truly explore and evaluate literary characters, you need to return to the formal aspects of the text and evaluate how the author has drawn these characters. The twentieth-century writer E. M. Forster coined the terms *flat* characters and *round* characters. Flat characters are static, one-dimensional characters who frequently represent a particular concept or idea. In contrast, round characters are fully drawn and much more realistic characters who frequently change and develop over the course of a work. Are the characters you are studying flat or round? What elements of the characters lead you to this conclusion? Why might the author have drawn characters like this? How does their development affect the meaning of the work? Similarly, you should explore the techniques the author uses to develop characters. Do we hear a character's own words, or do we hear only other characters' assessments of him or her? Or, does the author use an omniscient or limited omniscient narrator to allow us access to the workings of the characters' minds? If so, how does that help develop the characterization? Often you can even evaluate the narrator as a character. How trustworthy are the opinions and assessments of the narrator? You should also think about characters' names. Do they mean anything? If you encounter a hero named Sophia or Sophie, you should probably think about her wisdom (or lack thereof), since *sophia* means "wisdom" in Greek. Similarly, since the name *Sylvia* is derived from the word *sylvan,* meaning "of the wood," you might want to evaluate that character's relationship with nature. Once again, you might look to the title of the work. Does Herman Melville's "Bartleby, the Scrivener" signal anything about Bartleby himself? Is Bartleby adequately defined by his job as scrivener? Is this part of Melville's point? Pursuing questions like these can help you develop thorough papers about characters from psychological, sociological, or more formalistic perspectives.

WRITING ABOUT FORM AND GENRE

Genre, a word derived from French, means "type" or "class." Literary genres are distinctive classes or categories of literary composition. On the most general level, literary works can be divided into the genres of drama, poetry, fiction, and essays, yet in those genres there are classifications that are also referred to as genres. Tragedy and comedy, for example, are genres of drama. Epic, lyric, and pastoral are genres of poetry. *Form,* on the other hand, generally refers to the shape or structure of a work. There are many clearly defined forms of poetry that follow specific patterns of meter, rhyme, and stanza. Sonnets, for example, are poems that follow a fixed form of 14 lines. Sonnets generally follow one of two basic sonnet forms, each with its own distinct rhyme scheme. Haiku is another example of poetic form, traditionally consisting of three unrhymed lines of five, seven, and five syllables.

While you might think that writing about form or genre might leave little room for argument, many of these forms and genres are very fluid. Remember that literature is evolving and ever changing, and so are its forms. As you study poetry, you may find that poets, especially more modern poets, play with traditional poetic forms, bringing about new effects. Similarly, dramatic tragedy was once quite narrowly defined, but over the centuries playwrights have broadened and challenged traditional definitions, changing the shape of tragedy. When Arthur Miller wrote *Death of a Salesman,* many critics challenged the idea that tragic drama could encompass a common man like Willy Loman.

Evaluating how a work of literature fits into or challenges the boundaries of its form or genre can provide you with fruitful avenues of investigation. You might find it helpful to ask why the work does or does not fit into traditional categories. Why might Miller have thought it fitting to write a tragedy of the common man? Similarly, you might compare the content or theme of a work with its form. How well do they work together? Many of Emily Dickinson's poems, for instance, follow the meter of traditional hymns. While some of her poems seem to express traditional religious doctrines, many seem to challenge or strain against traditional conceptions of God and theology. What is the effect, then, of her use of traditional hymn meter?

WRITING ABOUT LANGUAGE, SYMBOLS, AND IMAGERY

No matter what the genre, writers use words as their most basic tool. Language is the most fundamental building block of literature. It is essential that you pay careful attention to the author's language and word choices as you read, reread, and analyze a text. Imagery is language that appeals to the senses. Most commonly, imagery appeals to our sense of vision, creating a mental picture, but authors also use language that appeals to our other senses. Images can be literal or figurative. Literal images use sensory language to describe an actual thing. In the broadest terms, figurative language uses one thing to speak about something else. For example, if I call my boss a snake, I am not saying that he is literally a reptile. Instead, I am using figurative language to communicate my opinions about him. Since we think of snakes as sneaky, slimy, and sinister, I am using the concrete image of a snake to communicate these abstract opinions and impressions.

The two most common figures of speech are similes and metaphors. Both are comparisons between two apparently dissimilar things. Similes are explicit comparisons using the words *like* or *as;* metaphors are implicit comparisons. To return to the previous example, if I say, "My boss, Bob, was waiting for me when I showed up to work five minutes late today—the snake!" I have constructed a metaphor. Writing about his experiences fighting in World War I, Wilfred Owen begins his poem "Dulce et decorum est," with a string of similes: "Bent double, like old beggars under sacks, / Knock-kneed, coughing like hags, we cursed through sludge." Owen's goal was to undercut clichéd notions that war and dying in battle were glorious. Certainly, comparing soldiers to coughing hags and to beggars underscores his point.

"Fog," a short poem by Carl Sandburg, provides a clear example of a metaphor. Sandburg's poem reads:

> The fog comes
> on little cat feet.
>
> It sits looking
> over harbor and city
> on silent haunches
> and then moves on.

Notice how effectively Sandburg conveys surprising impressions of the fog by comparing two seemingly disparate things—the fog and a cat.

Symbols, by contrast, are things that stand for, or represent, other things. Often they represent something intangible, such as concepts or ideas. In everyday life we use and understand symbols easily. Babies at christenings and brides at weddings wear white to represent purity. Think, too, of a dollar bill. The paper itself has no value in and of itself. Instead, that paper bill is a symbol of something else, the precious metal in a nation's coffers. Symbols in literature work similarly. Authors use symbols to evoke more than a simple, straightforward, literal meaning. Characters, objects, and places can all function as symbols. Famous literary examples of symbols include Moby Dick, the white whale of Herman Melville's novel, and the scarlet *A* of Nathaniel Hawthorne's *The Scarlet Letter*. As both of these symbols suggest, a literary symbol cannot be adequately defined or explained by any one meaning. Hester Prynne's Puritan community clearly intends her scarlet *A* as a symbol of her adultery, but as the novel progresses, even her own community reads the letter as representing not just *adultery*, but *able, angel*, and a host of other meanings.

Writing about imagery and symbols requires close attention to the author's language. To prepare a paper on symbolism or imagery in a work, identify and trace the images and symbols and then try to draw some conclusions about how they function. Ask yourself how any symbols or images help contribute to the themes or meanings of the work. What connotations do they carry? How do they affect your reception of the work? Do they shed light on characters or settings? A strong paper on imagery or symbolism will thoroughly consider the use of figures in the text and will try to reach some conclusions about how or why the author uses them.

WRITING ABOUT HISTORY AND CONTEXT

As previously noted, it is possible to write an analytical paper that also considers the work's context. After all, the text was not created in a vacuum. The author lived and wrote in a specific time period and in a specific cultural context and, like all of us, was shaped by that environment. Learning more about the historical and cultural circumstances that surround the author and the work can help illuminate a text and provide you with productive material for a paper. Remember, though, that when you write analytical papers, you should use the context to illuminate the text. Do not lose sight of your goal—to interpret the meaning of the literary work. Use historical or philosophical research as a tool to develop your textual evaluation.

Thoughtful readers often consider how history and culture affected the author's choice and treatment of his or her subject matter. Investigations into the history and context of a work could examine the work's relation to specific historical events, such as the Salem witch trials in seventeenth-century Massachusetts or the restoration of Charles to the British throne in 1660. Bear in mind that historical context is not limited to politics and world events. While knowing about the Vietnam War is certainly helpful in interpreting much of Tim O'Brien's fiction, and some knowledge of the French Revolution clearly illuminates the dynamics of Charles Dickens's *A Tale of Two Cities,* historical context also entails the fabric of daily life. Examining a text in light of gender roles, race relations, class boundaries, or working conditions can give rise to thoughtful and compelling papers. Exploring the conditions of the working class in nineteenth-century England, for example, can provide a particularly effective avenue for writing about Dickens's *Hard Times.*

You can begin thinking about these issues by asking broad questions at first. What do you know about the time period and about the author? What does the editorial apparatus in your text tell you? These might be starting places. Similarly, when specific historical events or dynamics are particularly important to understanding a work but might be somewhat obscure to modern readers, textbooks usually provide notes to explain historical background. These are a good place to start. With this information, ask yourself how these historical facts and circumstances might have affected the author, the presentation of theme, and the presentation of character. How does knowing more about the work's specific historical context illuminate the work? To take a well-known example, understanding the complex attitudes toward slavery during the time Mark Twain wrote *Adventures of Huckleberry Finn* should help you begin to examine issues of race in the text. Additionally, you might compare these attitudes to those of the time in which the novel was set. How might this comparison affect your interpretation of a work written after the abolition of slavery but set before the Civil War?

WRITING ABOUT PHILOSOPHY AND IDEAS

Philosophical concerns are closely related to both historical context and thematic issues. Like historical investigation, philosophical research can provide a useful tool as you analyze a text. For example, an investigation into the working class in Dickens's England might lead you to a topic on the philosophical doctrine of utilitarianism in *Hard Times*. Many other works explore philosophies and ideas quite explicitly. Mary Shelley's famous novel *Frankenstein*, for example, explores John Locke's tabula rasa theory of human knowledge as she portrays the intellectual and emotional development of Victor Frankenstein's creature. As this example indicates, philosophical issues are somewhat more abstract than investigations of theme or historical context. Some other examples of philosophical issues include human free will, the formation of human identity, the nature of sin, or questions of ethics.

Writing about philosophy and ideas might require some outside research, but usually the notes or other material in your text will provide you with basic information, and often footnotes and bibliographies suggest places you can go to read further about the subject. If you have identified a philosophical theme that runs through a text, you might ask yourself how the author develops this theme. Look at character development and the interactions of characters, for example. Similarly, you might examine whether the narrative voice in a work of fiction addresses the philosophical concerns of the text.

WRITING COMPARISON AND CONTRAST ESSAYS

Finally, you might find that comparing and contrasting the works or techniques of an author provides a useful tool for literary analysis. A comparison and contrast essay might compare two characters or themes in a single work, or it might compare the author's treatment of a theme in two works. It might also contrast methods of character development or analyze an author's differing treatment of a philosophical concern in two works. Writing comparison and contrast essays, though, requires some special consideration. While they generally provide you with plenty of material to use, they also come with a built-in trap: the laundry list. These papers often become mere lists of connections between the works. As this chapter will discuss, a strong thesis must make an assertion that you want to prove or validate. A strong comparison/contrast thesis, then, needs to comment on the significance of the similarities and differences you observe. It is not enough merely to assert that the works contain similarities and differences. You might, for example, assert why the similarities and differences are important and explain how they illuminate the works' treatment of theme. Remember, too, that a thesis should not be a statement of the obvious. A comparison/contrast paper that focuses only on very obvious similarities or differences does little to illuminate the connections between the works. Often, an effective method of shaping a strong thesis and argument is to begin your paper by noting the similarities between the works but then to develop a thesis that asserts how these apparently similar elements are different. If, for example, you observe that Emily Dickinson wrote a number of poems about spiders, you might analyze how she uses spider imagery differently in two poems. Similarly, many scholars have noted that Hawthorne created many "mad scientist" characters, men who are so devoted to their science or their art that they lose perspective on all else. A good thesis comparing two of these characters—Aylmer of "The Birth-mark" and Dr. Rappaccini of "Rappaccini's Daughter," for example—might initially identify both characters as examples of Hawthorne's mad scientist type but then argue that their motivations for scientific experimentation differ. If you strive to analyze the similarities or differences, discuss significances, and move beyond the obvious, your paper should move beyond the laundry list trap.

PREPARING TO WRITE

Armed with a clear sense of your task—illuminating the text—and with an understanding of theme, character, language, history, and philosophy, you are ready to approach the writing process. Remember that good writing is grounded in good reading and that close reading takes time, attention, and more than one reading of your text. Read for comprehension first. As you go back and review the work, mark the text to chart the details of the work as well as your reactions. Highlight important passages, repeated words, and image patterns. "Converse" with the text through marginal notes. Mark turns in the plot, ask questions, and make observations about characters, themes, and language. If you are reading from a book that does not belong to you, keep a record of your reactions in a journal or notebook. If you have read a work of literature carefully, paying attention to both the text and the context of the work, you have a leg up on the writing process. Admittedly, at this point, your ideas are probably very broad and undefined, but you have taken an important first step toward writing a strong paper.

Your next step is to focus, to take a broad, perhaps fuzzy, topic and define it more clearly. Even a topic provided by your instructor will need to be focused appropriately. Remember that good writers make the topic their own. There are a number of strategies—often called "invention"—that you can use to develop your own focus. In one such strategy, called *freewriting*, you spend 10 minutes or so just writing about your topic without referring back to the text or your notes. Write whatever comes to mind; the important thing is that you just keep writing. Often this process allows you to develop fresh ideas or approaches to your subject matter. You could also try *brainstorming:* Write down your topic and then list all the related points or ideas you can think of. Include questions, comments, words, important passages or events, and anything else that comes to mind. Let one idea lead to another. In the related technique of *clustering*, or *mapping*, write your topic on a sheet of paper and write related ideas around it. Then list related subpoints under each of these main ideas. Many people then draw arrows to show connections between points. This technique helps you narrow your topic and can also help you organize your ideas. Similarly, asking journalistic questions—Who? What? Where? When? Why? And how?—can develop ideas for topic development.

Thesis Statements

Once you have developed a focused topic, you can begin to think about your thesis statement, the main point or purpose of your paper. It is imperative that you craft a strong thesis, otherwise, your paper will likely be little more than random, disorganized observations about the text.

Think of your thesis statement as a kind of road map for your paper. It tells your reader where you are going and how you are going to get there.

To craft a good thesis, you must keep a number of things in mind. First, as the title of this subsection indicates, your paper's thesis should be a statement, an assertion about the text that you want to prove or validate. Beginning writers often formulate a question that they attempt to use as a thesis. For example, a writer exploring the theme of absence of a mother through most of Angelou's *I Know Why the Caged Bird Sings* might ask, "How does the young Marguerite try to compensate for the seeming abandonment by her mother?" While a question like this is a good strategy to use in the invention process to help narrow your topic and find your thesis, it cannot serve as the thesis statement because it does not tell your reader what you want to assert about the daughter-mother relationship. You might shape this question into a thesis by instead proposing an answer to that question: In *I Know Why the Caged Bird Sings*, the young child Marguerite Johnson suffers in self-image and self-actualization from being shipped by her parents, by train, with her brother, Bailey, from California to their paternal grandmother in Stamps, Arkansas. This first volume of Angelou's serial autobiography demonstrates both positive and negative compensations made by the young girl—a strong identification with the power of her grandmother, on the one hand, and her vulnerability later to sexual exploitation by her mother's boyfriend on the other. Notice that this thesis provides an initial plan or structure for the rest of the paper, and notice, too, that the thesis statement does not necessarily have to fit into one sentence. After discussing the young girl's poor self-image, you could examine the ways in which being Black and female aggravate the difficulty and then theorize about what Angelou is saying about early attachments more generally. Perhaps you could discuss how the common need for mothering may vary according to race and gender and, finally, the ways in which the autobiography spells this all out dramatically through the raped child's guilt and then silence until language and literature and the friendship with Mrs. Flowers release her.

Second, remember that a good thesis makes an assertion that you need to support. In other words, a good thesis does not state the obvious. If you tried to formulate a thesis about mothering by simply saying, Mothering is important in *I Know Why the Caged Bird Sings*, you have done nothing but rephrase the obvious. Since Angelou's autobiography is centered on her own story and struggle, there would be no point in spending three to five pages supporting that assertion. You might try to develop a thesis from that point by asking yourself some further questions: What does it mean that Marguerite's brother, Bailey, has different problems and vulnerabilities? Why are Momma's (Grandmother's) pacifist methods for dealing with self-image in a segregated South so admirable and yet so frustrating to the young narrator? Does each person deal differently with these difficulties, or are there some common denominators? Such a line of questioning might lead you to a more viable thesis, like the one in the preceding paragraph.

As the comparison with the road map also suggests, your thesis should appear near the beginning of the paper. In relatively short papers (three to six pages) the thesis almost always appears in the first paragraph. Some writers fall into the trap of saving their thesis for the end, trying to provide a surprise or a big moment of revelation, as if to say, "TA-DA! I've just proved that in *I Know Why the Caged Bird Sings* Angelou uses mothering to symbolize the difficulties of growing up in a racist society." Placing a thesis at the end of an essay can seriously mar the essay's effectiveness. If you fail to define your essay's point and purpose clearly at the beginning, your reader will find it difficult to assess the clarity of your argument and understand the points you are making. When your argument comes as a surprise at the end, you force your reader to reread your essay in order to assess its logic and effectiveness.

Finally, you should avoid using the first person ("I") as you present your thesis. Though it is not strictly wrong to write in the first person, it is difficult to do so gracefully. While writing in the first person, beginning writers often fall into the trap of writing self-reflexive prose (writing *about* their paper *in* their paper). Often this leads to the most dreaded of opening lines: "In this paper I am going to discuss . . ." Not only does this self-reflexive voice make for very awkward prose, but it frequently allows writers to boldly announce a topic while completely avoiding a thesis statement. An example might be a paper that begins as follows: *I Know Why the Caged Bird Sings,* Maya Angelou's first book in her serial autobiography, takes place over the first decade of her life's memory, as the child is separated from, reunited with, and then again separated from her mother. In this paper, I am going to discuss how Angelou reacts to this separation. The author of this paper has done little more than announce a general topic for the paper (the reaction of Angelou to the separations). While the last sentence might be a thesis, the writer fails to present an opinion about the significance of the reaction. To improve this "thesis," the writer would need to back up a couple of steps. First, the announced topic of the paper is too broad; it largely summarizes the events in the story, without saying anything about the ideas in the story. The writer should highlight what she considers the meaning of the story: What is the story about? The writer might conclude that the separation, added to the young Marguerite's large size and awkwardness, triggers the feeling of invisibility and physical rejection that opens the narrative. From here, the author could select the means by which Angelou communicates these ideas and then begin to craft a specific thesis. A writer who chooses to explore the positive and negative attachments the young child makes with her grandmother and her mother's boyfriend might, for example, craft a thesis that reads, *I Know Why the Caged Bird Sings* is a life story that explores the effects of a mother's absence and seeming rejection on the child. The child, in turn, both admires and despises her southern grandmother's means of coping with a segregated society and mistakes the advances of her mother's boyfriend for real love. The descriptions of language and literature—and silence—show the impact of her feelings of rejection, guilt, and ultimate release.

Outlines

While developing a strong, thoughtful thesis early in your writing process should help focus your paper, outlining provides an essential tool for logically shaping that paper. A good outline helps you see—and develop— the relationships among the points in your argument and assures you that your paper flows logically and coherently. Outlining not only helps place your points in a logical order but also helps you subordinate supporting points, weed out any irrelevant points, and decide if there are any necessary points that are missing from your argument. Most of us are familiar with formal outlines that use numerical and letter designations for each point. However, there are different types of outlines; you may find that an informal outline is a more useful tool for you. What is important, though, is that you spend the time to develop some sort of outline—formal or informal.

Remember that an outline is a tool to help you shape and write a strong paper. If you do not spend sufficient time planning your supporting points and shaping the arrangement of those points, you will most likely construct a vague, unfocused outline that provides little, if any, help with the writing of the paper. Consider the following example.

Thesis: *I Know Why the Caged Bird Sings* is a life story that explores the effects of a mother's absence and seeming rejection on the child. The child, in turn, both admires and despises her southern grandmother's means of coping with a segregated society and mistakes the advances of her mother's boyfriend for real love. The descriptions of language and literature—and silence— show the impact of her feelings of rejection, guilt, and ultimate release.

    I.   Introduction and thesis

   II.   Marguerite Johnson
        A. Relationship to brother
        B. Admiration for "Momma," her grandmother
        C. Frustration with Momma also
        D. Reintroduction to her mother

  III.   Guilt over death of mother's boyfriend
        A. Silence

   IV.   Mother's boyfriend

    V.   Conclusion
        A. Marguerite has a poor self-image, and we see this by observing her reactions to her grandmother and her mother's boyfriend

This outline has a number of flaws. First, the major topics labeled with the Roman numerals are not arranged in a logical order, with the death of the boyfriend appearing before his introduction. The thesis actually makes no mention of this death, yet it is given a prominent place in the organization of the outline. Second, if the paper's aim is to show how Marguerite has positive and negative compensations for her poor self-image, the writer should establish the particulars of that image and those compensations before showing how this is played out in the text with silence. Third, the four items under Roman numeral II are not of parallel importance or weight, and the reintroduction of the mother does not seem to belong here. Similarly, the narrator's relationship to her brother, Bailey, may come up in the essay as information, but it does not appear as part of the thesis and should not have such a prominent place in the outline. A fourth problem is the inclusion of only a section A in numeral III. An outline should not include an A without a B, a 1 without a 2, and so forth. The final problem with this outline is the overall lack of detail. None of the sections provide much information about the content of the argument, and it seems likely that the writer has not given sufficient thought to the content of the paper.

A better start to this outline might be the following:

Thesis: *I Know Why the Caged Bird Sings* is a life story that explores the effects of a mother's absence and seeming rejection on the child. The child both admires and despises her southern grandmother's means of coping with a segregated society and mistakes the advances of her mother's boyfriend for real love. The descriptions of language and literature—and silence—show the impact of her feelings of rejection, guilt, and ultimate release.

I.   Introduction and thesis

II.   Marguerite's poor self-image
      A. Opens the book—"What you looking at me for? / I didn't come to stay. . ."
      B. Revealed in physical descriptions of herself—too big and clumsy and dark
      C. Intensified with reintroduction to beautiful mother—"she was too beautiful to have children"

```
    III. Compensations for poor self-image
          A. Positive: Identifying with and learning
             from "Momma," or grandmother, while also
             frustrated with her pacifism
          B. Negative: Vulnerability to the seeming
             affection, cuddling, but subsequent rape
             by mother's boyfriend

    IV.  Outcomes of rape and trial
          A. Death of the rapist
          B. Guilt in the young Marguerite, with
             result of her not speaking for years
          C. Separation again from mother, returned
             to grandmother in Arkansas

    V.   Conclusion: Marguerite compensates for her
         poor self-image, at least in part stemming from
         separation from her mother, by identifying with
         her grandmother but also by being vulnerable
         to the advances and rape by her mother's
         boyfriend. Subsequent events lead to guilt,
         silence, and once again separation from her
         mother.
```

This new outline would prove much more helpful when it came time to write the paper; in fact, if you do a carefully thought-through and full outline, the paper is practically written.

An outline like this could be shaped into an even more useful tool if the writer fleshed out the argument by providing specific examples and/ or quotations from the text to support each point. Once you have listed your main point and your supporting ideas, develop this raw material by listing related supporting ideas and material under each of those main headings. From there, arrange the material in subsections and order the material logically. Note that the page numbers of the following quotes from the book are given after each quotation. These will be needed for documentation in the final paper, and it will save some time looking them up if they are included in the outline.

For example:

I. Introduction and thesis

II. Marguerite's poor self-image
    A. Opens the book—"What you looking at me for? / I didn't come to stay . . ." Repeated three times in first paragraph, and then we discover it is a fragment, and she has to be prompted for the rest: "I just come to tell you / it's Easter Day." (7–8)
    B. Revealed in physical descriptions of herself—too big and clumsy and dark. "The age-faded color made my skin look dirty like mud, and everyone in church was looking at my skinny legs." (8)
    C. Intensified with reintroduction to beautiful mother—"I knew immediately why she had sent me away. She was too beautiful to have children." (50)

III. Compensations for poor self-image
    A. Positive: Identifying with and learning from "Momma," or grandmother, while also frustrated with her pacifism. After extreme scorn by "po' white trash," Momma "stood another whole song through and then opened the screen door to look down on me crying in rage. . . . She was beautiful." (29)
    B. Negative: Vulnerability to the seeming affection, cuddling, but subsequent rape by mother's boyfriend. "Then came the nice part. He held me so softly that I wished he wouldn't ever let me go. I felt at home. From the way he was holding me I

knew he'd never let me go or let anything bad ever happen to me." (59–60)

IV. Outcomes of rape and trial
   C. Death of the rapist—kicked to death and dropped behind the slaughterhouse, probably by the uncles (69)
   D. Guilt in the young Marguerite, with result of her not speaking for years. "Just my breath, carrying my words out, might poison people and they'd curl up and die like the black fat slugs that only pretended. I had to stop talking." (70)
   E. Separation again from mother, with being returned to grandmother in Arkansas. "I have never known if Momma sent for us, or if the St. Louis family just got fed up with my grim presence. There is nothing more appalling than a constantly morose child." (71)

V. Conclusion: Marguerite compensates for her poor self-image, at least in part stemming from separation from her mother, by identifying with her grandmother but also by being vulnerable to the advances and rape by her mother's boyfriend. Subsequent events lead to guilt, silence, and once again separation from her mother.

For another example of formulating a useful outline, you might begin with a thesis about another of the volumes of Angelou's serial autobiography: In Maya Angelou's fifth autobiographical volume, *All God's Children Need Traveling Shoes*, the search for home permeates the text as the narrator and her son live in Ghana, West Africa, and the narrator eventually returns to the United States without her now-grown son, Guy. As noted above, this thesis already gives you the beginning of an organization: To demonstrate that the search for home permeates the book, it is logical to work our way through the text from beginning to end, selecting the places and ways in which the search for home appears. You might begin your outline, then, with three topic headings: (1) Epigraph (a statement, usually a quotation, that appears as a preface to a text): "Swing low, sweet chariot, coming for to carry me home." (2) Black Americans in Africa, searching for a racial home. (3) Integration of African, American, and acceptance of adulthood independence of son and return to America. Under each of those headings, you could list ideas that support the particular point. Be sure to include references to parts of the text that help build your case, and, if possible, note the page numbers of the edition you are using.

An informal outline might look like this:

Thesis: In Maya Angelou's fifth autobiographical volume, *All God's Children Need Traveling Shoes*, the search for home permeates the text as the narrator and her son live in Ghana, West Africa, and the narrator eventually returns to the United States without her now-grown son, Guy.

1. Epigraph: "Swing low, sweet chariot, / coming for to carry me home"
2. Black Americans in Africa, searching for a racial home
   - Surprised not welcomed with open arms
   - Some leave
   - Different customs on the role of women
     - Marriage offer as one of the wives
     - Women should "be seen and not heard"
   - Separation from the group of expatriates to see Africa on her own
     - Travel to west coast of Ghana alone
3. Integration of African, American, and acceptance of adulthood independence of son and return to America
   - Visit of Malcolm X to Ghana after his transforming visit to Mecca (scolds Angelou

about her attitude toward Shirley Graham Du
Bois after W.E.B. Du Bois's death)
- New independence of son, Guy
- Has "gotten all Africa had to give me"

4. Conclusion: We do not leave even when we leave

You would set about writing a formal, more developed outline with a similar process, though in the final stages you would label the headings differently. A formal outline for a paper that argues the thesis about *All God's Children Need Traveling Shoes* cited above—that the travel of the narrator to Africa and back to America is all part of integrating the sense of home and what it means—might look like this. (Note that page numbers are given for quotations, for subsequent convenience in documentation of the final paper. Quotes are also copied quite lengthily, to ensure accuracy, even though in the final paper they may be shortened or summarized or paraphrased. Words left out of quotes are indicated by three dots, or an ellipsis—four if the end of a sentence. There will be more on this to come in the documentation section.)

Thesis: In Maya Angelou's fifth autobiographical volume,
All God's Children Need Traveling Shoes, the search for
home permeates the text as the narrator and her son
live in Ghana, West Africa, and the narrator eventually
returns to the United States without her now-grown son,
Guy.

I. From the very beginning, the search for home
   permeates the text, though its sense evolves
   A. Epigraph: "Swing low, sweet chariot, /
      coming for to carry me home" (n.p.)
   B. Echoed in the dedication to "all the
      fallen ones who were passionately and
      earnestly looking for a home" (n.p.)
   C. A change in the sense of what "home"
      means: singing "Swing low . . ." with
      President Tubman of Liberia. Singing with

all other Africans—"I knew . . . that not one of them was fired with religious zeal, so for what chariot were they calling and what home could they possibly miss?" (1,031)

D. Understanding of the spirituals in relation to Africa and America. The Africans "were earnest and their voices were in tune, but they could not duplicate the haunting melody of our singing. . . . In the absence of my creative ancestors who picked that melody out of cotton sacks, I humbly bowed my head" (1,032).

II. Black Americans in Africa, searching for a racial home

A. Initial delight in Ghana, "For two days Guy and I laughed. We looked at the Ghanaian streets and laughed. We listened to the melodious languages and laughed. We looked at each other and laughed out loud" (890). "I was soon swept into an adoration for Ghana as a young girl falls in love. . . ; heaven and Africa were inextricably combined" (902). "Our arrival had little impact on anyone but us. We ogled the Ghanaians and few of them even noticed. The newcomers hid disappointment in quick repartee, in jokes and clenched jaws" (903). The black Americans "buzzed mothlike on the periphery of acceptance. . ." (905)

B. Eventual surprise American blacks not welcomed with open arms. "Were we only and vainly trying to kill that portion of our history which we could neither accept nor deny? The questions temporarily sobered my intoxication with Africa. . . . I examined whether in looking for a home I, and all the émigrés, were running from a bitter truth that rode lightly but forever at home on our shoulders." (914)

C. Some black Americans leave. Couple who have "'come to Mother Africa to suckle from her breasts,'" and Angelou says, "Africa doesn't need anybody as big as you pulling on her tits" (917). "They didn't want to know that they had not come home, but had left one familiar place of painful memory for another strange place with none." (918)

D. Role of women customs

1. Gets hair done and "is relieved that I looked like every other Ghanaian woman." (916)

2. Sheikhali (romantic interest) dates and proposes to her. He was "exotic, generous and physically satisfying, but we had trouble translating ourselves to each other. My upbringing had not fitted me for even a pretended reticence." (941)

3. Proposes marriage: "'You will be my second wife. . . . If I need more children I will take a young girl because you and my wife will have no more babies. . . . Our families will marry.'" (942)

E. Separation from the group of expatriates to see Africa on her own

1. An "outdooring," the "first African rite of passage" eight days after birth (921–928)

2. A "durbar," or "thanksgiving feast" outside of Accra

3. Travel to west coast of Ghana alone
    a. Cape Coast Castle—"holding forts for captured slaves," "history had invaded my little car. Pangs of self-pity and a sorrow for my unknown relatives suffused me." (963)
    b. Town of Dunkwa; is mistaken for a member of a tribe. "For the first time since my arrival, I was very nearly home. Not a Ghanaian, but at least accepted as an African. The sensation was worth a lie. . . . I felt the distance narrow between my past and present" (967)."I had proved that one of their descendants, at least one, could just briefly return to Africa, and that despite cruel betrayals, bitter ocean voyages and hurtful centuries, we were still recognizable." (969)

III. Integration of African, American, and acceptance of adulthood independence of son and return to the United States.
    A. "Ghana was beginning to tug at me and make me uncomfortable, like an ill-fitting coat. . . . I had to admit that I had begun to feel that I was not in my right place." (1,003)
    B. Visit of Malcolm X to Ghana after his transforming visit to Mecca
        1. Scolds Angelou about her attitude toward Shirley Graham Du Bois after W.E.B. Du Bois's death. Says "We need people on each level to fight our

battle. Don't be in such a hurry to condemn a person because he doesn't do what you do, or think as you think or as fast. There was a time when you didn't know what you know today." (1001)

  2. "Malcolm's presence had elevated us, but with his departure, we were what we had been before: a little group of Black folks, looking for a home." (1,002)

C. New independence of son, Guy: "How could his life be separate from my life. . . . His existence defined my own" (1005). Review of their lives, her teaching him, defending him: "I needed to get away from him and myself and the situation. Maybe to Europe, or Asia. I never thought of returning to America." (1,007)

D. "It seemed that I had gotten all Africa had to give me. . . . If the heart of Africa still remained elusive, my search for it had brought me closer to understanding myself and other human beings. The ache for home lives in all of us, the safe place where we can go as we are and not be questioned. It impels mighty ambitions and dangerous capers . . . We shout in Baptist churches, wear yarmulkes and wigs and argue even the tiniest points in the Torah, or worship the sun and refuse to kill cows for the starving. Hoping that by doing these things, home will find us acceptable or failing that, that we will forget our awful yearning for it." (1,041–42)

IV. Conclusion: We don't leave even when we leave. "I knew my people had never completely left

Africa. We had sung it in our blues, shouted it
in our gospel and danced the continent in our
breakdowns. As we carried it to Philadelphia,
Boston and Birmingham we had changed its color,
modified its rhythms, yet it was Africa which
rode in the bulges of our high calves, shook in
our protruding behinds and crackled in our wide
open laughter.
    I could nearly hear the old ones chuckling."
(1051)

As in the previous example outline, the thesis provided the seeds of a
structure, and the writer was careful to arrange the supporting points
in a logical manner, showing the relationships among the ideas in the
paper.

Body Paragraphs

Once your outline is complete, you can begin drafting your paper. Paragraphs, units of related sentences, are the building blocks of a good
paper, and as you draft you should keep in mind both the function and
the qualities of good paragraphs. Paragraphs help you chart and control
the shape and content of your essay, and they help the reader see your
organization and your logic. You should begin a new paragraph whenever you move from one major point to another. In longer, more complex
essays, you might use a group of related paragraphs to support major
points. Remember that in addition to being adequately developed, a good
paragraph is both unified and coherent.

Unified Paragraphs

Each paragraph must be centered on one idea or point, and a unified
paragraph carefully focuses on and develops this central idea without
including extraneous ideas or tangents. For beginning writers, the best
way to ensure that you are constructing unified paragraphs is to include
a topic sentence in each paragraph. This topic sentence should convey
the main point of the paragraph, and every sentence in the paragraph
should relate to that topic sentence. Any sentence that strays from the
central topic does not belong in the paragraph and needs to be revised or
deleted. Consider the following paragraph about the young Marguerite's

guilt after the death of her rapist in *I Know Why the Caged Bird Sings*. Notice how the paragraph veers away from the main point that it is her feelings of guilt that lead to her long silence.

> "Just my breath, carrying my words out, might poison people and they'd curl up and die like the black fat slugs that only pretended. I had to stop talking" (70). This is what the young Marguerite Johnson concludes after she lies on the witness stand and says that her mother's boyfriend had never touched her before the time of the rape. She is afraid that if she told the truth, that she had been held and touched and had liked it and kept it a secret, she would lose the love and affection of her brother, Bailey. Her older brother, Bailey, has been crucial to her life, from the time the two children were sent by train from their mother in California to their paternal grandmother in Stamps, Arkansas. In St. Louis, Bailey has grown more distant, finding his own niche, and to some extent, Marguerite feels abandoned by him. He also has an extreme love for their beautiful mother although at this stage of her young life, Marguerite almost fears her. When the two children are sent back to their grandmother in Stamps, Marguerite is much happier about it than Bailey is, and to some extent, this is the beginning of more independence of the young girl from her brother, though it takes her years to find her own way with the help of Mrs. Flowers and poetry.

Although the paragraph begins solidly, with the quotation and the second explanatory sentence, the author soon goes on a tangent, beginning somewhat with the reference to Bailey in the third sentence, and then losing the way in the rest of the paragraph. If the purpose of the paragraph is to demonstrate that Marguerite's feelings of guilt leads to her silence, the sentences about her changing relationship to Bailey are tangential here. They may find a place elsewhere in the paper, but they should not be in this paragraph.

Coherent Paragraphs

In addition to shaping unified paragraphs, you must also craft coherent paragraphs, paragraphs that develop their points logically with sentences that flow smoothly into one another. Coherence depends on the order of your sentences, but it is not strictly the order of the sentences that is important to paragraph coherence. You also need to craft your prose to help the reader see the relationship among the sentences.

Consider the following paragraph about the guilt of Marguerite Johnson (Maya Angelou) leading to her silence in *I Know Why the Caged Bird Sings*. Notice how the writer has achieved unity—that is, all the sentences relate to the main point of the paragraph—yet fails to help the reader see the relationships among the points.

"Just my breath, carrying my words out, might poison people and they'd curl up and die like the black fat slugs that only pretended. I had to stop talking" (70). The young Marguerite Johnson becomes silent after she lies on the witness stand. She said that her mother's boyfriend had never touched her before the time of the rape. Marguerite does not want to admit on the stand that Mr. Freeman had previously held and touched her and that she had liked it and kept it a secret under threat from the man. Marguerite feels she will lose the love and respect of her mother, her grandmother, but especially her brother, Bailey. She had never withheld a secret from Bailey. It is probable that her violent uncles took revenge for her rape by killing Mr. Freeman. Mr. Freeman had threatened that if she told anyone about his advances, he would kill Bailey. Words have the power to kill; it was better not to use them at all. First as the effect of the trauma and hospital stay, Marguerite is silent, but after many, many weeks it becomes inexplicable to others, who call her impudent and sullen. She received "thrashings, given by any relative who felt himself offended" (70). The children are sent from St. Louis back to their grandmother in Arkansas, with Bailey inconsolable at having to leave

```
"Mother Dear," but with Marguerite having "no more
thought of our destination than if I had simply been
heading for the toilet" (71). Stamps is a small town
compared with St. Louis.
```

This paragraph demonstrates that unity alone does not guarantee paragraph effectiveness. The argument is hard to follow because the author fails both to show connections between the sentences and to indicate how they work to support the overall point.

A number of techniques are available to aid paragraph coherence. Careful use of transitional words and phrases is essential. You can use transitional flags to introduce an example or an illustration (*for example, for instance*), to amplify a point or add another phase of the same idea (*additionally, furthermore, next, similarly, finally, then*), to indicate a conclusion or result (*therefore, as a result, thus, in other words*), to signal a contrast or a qualification (*on the other hand, nevertheless, despite this, on the contrary, still, however, conversely*), to signal a comparison (*likewise, in comparison, similarly*), and to indicate a movement in time (*afterward, earlier, eventually, finally, later, subsequently, until*).

In addition to transitional flags, careful use of pronouns aids coherence and flow. If you were writing about *The Wizard of Oz*, you would not want to keep repeating the phrase *the witch* or the name *Dorothy*. Careful substitution of the pronoun *she* in these instances can aid coherence. A word of warning, though: When you substitute pronouns for proper names, always be sure that your pronoun reference is clear. In a paragraph that discusses both Dorothy and the witch, substituting *she* could lead to confusion. Make sure that it is clear to whom the pronoun refers. Generally, the pronoun refers to the last proper noun you have used.

While repeating the same name over and over again can lead to awkward, boring prose, it is possible to use repetition to help your paragraph's coherence. Careful repetition of important words or phrases can lend coherence to your paragraph by reminding readers of your key points. Admittedly, it takes some practice to use this technique effectively. You may find that reading your prose aloud can help you develop an ear for effective use of repetition.

To see how helpful transitional aids are, compare the paragraph below to the preceding paragraph about the narrator's guilt leading to her prolonged silence in *I Know Why the Caged Bird Sings*. Notice how the author works with the same ideas and quotations but shapes them into a much more coherent paragraph whose point is clearer and easier to follow.

"Just my breath, carrying my words out, might poison people and they'd curl up and die like the black fat slugs that only pretended. I had to stop talking" (70). This is what the young Marguerite Johnson concludes after she lies on the witness stand, saying that her mother's boyfriend had never touched her before the time of the rape. Marguerite's reluctance to admit on the stand that Mr. Freeman had previously held and touched her and that she had liked it and kept it a secret under threat from the man is understandable, since she feels she will lose the love and respect of her mother, her grandmother, but especially her brother, Bailey, from whom she had not withheld a secret before in their lives. Yet her lie, she believes, is what has led her violent uncles to take revenge for her rape by killing Mr. Freeman. Mr. Freeman had threatened that if she told anyone about his advances, Bailey would be killed; but now Mr. Freeman himself was dead, so with the reasoning of a child, she sees that words—her words— have the power to kill. It is better, then, not to use them at all. Taken at first as the effect of the trauma and hospital stay, Marguerite's silence, after many, many weeks, becomes inexplicable to others, who call her impudent and sullen and "then came the thrashings, given by any relative who felt himself offended" (70). Finally both the girl and her beloved brother are sent from St. Louis back to their grandmother in Arkansas, with Bailey inconsolable at having to leave "Mother Dear," but with Marguerite having "no more thought of our destination than if I had simply been heading for the toilet" (71). It will be easier to pursue her vow of silence in the small town of Stamps.

Similarly, the following paragraph from a paper on Angelou's adjustment to the growing independence of her son, Guy, in *All God's Children Need Traveling Shoes,* demonstrates both unity and coherence. In it, the author argues that Angelou integrates leaving "Mother Africa" and leaving her grown son in such a way as to draw the best out of each experience.

Crucial to Angelou's decision to return to the United States is the new and full independence of her son, Guy. This separation into separate entities for the two of them reaches its climax after she confronts the nineteen-year-old about dating a woman a year older than Angelou herself. He "had the nerve," Angelou writes, to express his annoyance—"Oh, Mother, really. Don't you think it's time I had a life of my own?" (1005). At this stage, she cannot see how his life could be separate from hers, for "his existence had defined my own" (1005). Then she mentally reviews their lives, her teaching him, defending him, many of the events that are narrated in the previous autobiographies. She feels some guilt over the fact that he had gone to nineteen schools in eleven years, but when she had been told by a school psychologist that her son needed the security of "stability," Angelou had responded: "I am his security. Wherever we go, we go together. Wherever he is he knows that that six-foot-tall Black woman is not too far away. What I don't furnish in stability, I make up in love" (1006). But now Guy had "moved beyond" her reach "into the arms of a cradle robber." "I needed to get away from him and myself and the situation" (1007). A surprise invitation to tour Europe with a production of Genet's *The Blacks*, in which she had acted in New York City, fortunately gets her to Berlin and Venice and gives her new perspective. Back in Ghana again, she is still in her traveling clothes when Guy announces "'You have finished mothering a child. You did a very good job. Now, I am a man. Your life is your own, and mine belongs to me'" (1033). There is nothing to do but accept and take joy from what has been and from what has changed. Her leaving of Guy and leaving of Africa come together, and she makes a decision as a newly independent mother. "If the heart of Africa still remained elusive, my search for it had brought me closer to understanding myself and other human beings. The ache for home lives in all of us, the safe place where we can go as we are and not be questioned. . . . My mind was made up. I would go back to the United States as soon as possible" (1041–42).

Introductions

Introductions present particular challenges for writers. Generally, your introduction should do two things: capture your reader's attention and explain the main point of your essay. In other words, while your introduction should contain your thesis, it needs to do a bit more work than that. You are likely to find that starting that first paragraph is one of the most difficult parts of the paper. It is hard to face that blank page or screen, and as a result, many beginning writers, in desperation to start somewhere, start with overly broad, general statements. Sometimes, writers find that writing the introduction after the rest of the paper works. While it is often a good strategy to start with more general subject matter and narrow your focus, do not begin with broad, sweeping statements such as, Everyone likes to be creative and feel understood. Such sentences are nothing but empty filler. They begin to fill the blank page, but they do nothing to advance your argument. Instead, you should try to gain your readers' interest. Some writers like to begin with a pertinent quotation or with a relevant question. Or, you might begin with an introduction of the topic you will discuss. If you are writing about Angelou's positive and negative reactions to abandonment by her mother in *I Know Why the Caged Bird Sings,* for instance, you might begin by talking about how important the early years of life are to a child's sense of self. Another common trap to avoid is depending on your title to introduce the author and the text you are writing about. Always include the work's author and title in your opening paragraph.

Compare the effectiveness of the following introductions:

1) The early years of life are crucial to a child's self-image. Imagine what it would be like to feel that your mother had abandoned you! You would wonder if it was because you were not good enough, wouldn't you? In this book, Angelou describes what she went through as a child—how some of her adjustments, like admiring her grandmother, were positive but others not so good, like accepting her mother's boyfriend's advances just to be loved.

2) Psychologists are well aware that parents, and the mother in particular, are very powerful influences on the child's self-image. When that mother is absent, the child must make adjustments and create compensatory attachments in order to grow up psychologically healthy, and when the absence of the mother appears to be abandonment, such adjustments can be particularly problematic and difficult. Sigmund Freud, in fact, describes such "object loss" as leaving the child in a state of mourning. In the first volume of her serial autobiography, *I Know Why the Caged Bird Sings*, Maya Angelou, with amazing honesty and effectiveness, describes her own experiences as a child who has been sent by her mother on a train halfway across the United States to her paternal grandmother. When Angelou and her somewhat older brother are subsequently returned to their mother and her family, the insecure Angelou forms a disastrous attachment to her mother's boyfriend, which leads to rape, a trial, and the death of the boyfriend, Mr. Freeman.

The first introduction begins with a vague, overly broad sentence; cites unclear, undeveloped examples; and then moves abruptly to the thesis. Notice, too, how a reader deprived of the paper's title does not know the title of the book that the paper will analyze. The second introduction works with the same material and thesis but provides more detail and is consequently much more interesting. It begins by discussing psychological understandings of the child's attachment to the mother, gives specific examples, and then speaks briefly about one psychologist's depiction of object loss and the child. The paragraph ends with the thesis, which includes both the author and the title of the work to be discussed.

The paragraph below provides another example of an opening strategy. It begins by introducing the author and the text it will analyze, and then it moves on by briefly introducing relevant details of the story in order to set up its thesis.

> The first volume of Maya Angelou's serial autobiography, *I Know Why the Caged Bird Sings,* depicts the early, difficult life of the first-person narrator and author. Sent by her mother halfway across the United States to live with their paternal grandmother, the three-year-old Maya (then named Marguerite Johnson) and her brother, Bailey, five, find Stamps, Arkansas, in the days of the segregated South, a challenging place to grow and thrive. Their grandmother ("Momma") helps tremendously in this process, however, for she is an ambitious, religious, altruistic general store owner in the black section of town, a strong female role model. Able to endure and rise above even the ugliest taunts of the "po' white trash," Momma frustrates Angelou with her pacifism but serves as a positive and inspiring example of struggle. The young Marguerite's other compensation for a negative self-image is not such a happy one. When the two children are brought to St. Louis to live with their mother and her family, the mother's boyfriend befriends the lonely girl, then fondles her, and finally rapes her. The subsequent trial and death of Mr. Freeman, probably at her uncles' hands, causes Marguerite to take up silence, and after enduring months of this, her mother sends her back to Arkansas.

Conclusions

Conclusions present another series of challenges for writers. No doubt you have heard the adage about writing papers: "Tell us what you are going to say, say it, and then tell us what you've said." While this formula does not necessarily result in bad papers, it does not often result in good ones, either. It will almost certainly result in boring papers (especially boring conclusions). If you have done a good job establishing your points in the body of the paper, the reader already knows and understands your argument. There is no need to merely reiterate. Do not just summarize your main points in your conclusion. Such a boring and mechanical conclusion does nothing to advance your argument or interest your reader. Consider the following conclusion to the paper about the compensations the child makes to absence of her mother and her poor self-image in Angelou's *I Know Why the Caged Bird Sings.*

> In conclusion, Angelou shows that loss of a mother's presence can lead a child to positive and/or negative compensations. Marguerite takes up silence as a defense after she is raped, and silence sends her away from her mother once again. It is not easy for a child to grow up in difficult circumstances. We would all undoubtedly find that to be true.

Besides starting with a mechanical transitional device, this conclusion does little more than summarize the main points of the outline (and it does not even touch on all of them). It is incomplete and uninteresting (and a little too depressing).

Instead, your conclusion should add something to your paper. A good tactic is to build upon the points you have been arguing. Asking "why?" often helps you draw further conclusions. For example, in the paper on *All God's Children Need Traveling Shoes,* you might make observations about the theme of the search for home as it appears in the works of other black writers or the way that same longing and search manifests itself in the language and actions of Alzheimer's patients, even after specific memory is gone. Another method for successfully concluding a paper is to speculate on other directions in which to take your topic by tying it into larger issues. You might do this by envisioning your paper as just one section of a larger paper. Having established your points in this paper, how would you build upon this argument? Where would you go next? In the following conclusion to the paper on *All God's Children Need Travel-*

ing Shoes, the author reiterates some of the main points of the paper but does so in order to amplify the discussion of the story's central message and to connect it to other examples.

> Maya Angelou, looking back on her life, sees the search for home as a central theme. First, she feels that sense common to some black Americans that Africa represents "home" in some profound way that is part of the struggle for identity. And then, over time, she realizes that home and the longing for it is something we all carry with us always as human beings, even after other memory has gone. Caretakers and researchers of Alzheimer's patients, for example, often find the disoriented men and women heading out to "go home," even though they cannot articulate what or where "home" is.

Similarly, in the following conclusion to a paper on self-image and compensation for loss of the mother in *I Know Why the Caged Bird Sings,* the author draws a conclusion about what the autobiography is saying about self-image and compensation more broadly.

> *I Know Why the Caged Bird Sings* is the honest and moving story of a black girl growing up in the segregated American South of the 1930s, with the added difficulty of separation, even abandonment, by her mother and father. Young Marguerite Johnson, a natural fighter, admires but cannot bring herself to emulate the model of her religious, enduring, and pacifist grandmother, and when Marguerite and her brother, Bailey, are brought to St. Louis to their mother and her family, the girl finds appealing the advances of her mother's boyfriend. Those seemingly pleasant encounters of love and protection unfortunately lead to Marguerite's rape and a court trial in which she feels she must deny the pleasurable beginnings of her assault. This lie on the witness stand causes her to subsequently blame herself and her words for her rapist's death, and she adopts a vow of silence.

The self-image of this young girl suffers enormously from her surroundings and the events of her early life. She is big when tiny females are the standard of beauty; black before the advent of "Black is Beautiful"; clumsy when "feminine" images rule American culture; and she sees herself as a liar who has caused a man's death. That Marguerite ultimately, in this the first volume of Maya Angelou's autobiography, gains a measure of assurance, independence, and love of literature and releases herself from her vow of silence is a tribute to the human spirit, even or especially in the young and vulnerable.

Citations and Formatting

Using Primary Sources

As the examples included in this chapter indicate, strong papers on literary texts incorporate quotations from the text in order to support their points. It is not enough for you to assert your interpretation without providing support or evidence from the text. Without well-chosen quotations to support your argument you are, in effect, saying to the reader, "Take my word for it." It is important to use quotations thoughtfully and selectively. Remember that the paper presents *your* argument, so choose quotations that support *your* assertions. Do not let the author's voice overwhelm your own. With that caution in mind, there are some guidelines you should follow to ensure that you use quotations clearly and effectively.

Integrate Quotations

Quotations should always be integrated into your own prose. Do not just drop them into your paper without introduction or comment. Otherwise, it is unlikely that your reader will see their function. You can integrate textual support easily and clearly with identifying tags, short phrases that identify the speaker. For example:

In Angelou's description, black Americans in Ghana in the 1960s "buzzed moth-like on the periphery of acceptance."

While this tag appears before the quotation, you can also use tags after or in the middle of the quoted text, as the following examples demonstrate:

```
A "thanksgiving feast" is the way Angelou describes a
"durbar" in Ghana.
```

```
"It seemed that I had gotten all Africa had to give me,"
Angelou concludes, and the search for the heart of the
continent "brought me closer to understanding myself
and other human beings."
```

You can also use a colon to formally introduce a quotation:

```
Malcolm X tells Angelou: "Don't be in such a hurry to
condemn a person because he doesn't do what you do, or
think as you think or as fast."
```

When you quote brief sections of poems (three lines or fewer), use slash marks to indicate the line breaks in the poem:

```
As the poem ends, Angelou concludes that the state of
Arkansas "writhes in awful / waves of brooding."
```

Longer quotations (more than four lines of prose or three lines of poetry) should be set off from the rest of your paper in a block quotation. Double-space before you begin the passage, indent it 10 spaces from your left-hand margin, and double-space the passage itself. Because the indentation signals the inclusion of a quotation, do not use quotation marks around the cited passage. Use a colon to introduce the passage:

```
Angelou concludes this book about traveling and the
search for home with a survey of the ways all humankind
engages in that search:

    We shout in Baptist churches, wear yarmulkes and
    wigs and argue even the tiniest points in the
    Torah, or worship the sun and refuse to kill
```

cows for the starving. Hoping that by doing these
things, home will find us acceptable or failing
that, that we will forget our awful yearning for
it.

This broadening of the discussion enables the reader
to enjoy Angelou's own struggle and search for home
throughout the book and relate his or her own experience
to hers.

The last stanza of Angelou's poem looks to the past and
future:

Old hates and
ante-bellum lace, are rent
but not discarded.
Today is yet to come
in Arkansas.
It writhes. It writhes in awful
waves of brooding.

Clearly, she faces the difficulties of progress but
nevertheless hopes for it.

It is also important to interpret quotations after you introduce them
and explain how they help advance your point. You cannot assume that
your reader will interpret the quotations the same way that you do.

Quote Accurately

Always quote accurately. Anything within quotations marks must be the
author's exact words. There are, however, some rules to follow if you need
to modify the quotation to fit into your prose.

1. Use brackets to indicate any material that might have been
   added to the author's exact wording. For example, if you need
   to add any words to the quotation or alter it grammatically to
   allow it to fit into your prose, indicate your changes in brackets:

```
"For two days Guy [Angelou's son] and I laughed."
```

2. Conversely, if you choose to omit any words from the quotation, use ellipses (three spaced periods) to indicate missing words or phrases:

```
About singing the spiritual "Swing Low, Sweet
Chariot" with Africans, Angelou writes: "I
knew . . . that not one of them was fired
with religious zeal, so for what chariot were
they calling and what home could they possible
miss?"
```

3. If you delete a sentence or more, use the ellipses after a period:

```
They "could not duplicate the haunting melody
of our singing. . . . In the absence of my
creative ancestors who picked that melody out of
cotton sacks, I humbly bowed my head."
```

4. If you omit a line or more of poetry, or more than one paragraph of prose, use a single line of spaced periods to indicate the omission:

```
There is a deep brooding
in Arkansas

. . . . . . . . . . . . . . . . . .
The sullen earth
is much too
red for comfort.
```

Punctuate Properly

Punctuation of quotations often causes more trouble than it should. Once again, you just need to keep these simple rules in mind.

1. Periods and commas should be placed inside quotation marks, even if they are not part of the original quotation:

> Angelou and her son enjoy to the hilt their
> first experience of Africa: "We looked at each
> other and laughed out loud."

The only exception to this rule is when the quotation is followed by a parenthetical reference. In this case, the period or comma goes after the citation (more on these later in this chapter):

> Angelou and her son enjoy to the hilt their
> first experience of Africa: "We looked at each
> other and laughed out loud" (890).

2. Other marks of punctuation—colons, semicolons, question marks, and exclamation points—go outside the quotation marks unless they are part of the original quotation:

> The reader wonders, why is Angelou after her
> new hair styling "relieved that I looked like
> every other Ghanaian woman"?

> "Were we only and vainly trying to kill that
> portion of our history which we could neither
> accept nor deny?"

Documenting Primary Sources

Unless you are instructed otherwise, you should provide sufficient information for your reader to locate material you quote. Generally, literature papers follow the rules set forth by the Modern Language Association (MLA). These can be found in the *MLA Handbook for Writers of Research Papers* (sixth edition). You should be able to find this book in the reference section of your library. Additionally, its rules for citing both primary and secondary sources are widely available from reputable online sources. One of these is the Online Writing Lab (OWL) at Purdue University. OWL's guide to MLA style is available at http://owl.english. purdue.edu/owl/resource/557/01/. The Modern Language Association also offers answers to frequently asked questions about MLA style on this helpful Web page: http://www.mla.org/style_faq. Generally, when you are citing from literary works in papers, you should keep a few guidelines in mind.

Parenthetical Citations

MLA asks for parenthetical references in your text after quotations. When you are working with prose (short stories, novels, or essays) include page numbers in the parentheses:

> Angelou and her son enjoy to the hilt their first experience of Africa: "We looked at each other and laughed out loud" (890).

When you are quoting poetry, include line numbers:

> Angelou depicts, in "The Singer Will Not Sing," "The mouth seamed, voiceless" (140-41).

Works Cited Page

These parenthetical citations are linked to a separate works cited page at the end of the paper. The works cited page lists works alphabetically by the authors' last name. An entry for the above references to Angelou's *I Know Why the Caged Bird Sings* would read:

> Angelou, Maya. *I Know Why the Caged Bird Sings. The Collected Autobiographies of Maya Angelou.* New York: The Modern Library, 2004. 1-222.

The *MLA Handbook* includes a full listing of sample entries, as do many of the online explanations of MLA style.

Documenting Secondary Sources

To ensure that your paper is built entirely upon your own ideas and analysis, instructors often ask that you write interpretative papers without any outside research. If, on the other hand, your paper requires research, you must document any secondary sources you use. You need to document direct quotations, summaries or paraphrases of others' ideas, and factual information that is not common knowledge. Follow the guidelines above for quoting primary sources when you use direct quotations from secondary sources. Keep in mind that MLA style also includes specific guidelines for citing electronic sources. OWL's Web site provides a good summary: http://owl.english.purdue.edu/owl/resource/557/09/.

Parenthetical Citations

As with the documentation of primary sources, described above, MLA guidelines require in-text parenthetical references to your secondary sources. Unlike the research papers you might write for a history class, literary research papers following MLA style do not use footnotes as a means of documenting sources. Instead, after a quotation, you should cite the author's last name and the page number:

> "Although Angelou's grandmother owned a general merchandise store, her household suffered only a degree less than other families" (Hagen 14).

If you include the name of the author in your prose, then you would include only the page number in your citation. For example:

> Lyman Hagen reminds us that "although Angelou's grandmother owned a general merchandise store, her household suffered only a degree less than other families" (14).

If you are including more than one work by the same author, the parenthetical citation should include a shortened yet identifiable version of the title in order to indicate which of the author's works you cite. For example:

> Suzette A. Henke calls Angelou's six books about her life, beginning with *I Know Why the Caged Bird Sings*, "autobiographic novel[s] rather than autobiographies" ("Autobiography" 99).

Similarly, and just as important, if you summarize or paraphrase the particular ideas of your source, you must provide documentation:

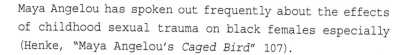

Maya Angelou has spoken out frequently about the effects
of childhood sexual trauma on black females especially
(Henke, "Maya Angelou's *Caged Bird*" 107).

Works Cited Page

Like the primary sources discussed above, the parenthetical references
to secondary sources are keyed to a separate works cited page at the end
of your paper. Here is an example of a works cited page that uses the
examples cited above. Note that when two or more works by the same
author are listed, you should use three hyphens followed by a period in
the subsequent entries. You can find a complete list of sample entries in
the *MLA Handbook* or from a reputable online summary of MLA style.

WORKS CITED

Hagen, Lyman B. *Heart of a Woman, Mind of a Writer, and
    Soul of a Poet: A Critical Analysis of the Writings
    of Maya Angelou.* Lanham, MD: University Press of
    America, 1997.

Henke, Suzette. "Autobiography as Revolutionary Writing."
    Readings on Maya Angelou. Ed. Mary E. Williams. San
    Diego, CA: Greenhaven Press, Inc. 1997. 99–104.

——. "Maya Angelou's *Caged Bird* as Trauma Narrative." In
    Harold Bloom, Ed., *Maya Angelou.* Bloom's Modern Critical
    Views. New York: Infobase Publishing, 2009. 107–120.

Plagiarism

Failure to document carefully and thoroughly can leave you open to
charges of stealing the ideas of others, which is known as plagiarism,
and this is a very serious matter. Remember that it is important to
include quotation marks when you use language from your source, even
if you use just one or two words. For example, if you wrote, Angelou's
grandmother and family suffered only a degree less than
other families, you would be guilty of plagiarism, since you used
Hagen's distinct language without acknowledging him as the source.
Instead, you should write: Angelou's grandmother and family
"suffered only a degree less than other families" (Hagen
14). In this case, you have properly credited Hagen.

Similarly, neither summarizing the ideas of an author nor changing or omitting just a few words means that you can omit a citation. Mary Jo Lupton's essay called "The Significance of Momma Henderson in Angelou's Autobiographies" contains the following passage about the mother figures in the book:

> In flux, in defiance of chronological time, the mother-child configuration forms the basic pattern against which other relationships are measured and around which episodes and volumes begin or end. Motherhood also provides the series with a literary unity, as Angelou shifts positions—from mother to granddaughter to child—in a non-ending text that, through its repetitions of maternal motifs, provides an ironic comment on mother love, is trapped in the conflicts between working and mothering, independence and nurturing—conflicts that echo her ambivalence towards her mother, Vivian Baxter, and her apparent sanctification of Grandmother Henderson, the major adult figure in *Caged Bird.*

Below are two examples of plagiarized passages:

> All the other relationships in *Caged Bird* and the following books revolve around the mother-child relationship. This theme gives the books a nice unity and seems to reflect Angelou's confused feeling about her mother and her idolization of her grandmother.

> What happens with the mother-child configuration in Angelou's books lends them a literary unity. Repetitions of maternal motifs reflect Angelou's ambivalence toward her mother, Vivian Baxter (Lupton 73–74).

While the first passage does not use Lupton's exact language, it does summarize the same ideas she proposes as critical to the books without citing her work. Since this interpretation is Lupton's distinct idea, this constitutes plagiarism. The second passage has shortened the original and changed some wording, and included a citation, but some of the phrasing is Lupton's. The first passage could be fixed with a parenthetical citation. Because some of the wording in the second remains the same, though, it would require the use of quotation marks, in addition to a parenthetical citation. The passage below represents an honestly and adequately documented use of the original passage:

> According to Mary Jane Lupton, a major element of Angelou's autobiographies is the repetition of the mother-child relationship in different forms. Lupton sees this repetition as giving the books a "literary unity" and "an ironic comment on [Angelou's] own sense of identity." The conflicts in these relationships— "working and mothering, independence and nurturing"— come directly from Angelou's relationship with her own mother, Vivian Baxter, toward whom the author's changing relationship remains one of "ambivalence" (73–74).

This passage acknowledges that the interpretation is derived from Lupton while appropriately using quotations to indicate her precise language.

While it is not necessary to document well-known facts, often referred to as "common knowledge," any ideas or language that you take from someone else must be properly documented. Common knowledge generally includes the birth and death dates of authors or other well-documented facts of their lives. An often-cited guideline is that if you can find the information in three sources, it is common knowledge. Despite this guideline, it is, admittedly, often difficult to know if the facts you uncover are common knowledge or not. When in doubt, document your source.

Sample Essay

Sven Peterson
Ms. Olsen
English II
March 19, 2012

Traveling Shoes: Maya Angelou's Search for Home
In Maya Angelou's fifth autobiographical volume, *All God's Children Need Traveling Shoes,* the search for home permeates the text, even as the word's sense

evolves, as the narrator and her son live in Ghana, West Africa, and the narrator eventually returns to the United States without the now-grown Guy. Lyman B. Hagen says it well: The book "contains a strong sense of home and a rediscovery of homeland" (113). The epigraph of the book is from an old Negro spiritual: "Swing low, sweet chariot, / coming for to carry me home" (n.p.). And longing for home is echoed in the dedication of the book to "all the fallen ones who were passionately and earnestly looking for a home" (n.p.)

Black Americans in Africa, including Angelou and Guy, initially find great joy in the racial belonging they feel. Ghana is a scrumptious delight; "For two days Guy and I laughed. We looked at the Ghanaian streets and laughed. We listened to the melodious languages and laughed. We looked at each other and laughed out loud" (890). If all of Angelou's autobiographical volumes depict her search for identity, then *All God's Children* is different because "here she looks physically like almost everyone else" (Saunders 12). Angelou likens the "adoration" she at first feels for the country to the way a "young girl falls in love . . . ; heaven and Africa were inextricably combined" (902). But soon they notice that the Ghanaians, on the other hand, pay no attention to the entranced newcomers and do not even seem to see them (903). With an image of futile activity, she says that the black Americans "buzzed moth-like on the periphery of acceptance . . ." (905). This shock causes her to examine "whether in looking for a home I, and all the émigrés, were running from a bitter truth that rode lightly but forever at home on our shoulders" (914).

As her stay lengthens and she is forced to find work at the university as a secretary and begins to know Ghana from the inside, Angelou grows impatient with the Americans seeking their roots. One visitor has come with his wife (they remain unnamed in Angelou's text, leading the reader to expect that their depiction will not be favorable). The man says that they have "'come to Mother Africa to suckle from her breasts,'" and Angelou retorts: "Africa doesn't need anybody as big as you pulling on her tits" (917). Who would tell them "that they had not come home, but had left one familiar place of painful memory for another strange place with none"? (918).

She has her hair done in the Ghanaian style and is "relieved that I looked like every other Ghanaian woman" (916). Yet she also recognizes that there are African customs that she does not want to accept and adjust to, customs that would deny her personhood and identity, not enhance them. A case in point is the businessman from Mali, Sheikhali, who repeatedly asks her to marry him: "'You will be my second wife. . . . If I need more children I will take a young girl because you and my wife will have no more babies. . . . Our families will marry'" (942). He was "exotic, generous and physically satisfying," Angelou comments, "but we had trouble translating ourselves to each other." She then adds an understatement about women's roles: "My upbringing had not fitted me for even a pretended reticence" (941).

Angelou's changing sense of belonging is repeatedly expressed in the image of "home"—what home means, whether it can change, whether we come to a deeper and deeper understanding of it, too, as we grow in experience and maybe even wisdom. She brings these questions out in relation to an event to which she is invited, with President Tubman of Liberia as the honored guest. She is asked to sing, and she complies with some of the spirituals. The Africans join in on "Swing Low, Sweet Chariot." Angelou "knew . . . that not one of them was fired with religious zeal, so for what chariot were they calling and what home could they possibly miss?" (1,031). The Africans "were earnest and their voices were in tune, but they could not duplicate the haunting melody of our singing. . . . In the absence of my creative ancestors who picked that melody out of cotton sacks, I humbly bowed my head" (1,032).

As Angelou separates her aspirations and sense of history from those of her African friends and co-workers and acquaintances, she is able to appreciate African culture, warts and all. She attends an "outdooring," the "first African rite of passage" eight days after birth (921–928), and a "durbar," or "thanksgiving feast," outside Accra. She takes leave of the other Americans to travel on her own to the west coast of Ghana, including to the infamous Cape Coast Castle—"holding forts for captured slaves," the part of the country's history that connected with her own history. She says it honestly and powerfully: "History had invaded my little car. Pangs of self-pity and a sorrow for my unknown relatives suffused me" (963). In the little village of Keta, she is mistaken for a member of the community, and a woman, in her gestures, suggests Angelou's grandmother Henderson back in Arkansas. "For the first time since my arrival, I was very nearly home. Not a Ghanaian, but at least accepted as an African. . . . I felt the distance narrow between my past and present" (967). But Angelou knows that it is a transient home: "I had proved that one of their descendants, at least one, could just briefly return to Africa, and that despite cruel betrayals, bitter ocean voyages and hurtful centuries, we were still recognizable" (969). As Joanne Braxton says, "for Angelou, Africa and the welcome table, will forever be within" (94).

Back in Accra, she senses that "Ghana was beginning to tug at me and make me uncomfortable, like an ill-fitting coat. . . . I had to admit that I had begun to feel that I was not in my right place" (1,003). Malcolm X visits Ghana after his transforming visit to Mecca and counsels her following the death of the revered W.E.B.

Du Bois and Angelou's criticism of the man's widow, Shirley Graham: "'We need people on each level to fight our battle. Don't be in such a hurry to condemn a person because he doesn't do what you do, or think as you think or as fast. There was a time when you didn't know what you know today'" (1,001). His presence "elevated us," Angelou reports, "but with his departure, we were what we had been before: a little group of Black folks, looking for a home" (1,002).

Even more crucial to Angelou's decision to return to the United States is the new and full independence of her son, Guy. The dividing into separate entities for the two of them reaches its climax after she confronts the nineteen-year-old about dating a woman a year older than Angelou herself. He "had the nerve," Angelou writes, to express his annoyance—"'Oh, Mother, really. Don't you think it's time I had a life of my own?'" (1,005). At this stage, she cannot see how his life could be separate from hers, for "his existence had defined my own" (1,005). Then she mentally reviews their lives, her teaching him, defending him, many of the events that are narrated in the previous autobiographies. She feels some guilt over the fact that he had gone to nineteen schools in eleven years, but when she had been told by a school psychologist that her son needed the security of "stability," Angelou had responded: "I am his security. Wherever we go, we go together. Wherever he is he knows that that six-foot-tall Black woman is not too far away. What I don't furnish in stability, I make up in love" (1,006). But now Guy had "moved beyond" her reach "into the arms of a cradle robber." Angelou notes, "I needed to get away from him and myself and the situation" (1,007).

A surprise invitation to tour Europe with a production of Genet's *The Blacks,* in which she had acted in New York City, fortunately gets her to Berlin and Venice and gives her new perspective. Back in Ghana again, she is still in her traveling clothes when Guy announces "'You have finished mothering a child. You did a very good job. Now, I am a man. Your life is your own, and mine belongs to me" (1,033). There is nothing to do but accept and take joy from what has been and from what has changed. Her leaving of Guy and leaving of Africa come together and she makes a decision as a newly independent mother.

> If the heart of Africa still remained elusive, my search for it had brought me closer to understanding myself and other human beings. The ache for home lives in all of us, the safe place where we can go as we are and not be questioned. . . . My mind was made up. I would go back to the United States as soon as possible" (1,041–42).

All God's Children Need Traveling Shoes concludes with the narrator's leave taking, full in the knowledge that

> my people had never completely left Africa. We had sung it in our blues, shouted it in our gospel and danced the continent in our breakdowns. As we carried it to Philadelphia, Boston and Birmingham, we had changed its color, modified its rhythms, yet it was Africa which rode in the bulges of our high calves, shook in our protruding behinds and crackled in our wide open laughter.

> I could nearly hear the old ones chuckling (1,051).

Maya Angelou, looking back on her life, sees the search for home as a central theme. First, she feels that sense common to black Americans that Africa represents "home" in some profound way that is part of the struggle for identity. And then, over time, she realizes that home and the longing for it is something we all carry with us always as human beings, even after other memory has gone. Caretakers and researchers of Alzheimer's patients, for example, often find the disoriented men and women heading out to "go home," even though they cannot articulate what or where "home" is. The one thing that is sure: Home is a yearning we share as human beings.

WORKS CITED

Angelou, Maya. *All God's Children Need Traveling Shoes. The Collected Autobiographies of Maya Angelou.* New York: The Modern Library, 2004. 881–1,051.

Braxton, Joanne. "Angelou's Multivolume Autobiography Is 'a Poetic Adventure.'" In *Readings on Maya Angelou.* Ed. Mary E. Williams. San Diego, CA: Greenhaven Press. 87–94.

Hagen, Lyman B. *Heart of a Woman, Mind of a Writer, and Soul of a Poet: A Critical Analysis of the Writings of Maya Angelou.* Lanham, MD: University Press of America, 1997.

Saunders, James Robert. "Breaking Out of the Cage: The Autobiographical Writings of Maya Angelou." In *Bloom's Modern Critical Views: Maya Angelou—New Edition.* Ed. Harold Bloom. New York: Chelsea House Publishers, 2009. 3–15.

HOW TO WRITE ABOUT MAYA ANGELOU

MAYA ANGELOU was born as Marguerite Ann Johnson in St. Louis, Missouri, on April 4, 1928. Given the name "Maya" by her brother, Bailey, she later added the modified version of the name of her first husband, Tosh Angelos. Angelou is a hardworking, accomplished author of autobiography, poetry, essay, and children's books. Though she did not attend college, she now has many honorary doctoral degrees and has held many distinguished visiting professor positions at major universities. Additionally, she is a popular and effective speaker, singer, actress, and television and movie personality.

As a writer, Angelou is best known for her six autobiographies, especially the first, *I Know Why the Caged Bird Sings* (1970). The six, with the last one published in 2002, are a series of books that cover her eventful life consecutively from a few years after her birth to 1968. (One can also consider Angelou's delightful *Hallelujah! The Welcome Table: A Lifetime of Memories with Recipes* [2004] an autobiography. Here she intersperses life stories, some of which appear in the six serial autobiographies and some not, with recipes and photographs from her very social home and heart, such as the chapters "Assurance of Caramel Cake" and "Potato Salad Towers over Difficulties.") Understandably, the years covered by these books are marked by crucial events in American and world history, from thoroughgoing segregation in the American South through World War II and its aftermath into the civil rights, Black Power, Black Is Beautiful, and Black Muslim movements, culminating in the assassination of Martin Luther King Jr., an event that occurred on Angelou's fortieth birthday, just as she was planning to work for the second time in King's organization, the Southern Christian Leadership Conference (SCLC). By bringing an experiential perspective to these periods, Angelou's books give us unique insights into them from the point of view of a struggling but determined, talented black woman.

Angelou's writing and publishing production is vast beyond these six or seven autobiographies, amazing in part because she says, now in her eighties, that she does not habitually write on her computer in her spacious redbrick colonial home in Winston-Salem, North Carolina, where she has been, since 1981, Reynolds Professor of American Studies at Wake Forest University. Instead, she rents a hotel room, where she has a thesaurus, a Bible, a dictionary, a pack of cards, and yellow legal pads on which she composes with a pen. Her collections of short essays include *Wouldn't Take Nothing for My Journey Now* (1993) and *Even the Stars Look Lonesome* (1997); her children's books include *Life Doesn't Frighten Me* (1993), *My Painted House, My Friendly Chicken, and Me* (1994), *Kofi and His Magic* (1996), and four volumes of *Maya's World* (2004) on children in Lapland, Italy, France, and Hawaii. She has also written plays, screenplays, and short stories and has done many recordings and spoken word albums.

Many people are introduced to Angelou through her poetry, which is accessible and which she performs dramatically. She has published six collections between *Just Give Me a Cool Drink of Water 'Fore I Diiie* (1971), which was nominated for a Pulitzer Prize, and *I Shall Not Be Moved* (1990), with a volume of her collected poems issued in 1994. Most people are aware of Angelou as the author and performer of "On the Pulse of Morning," written and read at the request of the forty-second president of the United States, William Jefferson Clinton, at his inauguration on January 20, 1993. After that event, Angelou became a popular presenter of poems for special occasions, including "A Brave and Startling Truth" at the fiftieth anniversary of the United Nations on June 26, 1995; "From a Black Woman to a Black Man" at the Million Man March on October 16, 1995; and "Amazing Peace" at the National Christmas Tree Ceremony at the White House on December 1, 2005.

In the following chapters, we will look separately at issues related to Angelou's autobiographical writing, her poetry, her essays, her children's books, and her performance work in television and movies. The chances are that a student working on a paper on Angelou would be introduced to and/or attracted to one or another of these modes of her writing, but there are some overriding topics that might be considered as well. First of all, her work in all its range of genre, or form, represents one person's attempt to translate her experience and thought into creations accessible to a wide range of audiences—black and white, young and old, male and female, schooled and unschooled, American and international. Questions arising from this sense of audience include: Does this attempt to appeal to so many people dilute her writing or enhance it? Does awareness of a particular audience show up in her various works? Has she left anyone out? Literary critics have not exactly ignored her, but she is generally considered by academics to be more a popular than a literary writer. (See, for example, Harold Bloom's "Editor's Note" in *Maya Angelou*, Bloom's Modern Critical Views, Chelsea House Publishers: New York, 2009, p. vii, in which he says that "formal analysis" is not for the most part "relevant" to Angelou's work, but the authors of the essays in his book "do explore most of the contours of their author as a benign contribution to our era's espousal of societal equality." In the introduction to the same collection, Bloom is even more direct: "Her poetry has a large public, but very little critical esteem. It is, in every sense, 'popular poetry,' and makes no formal or cognitive demands upon the reader" [1–2].) Does being popular automatically exclude a writer from the literary canon, that group of authors and works highly regarded by critics and often taught in university literature courses? Does being living or dead make a difference? Does writing in several forms tend to exclude an author? Does writing to include a white audience exclude a black audience for a black writer, or writing to include a male audience tend to exclude some portion of the female audience for a woman writer?

When we turn to Angelou's autobiographical works, other questions occur. First of all, the whole category of writing and publishing in the form referred to as a memoir or autobiography has changed over the years since Angelou published *I Know Why the Caged Bird Sings* in 1970, some of that change due to her own work. Personal narratives of all kinds now receive considerable critical attention in courses on "life writing," in books and journals and literary conferences, on the Internet in blogs, and elsewhere, and publishers are known to push writers into changing what is written as a novel into a memoir, since the latter is more marketable. Jay Neugeboren says it well in a review of Michael Greenberg's *Beg, Borrow, Steal: A Writer's Life* (Other Press, 2009): "Greenberg writes about what has become a minor literary plague—writers inventing tales they purvey as memoirs—and directs our attention to issues beyond deceit and plagiarism, to concerns, literary and ethical, that arise whenever we write about people we know" (66). Introducing his collection of essays titled *The Ethics of Life Writing,* Paul John Eakin says we live in an age of "personal exposure" and "a pervasive culture of confession." Naturally some of the questions that arise now about Angelou's serial autobiographies come out of this later deep and wide critical examination of autobiography in its broader context. How does she depict family members—her mother, her brother, her grandmother, her father, her husbands? Is there progression in their treatment throughout the books, and why do some of them disappear from the narrative for a time? In her depiction of the famous, does Angelou strike a balance between what is known historically or publicly about a person and her personal relationship with him or her? Is she too open about her sexual encounters, including her rape at age eight, her pregnancy and childbirth at age sixteen, her liaisons and marriages?

Mary Jane Lupton, introducing "The Life and Works of Maya Angelou" in her *Maya Angelou: A Critical Companion,* says that Angelou's writing "transcends the autobiographical tradition, enriching it with contemporary experience and female sensibility" (1). Female autobiography, and especially black female autobiography, has become increasingly important in black literary history. The autobiographical form has always been very strong in black history and writing, dating back to slave days in the mid-nineteenth century, when slave narratives told the dramatic stories of bondage, escape, freedom, often in "as told to" narratives by illiterate slaves and recorded by white abolitionists. Some have thought, with considerable support, that the great preponderance of male slave narratives over female is because so many more men than women were able to escape, the women being unwilling to leave their children or risk their lives in consideration of their children. In the female stories that exist, such as Harriet Jacobs's *Incidents in the Life of a Slave Girl,* it is instructive to compare and contrast a young woman's experience with that of a male, such as in the well-known well-written *Narrative of the Life of Frederick Douglass*. Such considerations lead to questions that occur in relation to Angelou's writing; for example, she is direct about the influence of black poets on her life and her work, such as her adopting a line from Paul Laurence Dunbar's "Sympathy" as the title *I Know Why the Caged Bird Sings*. Is there also evidence of influence of other earlier black writing, such as the slave narratives? Does Angelou's work in a sense follow the sequence of the slave narrative—bondage, escape, freedom? In what ways does Angelou distinguish the female from the male experience? Does she overdo it?

TOPICS AND STRATEGIES
Themes

Maya Angelou's life has spanned some significant events—the early 1930s Great Depression, which deeply affected segregated black communities in the rural South; World War II and the surge in the home-front employment of women (Angelou broke two barriers at the time, by becoming San Francisco's first and only black female streetcar conductor); the civil rights and African liberation movements in the 1960s; violence and protest, including the assassination of Malcolm X; the March on Washington; the death of W.E.B. Du Bois in Ghana, where Angelou lived at the time; and the assassination of Martin Luther King Jr. By giving us a black female perspective on these events, Angelou's story and creations become representative of changes in the larger culture.

At the same time, we find in her work a very personal, private story of early trauma, young pregnancy and childbirth, single motherhood, and continuous attempts to juggle work and child care before discussion of this "woman's problem" was commonplace in the larger culture. African American women have long worked outside the home in larger percentages than white women, often in the kinds of jobs, such as cooking, Angelou takes on. Amazingly, reading about her long struggle to eventually make a living with her singing and dancing does not drag the reader down but entertains, lends insight, and inspires. Much like Angelou's own positive demeanor and presentations, her writing reflects a great deal of struggle but also a great deal of strength, much of it learned from her Grandmother Henderson, or "Momma," in Stamps, Arkansas, and her mother, Vivian Baxter, mostly in San Francisco. Most readers of Maya Angelou will have a strong feeling about particular pieces of her writing; assessing and analyzing those reactions will be a good way to start with a writing topic or assignment. If you pick something that resonates with you, and then step back and ask how Angelou has achieved this sympathy, you will have a start on defining a topic. The following sample topic suggestions are intended not to give you a final topic but to get you going in some directions you might not have thought of or known much about.

Sample Topics:

1. **The search for self:** By covering the formative years of her life in such honest and thoroughgoing detail, Angelou gives us not only a story of struggle and survival and success but an example of how one can work through difficulties and come out a better, stronger person. Through searching for an understanding of who she is and where she is going, a writer, a user of words to convey experience, can find some of the answer. Black when the standard of feminine beauty was white, even in the black community, which was still wont to place people in a hierarchy according to the lightness of their skin; tall when the notion of feminine beauty was small and delicate; a mother when she was barely more than a child herself; a talented and enthusiastic dancer, singer, and actress when such women were often used and abused by ambitious men, Angelou nevertheless kept going and searching to become herself.

2. **The search for home:** Ira Berlin has published a book that attempts to change the African American story from one emphasizing slavery to freedom to the story of an uprooted people's search for a home. Berlin studies four great migration movements—the Middle Passage, or transportation of slaves from Africa to the Americas; the movement of slaves from coastal regions to the isolated plantations of the American South; the great surge of movement from the rural South to the urban North during the second decade of the twentieth century; and the current influx of Africans into the United States. A sense

of uprootedness and the search for home permeate Angelou's work, especially her autobiographies. The young child in *I Know Why the Caged Bird Sings* has been sent far away, alone with her slightly older brother, by their parents. The rest of her journey in this book, until age 16 and the birth of her son, Clyde (or Guy), is a search for a place of belonging and security. In the fifth book in the serial autobiography, *All God's Children Need Traveling Shoes*, the search for home is played out in an international setting from beginning to end, from America "back to Africa" and back to America. The work opens with the words of a spiritual, "Swing low, sweet chariot, coming for to carry me home." Is this a universal theme Angelou is attempting to articulate? Does Angelou add a unique perspective to it?

3. **The search for artistic expression:** Angelou's multiplicity of writing forms, in addition to her acting, directing, singing and performing, suggests a talented woman who has much to say and is looking for ways to convey her message to a wide audience. She is not exactly experimental in her prose or poetry, but she is searching and venturesome. A case in point is the autobiographical cookbook, *The Welcome Table*, a kind of ultimate coming home to finding comfort and fellowship, suggestive of the hard-won lifetime appointment she holds at Wake Forest and her secure sense of identity as a woman in her eighties. Angelou's descriptions of the Harlem Writer's Club and its meetings are fascinating to a writer or a student of African American history and literature. Why is everyone so fearful about reading before the group? Does the group help Angelou break into writing and publishing? Do you recognize, or can you find out about, some of the other writers she mentions from this group?

Characters

Sample Topics:

1. **Mother models:** Angelou's mother and grandmother thread their ways through most of the autobiographies, setting a background of modeling and questioning for Angelou's own mothering of her son. The relationship with her mother is particularly

long and difficult in its development, beginning with essentially the mother's abandonment of the child Marguerite at a young age. Vivian Baxter was "too beautiful to have children," Angelou thought as a girl. Grandma Henderson in Stamps as a model is another frustration to the young child, both inspiring and disturbing, especially in her ability to withstand and take victory from tolerating the scorn and disrespect of "poor white" children, while Angelou rages inside, wanting and dreaming of narratives where Momma not only stands up but fights back. It is, of course, in her own mothering that Angelou finds both humility and growth, culminating in book five, *All God's Children Need Traveling Shoes*, when her son declares his independence of her. Are models important in human growth? What are the most difficult things about mothering presented in the books, and what keeps recurring? Are any of these problems you or someone you know has also run into? Have things gotten easier for women who raise children as single mothers and have to work for their income?

2. **Black men and history:** It is clear that Angelou recognizes the nation's slave history as marking the origin of many of the challenges faced by the black men in her Million Man March poem, recited at the event in Washington, D.C., in 1995. "Under a dead blue sky on a distant beach, / I was dragged by my braids just beyond your reach. / Your hands were tied, your mouth was bound / . . . You were helpless and so was I. . . ." The second stanza goes on to assert that black men are the ones who have borne the heaviest "badge of shame" of enslavement. What other examples in Angelou's writing do you find that suggest that she has this difficult history of the American black man in mind?

3. **Black men as brothers, fathers, uncles:** Angelou depicts the difficulties faced by many black males through some of the men who entered her life. Her brother, Bailey, is closest to her, especially in the first of her serial autobiographies, when he is the slightly older big brother who protects her, serves as her confidant, and impresses her with his attractive demeanor and intelligence. But Bailey as an adult ends up in prison, at least for a time, and he pretty much disappears from the later books, apparently

according to his wishes. How does Bailey's role change in the six books? Next we have Angelou's father, also Bailey Johnson, a man of impeccable manners and language but reliant, the writer suggests, much too much on charm as a means to his ends. He takes Angelou as a fourteen-year-old to his haunts in Mexico, gets drunk, and has to be driven out of danger by this girl who has never before driven a car. Bailey senior also disappears from the series, and, by the time her mother, Vivian Baxter, has been rehabilitated in Angelou's mind and actions, her father is gone. Does Angelou seem to model her life as a single mother supporting a child on what she does not want to be, that is, like her father? A third family member to whom Angelou relates is her Uncle Willie in Stamps. Does the physically disabled Willie represent the black man made helpless by women's confidence and economic power, especially since he still lives with his mother, Angelou's grandmother, Annie Henderson? In *Caged Bird*, only in one incident does Angelou mention Willie's attempting to hide his disability, and that is when white men come in the store. In her poem called "Willie," Angelou piles up words and phrases such as *without fame, crippled, limping, pain, solitude,* and *emptiness* (*The Complete . . .* 150–51). Where does Willie find refuge in the poem and in the autobiographies?

4. **Black men as sons:** Many other black males appear in Angelou's works, many who try to use her and many who try to win her affections. The only one who gains prominence as he gains in stature and years is her son, Guy. In *All God's Children Need Traveling Shoes,* he sends his mother from Ghana back to the United States by reassuring and suggesting to her: You are a good mother, you did a good job, your job is done now, I am a grown man, and I must have my own life. The only thing that can compensate for the sense of loss felt by a mother at this stage is seeing the child become strong, independent, and happy. That Angelou has seen. Do you see the presence of her growing son as a changing reality that ties her life and her autobiographical books together?

5. **Artists, writers, and performers:** Angelou has longstanding friendships and working relationships with a variety of perform-

ers, from the scrabbling nightclub hoofers in 1950s California to productions of *Porgy and Bess* and *The Blacks* in New York City and on tour in Europe to ancient Greek theater produced in Ghana, Africa. She also comes to know many writers and is especially close to James Baldwin and his family. Most interesting is where performing for art becomes mixed with performing for a cause, such as Cabaret for Freedom, which Angelou helps write and perform to raise money for Martin Luther King Jr.'s Southern Christian Leadership Conference. Where does art leave off and propaganda begin? Can a writer only do his or her best work alone with that blank sheet of paper, or should the well-known writer with an audience speak and march for the cause? Much as James Baldwin struggled with these questions during the civil rights movement of the 1960s, so did Angelou, seeming to conclude, especially after the deaths of first Malcolm X and then Martin Luther King Jr. just before she was set to work for each of them, that her right work and true contribution was found in her writing. W.E.B. Du Bois, whom Angelou knew in his final years in Ghana, once said that the best art is the best propaganda. Does Angelou seem to agree?

History and Context

The time period that Angelou covers in her six autobiographies is both tragic in events and exciting with new possibilities in American life. A writer discussing and analyzing any of her work might well look at historical documents and materials as relevant background to her writing and thinking, whether her treatment of the events is direct or indirect. An example of a useful and convenient collection of such materials is in the book by Joanne Megna-Wallace called *Understanding* I Know Why the Caged Bird Sings: *A Student Casebook to Issues, Sources, and Historical Documents*. Part of the Greenwood Press Literature in Context series, this book groups articles and documents under seven topical headings: "Violence and Intimidation as a Means of Social Control: A Historical Overview of Race Relations in the South," "Segregated Schools: An Institutional Method of Social Control," "The African American Church," "The African American Family and Other Role Models," "Child Sexual Abuse," and "Censorship." Much of this material would be useful to an essay on other Angelou writings as well as to *Caged Bird*.

An interesting and useful way to get a feel for the times about which Angelou is writing is to look at news or other magazine articles of the period—look at what is on the covers and would be seen by someone passing a newsstand; look at the ads and see what images they convey of women and of minority groups; access publications designed for a black audience, such as *Ebony,* and compare and contrast what you find there with those periodicals, such as *Life,* aimed primarily at white audiences of the time. Finally, we will frequently make use in this volume of a recent reference publication, the five volumes of the *Encyclopedia of African American History: 1896 to the Present* (Oxford: New York 2009). The thorough index for this set is in volume V (273–517); there, you will also find a helpful "Thematic Outline of Entries" (229–43) and a chronology of events by year from 1896 to 2009. Additionally, each entry is followed by an annotated list of further works to consult, a helpful feature whether you are looking for material about blacks in the Great Depression in the Deep South or about one of the authors or show business people Angelou comes to know.

Sample Topics:

1. **Civil rights and change:** Much occurred historically during the time Angelou writes of, nationally and legally, but also personally and intimately, in racial equality. Ongoing questions might include, how do those things go together in her work—that is the national events and the personal life? Do Angelou's actions and creations have a role in positive changes? Do you see a kind of trajectory of events and attitudes that would lead eventually to the election of the nation's first black president in 2008?

2. **Violence and change:** Do lynchings, assassinations, and riots make positive change more or less likely? In what ways are these things setbacks, and in what ways are they spurs to improve existing conditions? Do you see both kinds of violence in Angelou's writing?

3. **African American literature and art and change:** A useful book as background to this topic is Stacy I. Morgan's *Rethinking Social Realism: African American Art and Literature 1930–1953.* What are the roles of authors, artists, and performers in creating or inspiring change? Is this a primary Angelou concern? Does the material in the case of written work have to be contemporaneous,

or can things written long ago and far away have an enduring impact? Since Angelou speaks of Shakespeare as her "first love" and of many other classic white writers, what is the role of black art particularly in reaching a black audience? A white audience?

Philosophy and Ideas

Many topic suggestions will be discussed in the following chapters in relation to specific Angelou books and collections, but here we will indicate just three that would be relevant in dealing with any of her works. For someone who has the time to read all of the work, particularly the autobiographies, it would be especially interesting to trace and follow one of these topics through each of the books.

Sample Topics:

1. **Militancy ("by any means necessary") and nonviolent civil disobedience:** These usually conflicting ideas of how to create positive change are especially relevant in books three to five of the autobiographies, when Angelou and her readers are introduced to Malcolm X and Martin Luther King Jr. But the difference in tactics precedes this period and continues today, so it can be useful to trace it in its more subtle expressions as well. Does Angelou lean toward one or the other of these tactics? Does she change her mind about them? Is the former often the stance of the young, the latter of the older person?

2. **Feminism:** Many questions have been raised about Angelou's commitment to feminism, particularly in its more militant forms. She herself has come to use the word *womanist* instead of *feminist* to describe herself. What are the elements of her beliefs about women and men? Even if she does not express verbal support for the women's movement, do her actions exemplify someone who assumes equality between the sexes? To what extent is her attitude toward lesbianism a part of her attitude toward feminism? Does this attitude change?

3. **Christianity:** While direct depictions of the church and its teachings appear mostly in the first and third autobiographies, the indirect reflection of some key principles of Christianity, such as altruism, nonviolence, and "turning the other cheek," seem to reappear with some regularity and with consider-

able questioning by Angelou. How do you see the phases she goes through? Are the teachings of the church in her early life reflected in her later writings?

Bibliography and Online Resources

Angelou, Maya. *The Collected Autobiographies of Maya Angelou.* New York: Modern Library, 2004. Includes the full texts of the six autobiographies.

———. *The Complete Collected Poems of Maya Angelou.* New York: Random House, 1994. Thirty-eight poems from *Just Give Me a Cool Drink of Water 'Fore I Diiie,* 36 from *O Pray My Wings Are Gonna Fit Me Well,* 32 from *And Still I Rise,* 28 from *Shaker, Why Don't You Sing,* 32 from *I Shall Not Be Moved,* and "On the Pulse of Morning" from the Clinton inauguration.

———. *Hallelujah! The Welcome Table: A Lifetime of Memories with Recipes.* New York: Random House, 2004.

Baisnée, Valérie. *Gendered Resistance: The Autobiographies of Simone de Beauvoir, Maya Angelou, Janet Frame, and Marguerite Duras.* Amsterdam and Atlanta: Rodopi, 1997.

Berlin, Ira. *The Making of America: Four Great Migrations.* New York: Viking, 2010.

Braxton, Joanne. "Maya Angelou." In *Modern American Women Writers.* Ed. Elaine Showalter, Lea Baechler, and A. Walton Litz. New York: Collier, 1993. 1–7.

Burr, Zofia. "Maya Angelou on the Inaugural Stage." In *Of Women, Poetry, and Power: Strategies of Address in Dickinson, Miles, Brooks, Lorde, and Angelou.* Urbana: University of Illinois Press, 2002. 180–194.

Douglass, Frederick. *Narrative of the Life of Frederick Douglass.* Boston, New York: Bedford/St. Martins, 2002.

Eakin, Paul John. *The Ethics of Life Writing.* Ithaca, NY: Cornell University Press, 2004.

Elliot, Jeffrey M., ed. *Conversations with Maya Angelou.* Jackson: University Press of Mississippi, 1989.

Finkelman, Paul et al., eds. *Encyclopedia of African American History, 1896 to the Present.* Volumes I–V. New York: Oxford University Press, 2009.

Jacobs, Harriet. *Incidents in the Life of a Slave Girl.* Boston, New York: Bedford/St. Martins, 2009.

Landrum, Gene N. "Maya Angelou—Assertive; Author, Actress, Educator." In *Profiles of Black Success: Thirteen Creative Geniuses Who Changed the World,* Amherst, NY: Prometheus, 1997. 109–125.

Lupton, Mary Jane. *Maya Angelou: A Critical Companion*. Westport, CT: Greenwood Press, 1998.

www.Mayaangelou.com Angelou's official Web site. Here you can find her latest work, news articles about her, photographs and short videos and can purchase options for her books.

Megna-Wallace, Joanne. *Understanding* I Know Why the Caged Bird Sings: *A Student Casebook to Issues, Sources, and Historical Documents*. Westport, CT and London: Greenwood Press, 1998.

Morgan, Stacy I. *Rethinking Social Realism: African American Art and Literature 1930–1953*. Athens: University of Georgia Press, 2004.

Neugeboren, Jay. "Dark Comedies of the City." Rev. of *Beg, Borrow, Steal: A Writer's Life* by Michael Greenberg. *New York Review of Books* December 17, 2009: 66–68.

I KNOW WHY THE
CAGED BIRD SINGS

READING TO WRITE

MAYA ANGELOU'S six autobiographies or as some have called them, autobiographical novels, cover the years 1931 to 1969, with the first of the books, *I Know Why the Caged Bird Sings* (published in 1971) covering 1931 to 1944. At the beginning of the book, the young Marguerite Johnson, as Angelou was then called, is three years old and by the end she has turned sixteen and become a mother herself. In between, she moves from California to rural Arkansas to St. Louis, back to Stamps, Arkansas, and then again to California. Conceptually, at the center of the book is the trauma of her rape at age eight by her mother's boyfriend in St. Louis, with a subsequent court trial and then murder of the rapist by Marguerite's uncles. The tracing of the maturing of a young person is often called by a German term, a *bildungsroman,* or a story of education. In addition, a narrative that follows the main character from place to place in a series of episodes is referred to as picaresque. *Caged Bird,* in the time and locations of its settings, calls up many questions that might serve as the beginning of an essay topic. What exactly does she learn over these first sixteen years of her life? What are the differences between the South, North, and West and the rural and urban settings? How does history play a role in the book—the Great Depression of the 1930s and the beginnings of World War II in the 1940s? Are there other instances of violence in the book besides the rape and murder? Are any of these things different because the author, or protagonist, is black? Female?

A strong essay begins with a good, careful reading of the text being studied and written about. It is always helpful to read a narrative at least twice, the first time becoming acquainted with the characters, the order of events, and the beginning, middle, and end and the second time repeatedly asking, "Why does the author do or say this?" and "How does the author manage to convey this?" As you read, particularly the second time, jot down notes of things you notice, and if the book belongs to you, mark passages with comments, summary subjects, or question marks. If you have a strong reaction, positive or negative, to any part, or if any part reminds you of something else you have read, take note of that, too, for the best essays often come out of the writer's reactions to the text under consideration.

We gain impressions of a book immediately from its title. What does this title lead you to expect? Why would a caged bird sing? What are some of the possible cages that might entrap a young black girl growing up in the American South of the difficult 1930s? In this case, the title is an allusion or a reference to a prominent poem in black American literature. Already with the title, Angelou sets up the work to convey two equally balanced moods, entrapment and singing, by adopting a repeated line of Paul Laurence Dunbar's poem "Sympathy." The poem begins with "I know what the caged bird feels, alas!" and continues in the second stanza with "I know why the caged bird beats his wing / Till its blood is red on the cruel bars." Then the final stanza brings it together:

> I know why the caged bird sings, ah me,
> When his wing is bruised and his bosom sore,—
> . . . .
> It is not a carol of joy or glee,
> But a prayer that he sends from his heart's deep core,
> But a plea, that upward to Heaven he flings—
> I know why the caged bird sings!

A reader not knowing the poem will anticipate in Angelou's book contrasting moods of pain and joy, but a reader familiar with the Dunbar poem will go somewhat beyond that to see that the singing is more a survival tactic, a prayer, a plea (for understanding or sympathy?), than it is a song of happiness. Angelou dedicated this book to "My Son, GUY JOHNSON, and all the Strong Black Birds of Promise Who Defy the

Odds and Gods and Sing Their Songs," adding to the feeling of survival a note of defiance.

The text opens with a prologue, a preface or introduction to the body of the work. Angelou will use prologues again in the next book in the series of autobiographies, *Gather Together in My Name*, and in the later *Heart of a Woman*. Here, in the first book, the prologue is short, two pages, and, with its repeated partial Easter poem, which the child Marguerite cannot manage to complete in front of the Colored Methodist Episcopal Church congregation in Stamps, sets up a wistful tone: "What you looking at me for? / I didn't come to stay. . . ." Interspersed with the repetition of this fragment, Angelou conveys the sense of entrapment in her dark, lanky, skinny frame in a made-over dress, or as she writes: "a too-big Negro girl, with nappy black hair, broad feet and a space between her teeth that would hold a number-two pencil" (Angelou, *I Know Why the Caged Bird Sings*, 7. Subsequent references to this book will be indicated by page number only). We right away get a sense that this child lives in a dream world, as most children do, for while her grandmother, or Momma, was making it, the dress "had made me go around with angel's dust sprinkled over my face." But the dream world she lives in is sadly based on rejection of her own race: "because I was really white," with blond hair and blue eyes, and "a cruel fairy stepmother, who was understandably jealous of my beauty," had, Maya believes, turned her into the stumbling, forgetful, awkward child who stood before the congregation. Then the experience reciting and forgetting parts of the poem in front of the church breaks the shining bubble of her dream. For the wonderful dress, in the bright sunlight of Easter morning, is revealed to be "a plain ugly cut-down from a white woman's once-was-purple throwaway" (8).

The prologue re-creates the child's humiliation (she not only could not complete the poem without help but also could not get to the bathroom in time to prevent "the sting . . . burning down my legs and into my Sunday socks" [9]). By also re-creating the child's dream world, it sets up the reader with an understanding of the meaning of the title. Not only do we expect the "singing" to be for survival, we expect to experience the bars of the cage. In case we have not caught the indirect conveying of this theme for the book, Angelou states it explicitly, making clear that her book will be about not just the black experience but the black female experience. The prologue ends, "If growing up is painful for the Southern

Black girl, being aware of her displacement is the rust on the razor that threatens the throat. It is an unnecessary insult" (9).

Before exploring possible topics for papers related to *Caged Bird*, it is good to recognize that this book, more than any other Angelou work, has had an enormous amount of critical commentary written about it. Many of these articles or book chapters have been collected into single volumes, such as Greenhaven Press's Angelou-themed entry in its series Literary Companions to American Authors and the several books under the auspices of Harold Bloom and Chelsea House Publishers—*Maya Angelou, New Edition* (part of the series Bloom's Modern Critical Views); *I Know Why the Caged Bird Sings, New Edition* (part of the series Bloom's Modern Critical Interpretations) and *Maya Angelou* (part of the series Bloom's BioCritiques). On one hand, having so much analysis by others collected in these convenient volumes makes writing a paper somewhat easier; on the other hand, it also has its dangers. The primary caution in reading and/or using what others have said is that you do not want to look at these article and essays by someone else before you have carefully read the work itself, twice, and recorded your own thoughts and comments on it. One of the big advantages in writing a paper about a piece of literature is that you have before you what is called a primary source, while the articles by others are secondary sources. This would be rare for something like a history paper, where to use primary sources you would need to spend a great deal of time in archives looking at old documents, including letters, diaries, and office records. So think of yourself as an inquiring reader who is the equal of anyone else analyzing the book—all will bring their own experience and training to the material. Thus if you read someone else's thoughts before you form your own, your unique interaction with the text will be compromised and influenced, for you run the risk of noting only what the other critic has noticed in his or her own assessment. With this precaution in mind, let us look at some questions to get you started on shaping your own reading and thinking into a good paper.

TOPICS AND STRATEGIES
Themes

Themes can be called the "messages," the philosophy or learning experience a text conveys in its entirety, through the combined effect of its plot, characters, setting, language, form, and style. When someone asks us "What is the book about?" we tend to give the plot or the order of events of the book. However, a book is "about" much more than the elements that make up its central storyline, and it is helpful to stop and think about themes for a while after a careful reading, or two readings, of a text. Discovering a theme of the book and then finding the material that leads the reader to that theme can be an effective approach to a writing assignment.

Sample Topics:

1. **Identity:** What do the prologue to *I Know Why the Caged Bird Sings*, its overall structure, and its ending suggest about the struggles of a black female child to develop a positive self-image and a productive place in a segregated society? What roles do other people play in this process, good or bad? Is Marguerite's feeling of uncertainty related to the abandonment by her parents? Does her loneliness and feeling of loss of identity cause her to "lead Mr. Freeman on"? Does her brother, Bailey's, struggle differ from hers? In what ways? Is identity confusion related to developing sexuality as we move toward the end of the book?

2. **Coping:** How does Angelou convey the way a child deals with difficult realities? Is living in an inner and outer world simultaneously one of those ways? Think of a scene like that in chapter 24, with Momma taking Marguerite to a white dentist, and note the two ways the text is printed, in regular type and italics. What part is italicized? How does it differ from the part appearing in regular typeface? Is her silence after the rape a way of coping? Is it a healthy way of coping?

3. **Maturation:** As the book proceeds, Marguerite takes more notice of the outer world, as that world expands for her. As we move physically through the book from the South—Arkansas—to the North—St. Louis—to the West—California—what are the differences in the segregated culture of the time? Does it take motherhood to set Angelou on the start of her path to maturity? What role does her own mother play in this process?

4. **The "march of history":** Why does Angelou spend so much time and space describing the cotton workers and others who frequent her grandmother's store? Are the "poor white" chil-

dren who insult and tease Momma also suffering from the Depression? Does their position during segregation on the social ladder above the blacks make it impossible for the poor to challenge the wealthy? Do difficult economic times make for more altruism and cooperation? For more violence? Do the former, positive reactions tend to take place within one's group in a segregated society and the latter, negative reactions between the more powerful and less powerful groups? What are some of the changes wrought by the advent of World War II after the Great Depression? Would Angelou's being hired as the first black female conductor on San Francisco's streetcars have been possible before the war?

5. **Tolerance:** Can the book as a whole be seen as a plea for sympathy on many levels, for tolerance and understanding, one person to another, family or not family, adult or child, black or white, religious or nonreligious? What role does living with other young homeless people in the junkyard play in the narrator's developing tolerance? Is it a struggle for Angelou to see white people as fully human? To see men as possibly sympathetic rather than out for what they can get? Can you see her attitudes toward whites and toward men as outgrowths of her experiences?

6. **Censorship:** *I Know Why the Caged Bird Sings* has, despite its many awards and appearances on "best books" lists, also appeared on many "most commonly banned" lists, especially for young people. (See, for example, Teri S. Lesesne and Rosemary Chance, *Hit List for Young Adults: Frequently Challenged Books*, Washington, D.C.: American Library Association, 2002, and also the background materials on "Censorship" in the Joanne Megna-Wallace work previously cited, *Understanding* I Know Why the Caged Bird Sings.) What age do you think is appropriate for readers of this book? If the banning is for its honest depiction of the child's molestation by Mr. Freeman and for the unwed motherhood presented at the end, do you think these depictions are framed in a positive way that would negate some of the criticism if the whole book is considered? Do you see a value in Angelou's honesty about these events? As a parent, would you seek to ban the book from a junior high or middle

school library or classroom? From a high school library or classroom? Why or why not?

Character

In the best works of literature, we come to know the characters as well as we know the people around us, maybe better, for we can gauge their motives, actions, and development over time, all guided by the author's selectivity. In an autobiography, the "characters" are real people, and this leads to additional questions about the author's depictions. As one would expect with an autobiography about childhood and young adulthood, the central character is the narrator, Angelou, or Marguerite, as she was then called. Next in importance to a growing child will be family, especially family who live in the same household as the child and serve as caretakers, no matter if they are parents or other close relatives. As the child grows, nonfamily members will come to play a role—teachers, informal and formal, neighbors and friends. In *I Know Why the Caged Bird Sings,* the expected chronological order of introduction of characters from parental care and closeness to others is reversed—Marguerite's parents appear after the brother and grandmother and uncle—and it is not until near the end of the book that our protagonist (as Angelou would be called as the main character, if this were a novel) grows close to her mother. In writing an essay about a character, it may be interesting to ask oneself, "Is this someone I would like for a parent? Grandparent? Sibling? Teacher? Minister? Friend? Why or why not?" These questions will lead us to searching the text to document the passages that have led us to our conclusions, an essential part of any character analysis.

Sample Topics:

1. **Bailey Jr.:** Bailey is four years old, with Marguerite, three, when they are put on a train from California to Arkansas, their tickets pinned inside Bailey's pocket, a label "To Whom it May Concern" on their jackets. Is this the beginning of the strong bond between the siblings? Does Marguerite's dependence on her "big brother" as a refuge from all things strange and frightening become too much reliance as she grows older—too much for Bailey? What are Bailey's struggles as a young black male in the segregated South? (See Richard Wright's autobiographical essay,

"The Ethics of Living Jim Crow" for illustrations of the situations a young man could find himself in.)

2. **Mrs. Annie Henderson, or "Momma"**: Next in importance in the work is the children's paternal grandmother in Arkansas. She and her "Store" (always written with a capital *S*) in the black, segregated section of Stamps are introduced immediately in chapter 1—in fact, the store is introduced first, almost like a character itself, and its customers, especially the cotton pickers, frame the story with their associations of poverty and struggle. How does Momma handle her high position in the black community as the general store owner and operator? How important is religion in her life? In her child rearing? Can you explain her actions of humility and acquiescence that frustrate the young Angelou, for example when Momma is teased by the poor white girls or when she takes Marguerite to a white dentist? Since we all learn from both positive and negative models ("I want to be just like ——" or "I never want to be like ——"), what characteristics of Momma does Angelou adopt as she grows, and what ones does she reject or modify?

3. **Uncle Willie**: How does he compensate for his physical limitations? How is his condition described (Angelou calls him *crippled*, a word no longer considered politically correct or polite)? Is he too tough on his nephew and niece about their school lessons? Do his handicaps mean he is treated better by powerful whites, like the members of the Ku Klux Klan? How do you explain the way he becomes the butt of the jokes of customers at the store and even Bailey Jr. and Marguerite? Only once does the young Marguerite see Uncle Willie pretend to be something he is not—strong, able, and upright—when a strange white couple comes to the store. How does Angelou explain this action? How would you explain it? Does Willie become for the author a kind of extreme example of the struggle for dignity of the black male? Is Uncle Willie, in a sense, the narrator's first lesson in tolerance?

4. **Bailey Johnson Sr.**: The children's father briefly appears on the scene four years after they are sent to Stamps, when they are seven and eight. He takes them to St. Louis, to their mother and her family. Then he appears again in the text near the end, when

Marguerite visits him and his girlfriend in Los Angeles, and he takes his daughter on a wild trip into Mexico. This marks the end of her father's involvement with her and the end of Angelou's inclusion of her father in her autobiographies. What is the young Angelou's impression of him? Since our first impressions are often based on appearance, clothing, and speech, how does he dress, talk, look? What kind of car does he drive, and is this significant? Does Marguerite's impression differ from Bailey Jr.'s? Does Angelou ever see her father sympathetically? Why or why not? Is he another black male trying to cope with Jim Crow segregation? Can she not get past his abandonment of his responsibility to his children?

5. **Vivian Baxter:** "Mother Dear," is what Marguerite and Bailey Jr. call their mother when they are introduced to her rather formally by their "nearly-white" German Grandmother Baxter in St. Louis. Mother Dear is spectacular—like a hurricane or a waterfall—and her daughter feels she now knows why their mother abandoned them—Vivian Baxter was "too beautiful to have children" (50). By the end of the book, we are back with Mother Dear in San Francisco, and with Angelou's pregnancy and childbirth, we have the beginnings of the strong relationship between daughter and mother that will come to the fore in the following autobiographies. How does Vivian Baxter react to the rape of her daughter? Later to her pregnancy? Does Vivian's character change when she gets away from her parents and brothers in St. Louis?

6. **Mrs. Flowers and Louise Kendricks:** How important is the friendship of the beautiful and cultured Mrs. Flowers to Marguerite after her rape and return to Stamps? How do these interactions bring the girl out of her silence? What means does Mrs. Flowers use? Why is the friendship of Louise Kendricks, who comes upon Angelou communing with nature at a church picnic, important to the girl?

History and Context

The narrative of *I Know Why the Caged Bird Sings* covers the years 1931 to 1944; in other words, its personal story is played out against the backdrop of the Great Depression and then the beginning of another fraught period, World War II. It is useful and revealing to recognize something of the situation for black people in the United States during this period, particularly in Arkansas and the South. As an example of a monograph (a book that is dedicated to a single topic) that could be used as background reading, historian Cheryl Lynn Greenberg has given a concise exploration of the economic and cultural situation during these years in her book, *To Ask for an Equal Chance: African Americans in the Great Depression* (Lanham, MD: Rowman and Littlefield, 2009). When we turn briefly to World War II, which forms the backdrop for the final section of the book, in California, there have been some clear advances in the status and opportunities for blacks, illustrated by Angelou's job as the first black streetcar conductor in San Francisco. In another monograph, by Emily Yellin, *Our Mothers' War: American Women at Home and at the Front During World War II* (New York: Free Press, 2004), a chapter appropriately called "Jane Crow" in included in which Yellin looks at the case of black women. Keep in mind that whenever you use a scholarly monograph, you will find a list of books used in the work or additional books on the subject listed alphabetically by author in the bibliography in the back of the book, and there you may find suggestions for additional books you may want to consult. Also, if your library has open stacks, where you can go and select your books rather than having a librarian find them, and you find the call number and the location of one of these books, look around at the nearby volumes; you might find useful material there.

For most writers of essays on this first of Angelou's autobiographies, the most helpful background source is likely to be a reference book, found in the reference section of the library, and something you will normally not be able to check out. The five volumes of the *Encyclopedia of African American History: 1896 to the Present* (New York: Oxford, 2009) is a good possibility. The thorough index is found in volume V (273–517), where you will also find a helpful "Thematic Outline of Entries" (229–43) and a chronology of events by year from 1896 to 2009. There you will find an overview of all of Angelou's work, articles on Arkansas, the Great Depression and New Deal programs, World War II, violence, and many topics that come up in Angelou, such as the victory of Joe Louis over Max Schmeling in 1938. Each article also includes a bibliography, which can lead you to further useful sources.

Sample Topics:

1. **The Great Depression:** How does the Great Depression affect the black community in Stamps? Since difficulties of hunger, homelessness, and illness ran rampant across the whole country, does it come through in Angelou's narrative that blacks fared worse than whites? Do we see any impact of the New Deal programs of President Franklin Roosevelt and the federal government in Stamps? If not, why not?

2. **Momma's store:** How important is Momma's store in Stamps as a support for the family during this time? Is black ownership, especially female ownership, of a profitable and sustaining business unusual? Does Momma use the store to help the whole community? How? In what ways are the grandchildren involved in the store and in helping the community?

3. **Community:** Black neighborhoods and black towns were just some of the places where black culture could support and help people in their difficulties. What are some examples of community gatherings in *I Know Why the Caged Bird Sings*? Think of church and school events and of such things as the summer picnic fish fry and the gathering to watch the Joe Louis fight. How do these events help people? How do they help Angelou in her maturing process?

4. **Folklore:** Scholars, especially Lyman Hagen, have pointed out that *Caged Bird* is strong in its use of folklore, stories (such as Mr. Taylor's ghost story in chapter 22), and expression of folk wisdom. Pick out some examples of folk material in the book. Why does Angelou use them? Are they effective? Are they related to compensation in the black community in Stamps for the difficulties people have? Are there as many of them in the city, after Angelou moves from Stamps?

5. **World War II:** When opportunities opened up for them (after black men and white women), black women left domestic service jobs and farm work and, in many cases, the South for the North to move into better-paying industrial work and other kinds of jobs previously unavailable to them. Yellin uses Angelou's successful and hard-fought campaign (with her mother's vehement encouragement) to get the San Francisco streetcar

conductor's job as a way of illustrating new opportunities in many areas. How does this situation fit with the rest of *I Know Why the Caged Bird Sings*? Is its placement near the end of the book (chapter 34 of 36) a way to place emphasis on its importance? (The most important positions in everything from a sentence to a full book or magazine are, first, the beginning and, second, the end. This is something worth thinking about in your own writing too.)

6. **Violence:** The 1930s and early 1940s saw an upsurge in violence against blacks, including lynching and riots. "Legal lynching" at the hands of the criminal justice system and the fight against this injustice was illustrated by the Scottsboro case when eight young men were accused by two white women of assault in a boxcar aboard a train passing through northern Alabama. The South also saw confrontations over sharecroppers attempting to organize in unions. What are examples of violence against blacks in *Caged Bird*? Are the dangers for black men and boys, such as Uncle Willie and Bailey, different than those for black women and girls? Is the North safer than the South, as Angelou depicts them? Do any of the examples of violence seem to be attempts to keep poor blacks and poor whites from uniting to protest their situation?

Philosophy and Ideas

When we turn from the historical to the philosophical and the ideas emerging from individual and group experiences, one of the topics relevant to Angelou's first autobiography is violence in the social and psychological sense, especially as related to black women and how they deal with it. Recent studies are useful in gaining an understanding of this issue, first of all in its broad, American context and then, more specifically, from a black feminist perspective. Two books by social scientists are useful: the recent *Behavior and the Social Environment*, by Charles Zastrow and Karen K. Kirst-Ashman, which asks the question, "Why do people behave the way they do?" (1) and a collection of essays, *Violence in the Lives of Black Women: Battered, Black, and Blue*, edited and introduced by Carolyn M. West, a psychologist, which includes entries on childhood sexual abuse, racism, sexism, black rape survivors, and resistance and healing—all topics relevant to a study of Angelou. Throughout the maturing process, female (and male) role models are an important help for a girl becoming a woman, and reading all kinds of literature can expand the number of role models significantly.

Sample Topics:

1. **Violence and psychology:** Does Angelou succeed in conveying what the experience of rape was like, physically and mentally, for an eight-year-old? Is Marguerite's compensation through silence a logical one for someone her age? A healthy one? How do the people of her family deal with the rape? With her silence? Which reactions and actions are helpful and which are not? Is her recovery largely a matter of time, or do other things play important roles?

2. **Female role models:** Why does her mother, Vivian Baxter, seem to be especially inept in dealing with Marguerite's rape and the aftereffects? Is she a better role model for Angelou when she is older, for example, when Angelou becomes pregnant? Is Momma better, of more help with the rape but less so with the pregnancy? What makes Mrs. Flowers such a powerful role model for the young Angelou?

3. **Literature as solace and teacher:** Early in the book, at the end of chapter 2, Angelou lists her early reading, including William Shakespeare, her "first white love." How many of these authors do you know? Kipling, Poe, Butler, Thackeray, and Henley, are listed among the white authors, and Paul Laurence Dunbar, Langston Hughes, James Weldon Johnson, and W.E.B. Du Bois are cited among the black. Why do you think Angelou reserved particular passion for the black authors? Why so much emphasis on poetry rather than prose? In chapter 15, Mrs. Flowers tells the post-trauma, silent Angelou that for literature to truly mean what it is capable of, it must be read or recited aloud. Do you believe this is true? Have you memorized any literature? (Keep in mind that the poetry of song lyrics can be included here, and the chances are great that you know many of those.) What are the benefits of reading something aloud and/or memorizing it?

Form and Genre

It is sometimes helpful to see how a book is constructed overall by look-ing at the number of chapters and their respective lengths. Then, one can look at any divisions the author has made through parts or sec-tions, whether explicit, or stated directly, or implicit, that is, indirectly. With *Caged Bird,* the text seems to fall implicitly into several parts, even though the parts are not given directly as divisions in the text. In chapter 2 of this book on writing about Maya Angelou, we looked at the question of autobiography and mentioned that some people have called what Angelou writes "autobiographical novels." Here, it may be helpful to examine more closely the ways in which *Caged Bird* resembles the genre of autobiography and the ways in which it adopts the typical form of the novel.

Sample Topics:

1. **Chapter division:** How many chapters does the book have? Which is the longest and which the shortest of the chapters? If the chapters are fairly numerous and short, why does Angelou choose to divide the book this way? Is it a help to the reader? The author? Does it fit with the content of the chapters? Are the chapters arranged chronologically, that is, according to their actual time sequence, or some other way, for example with flashbacks, going backward in time? Can some chapters stand alone, like set pieces, as short stories or essays? (Consider, for example, chapter 23 on her graduation from grammar school.)

2. **Grouping of chapters:** Does the book seem to divide into sev-eral sections? If so, what are they? Do they take place in differ-ent geographic locations? Does this grouping convey any sense of the growth of the main character, Marguerite or Angelou? What is conveyed or suggested by the final chapter, the conclu-sion of the book? Does it sum up a theme explored in the book in some way? Does it anticipate the next volume?

3. **Autobiography or novel or both?:** Look at some other auto-biographies published before 1971, when Angelou published *Caged Bird.* Do they typically contain as much dialogue as Angelou's do? If the autobiographies often open with a kind of family history or genealogy, why do you think Angelou does

not do this? *Caged Bird* can be called episodic, or composed of a series of separate episodes. Is this typical of the other autobiographies you examine? Do the other autobiographies cover more of the person's life span than Angelou's does? Today many autobiographical works are called memoirs, which suggests a shorter or more concentrated part of a person's life and a more idiosyncratic personal view of the author. Is Angelou's work in a sense an early form of the memoir? Do you see other differences or similarities between Angelou's work and the autobiographies you examined?

4. **The ethics of writing a "life story":** One of the reasons memoirs have taken the place of autobiographies is perhaps that the former is much more assumed to be the author's personal memory and not so much an attempt at accuracy from other perspectives. This has led to much publishing and reader turmoil about truthfulness in memoirs and much dismay from family and friends who find themselves or events depicted in ways they do not believe are accurate or they would not themselves choose. Does Angelou in *Caged Bird* create negative depictions that some might object to? Is she careful not to identify too clearly the people depicted in a negative light? Do you think that an author should consult and take into consideration the views of others, particularly family and friends, before publishing something that includes them?

Language, Symbols, and Imagery

One of the most immediately noticeable characteristics of Angelou's writing, especially in *Caged Bird*, is her fulsome use of similes and metaphors. These kinds of comparisons of unlike things seem to come to her naturally. Often these figurative comparisons are witty, humorous, or self-mocking, also characteristics of Angelou's prose style, and lead to an intimate and informal tone, as do her imitations of many conversational characteristics of a wide variety of people.

Sample Topics:

1. **Simile:** Pick out some examples of Angelou's use of simile you find particularly interesting or effective and analyze them in

context. An effective simile can be said to have two dimensions. It both makes one thing clearer by comparing it to something else while also revealing the mood or attitude of the speaker or writer. Do Angelou's similes typically work this way? As an example, early in the prologue of *Caged Bird*, Angelou uses an extended simile: "The truth of the statement [I didn't come to stay] was like a wadded-up handkerchief sopping wet in my fists, and the sooner they accepted it the quicker I could let my hands open and the air would cool my palms" (7). This tells us not just what truth is like but what it is like to this frightened, embarrassed child in the front of a church congregation. Can you find other similes that seem to have this power, effectiveness, and resonance?

2. **Symbol:** Some items and actions become more than themselves; they become symbolic of a repeated idea or struggle. Such are the gifts the child Marguerite receives from her absent mother at Christmastime in Stamps, a tea set and a doll with yellow hair. What makes these gifts so incongruous to the girl? What are some of the possible things they symbolize? What do Marguerite and her brother, Bailey, do to the gifts, and why? (One could say that their actions are also symbolic. What do those actions symbolize?) For more on the gifts as symbol, see Lupton, page 3 and Arensberg, page 281.

3. **Self-deprecation:** Pick out some passages where Angelou makes fun of herself and consider them closely. What is the effect on the reader? Do the examples further the story of self-discovery and maturation? Do the examples diminish in number as the book proceeds and the narrator grows?

4. **Humor:** Find passages that you find particularly entertaining or funny. What makes them that way? How do they fit with their context? Are they palatable to a reader and why or why not? Is humor ever employed at someone else's expense? Do the examples help make a point of some kind and, if so, what?

5. **Conversational language:** Find examples of speech in the work. Do people speak differently from one another? Does Angelou try to hide or to duplicate dialect of especially the unschooled characters, like Momma?

Compare and Contrast Essays

A comparison is finding how things are alike, and a contrast reveals how they are different. Typically in an essay, one would do some of each. One can compare and contrast characters, events, places, or actions within a single text, or one might compare and contrast these things between two different texts, such as two of Angelou's six autobiographies. One might also pick a non-Angelou text to compare and contrast to hers, such as the autobiography that is often considered an early model for much that has come after, Benjamin Franklin's, or one of the slave narratives of early black literature, such as Harriet Jacobs's *Incidents in the Life of a Slave Girl* or Frederick Douglass's *Narrative of the Life of Frederick Douglass.*

Sample Topics:

1. **Annie Henderson and Vivian Baxter:** Compare and contrast the nurturing styles of Angelou's grandmother, Momma, and her mother, Vivian Baxter. Does their difference have to do with their ages? With their religiosity? With their living in the South versus the North? In a rural area as opposed to an urban one? With Vivian having been raised by a mother, Grandmother Baxter, who is "almost white"? Is one scenario or situation better and one worse for the young Marguerite, and does this relationship change as she matures and lives in other parts of the country? Is it possible to say which woman has the greatest influence on the girl?

2. **Mrs. Flowers and the rest of the black community in Stamps:** How is Mrs. Flowers different than the other people in her community? How is she different than Momma? In what ways are she and Momma alike? Is it the likenesses or the differences that help establish a strong friendship between the two women? Is it because of her differences from those around her that Mrs. Flowers has such an influence on Marguerite?

3. **The South and the North, rural and urban:** What differences does the child notice, or do you notice, between Stamps and St. Louis and between Stamps and California? Are Angelou's opportunities for jobs greater in the North? Opportunities for friends? Does the North have a kind of self-imposed separation between the races comparable to the South's segregation as

imposed by law and custom? Do you see changes in these places during the times covered by the book?

4. *Caged Bird* **and another Angelou autobiography:** Compare and contrast two of her books as to both content and style. Do the themes differ? Do some family characters disappear? How important is the historical background? What difference do the times make? Does Angelou form the book in the same way, with episodic chapters, or differently? You could also look at differences and similarities in the settings, especially in the books in which she tours Europe and moves to Africa, and ask if her assumed audience has changed between the books.

5. *Caged Bird* **and another black autobiography or novel:** Compare and contrast Angelou's book with an early slave narrative, an autobiographical work to come out of the Harlem Renaissance of the 1920s, an autobiography published since 1971, with a book billed as a memoir rather than an autobiography, or with an autobiographical novel about childhood, such as James Baldwin's *Go Tell It on the Mountain*. In all cases, try to include both elements of the content of the books and elements of form, or how the book is written and constructed. If you choose to write comparing and contrasting *Caged Bird* with Harriet Jacobs's nineteenth-century book, *Incidents in the Life of a Slave Girl*, one of the references you might want to consult is Mary Vermillion's article, first published in *Biography*, "Re-embodying the Self: Representations of Rape in *Incidents in the Life of a Slave Girl* and *I Know Why the Caged Bird Sings*."

Bibliography and Online Resources for *I Know Why the Caged Bird Sings*

Angelou, Maya. *I Know Why the Caged Bird Sings*. In *The Collected Autobiographies of Maya Angelou*. New York: Modern Library, 2004. 1–222.

Arensberg, Liliane K. "Death as Metaphor of Self in *I Know Why the Caged Bird Sings*." *CLA Journal* 20 (1976): 273–96.

Barnwell, Cherron A. "Singin' de Blues, Writing Black Female Survival in *I Know Why the Caged Bird Sings*." In *Maya Angelou*. Bloom's Modern Critical Views. Ed. Harold Bloom. New York: Chelsea House Publishers, 2009. 133–46.

Bejan, Remus. "Nigrescence: Mapping the Journey in Maya Angelou's *I Know Why the Caged Bird Sings.*" In *Maya Angelou.* Bloom's Modern Critical Views. Ed. Harold Bloom. New York: Chelsea House Publishers 2009. 147–55.

Braxton, Joanne M. *Black Women Writing Autobiography.* Philadelphia: Temple University Press, 1989.

———, ed. *Maya Angelou's I Know Why the Caged Bird Sings: A Casebook.* New York: Oxford University Press, 1999.

Douglas, Kate. *Contesting Childhood: Autobiography, Trauma, and Memory.* Piscataway, NJ: Rutgers University Press, 2010.

Dunbar, Paul Laurence. "Sympathy." *Black Voices: An Anthology of Afro-American Literature,* Ed. Abraham Chapman. New York: Mentor, 1968. 356–57.

Finkelman, Paul et al., eds. *Encyclopedia of African American History, 1896 to the Present.* Volumes I–V. New York: Oxford University Press, 2009.

Fox-Genovese, Elizabeth. "Angelou's Autobiographical Emphasis on Community in *Caged Bird.*" In *Readings on Maya Angelou,* Ed. Mary Williams. San Diego: Greenhaven Press, 1997. 52–58.

Greenberg, Cheryl Lynn. *To Ask for an Equal Chance: African Americans in the Great Depression.* Lanham, MD: Rowman and Littlefield, 2009.

Hagen, Lyman B. *Heart of a Woman, Mind of a Writer, and Soul of a Poet: A Critical Analysis of the Writings of Maya Angelou.* Lanham, MD: University Press of America, 1997.

Henke, Suzette A. "Maya Angelou's *Caged Bird* as Trauma Narrative." In *Maya Angelou.* Bloom's Modern Critical Views. Ed. Harold Bloom. New York: Chelsea House Publishers, 2009. 107–20.

Kent, George E. "Maya Angelou's I Know Why the Caged Bird Sings and Black Autobiographical Tradition." 7:3 *Kansas Quarterly* (1974), 72–78. Reprinted in *Maya Angelou's I Know Why the Caged Bird Sings.* Bloom's Modern Critical Interpretations. Ed. Harold Bloom. Philadelphia: Chelsea House Publishers, 1998. 15–24.

Koyana, Siphokazi. "The Heart of the Matter: Motherhood and Marriage in the Autobiographies of Maya Angelou." In *Maya Angelou.* Bloom's Modern Critical Views. Ed. Harold Bloom. New York: Chelsea House Publishers, 2009. 67–83.

Lesesne, Teri S., and Rosemary Chance. *Hit List for Young Adults: Frequently Challenged Books.* Washington, D.C.: American Library Association, 2002.

Lupton, Mary Jane. *Maya Angelou: A Critical Companion.* Westport, CT: Greenwood Press, 1998.

———. "Singing the Black Mother: Maya Angelou and Autobiographical Continuity." *Black American Literature Forum* 24:2 (1990): 257–76. Page numbers
in the text here will be to the EBSCO host online printout version, 1–14.

Megna-Wallace, Joanne. *Understanding* I Know Why the Caged Bird Sings: A
Student Casebook to Issues, Sources, and Historical Documents. Westport,
CT and London: Greenwood Press, 1998.

Saunders, James Robert. "Breaking Out of the Cage: The Autobiographical Writings of Maya Angelou." In *Maya Angelou.* Bloom's Modern Critical Views.
Ed. Harold Bloom. New York: Chelsea House Publishers, 2009. 3–15.

Smith, Sidonie Ann. "The Quest for Self-Acceptance in *I Know Why the Caged
Bird Sings.*" In *Readings on Maya Angelou,* Ed. Mary E. Williams. San Diego:
Greenhaven Press, 1997. 120–27.

Tangum, Marion M., and Marjorie Smelstor. "Hurston's and Angelou's Visual
Art: The Distancing Vision and the Beaconing Gaze." In *Maya Angelou.*
Bloom's Modern Critical Views. Ed. Harold Bloom. New York: Chelsea
House Publishers, 2009. 49–65.

Vermillion, Mary. "Reembodying the Self: Representations of Rape in *Incidents
in the Life of a Slave Girl* and *I Know Why the Caged Bird Sings.*" In *Maya
Angelou.* Bloom's BioCritiques. Ed. Harold Bloom. New York: Chelsea House
Publishers, 2002.

Walker, Pierre A. "Racial Protest, Identity, Words, and Form in Maya Angelou's
I Know Why the Caged Bird Sings." In *Maya Angelou.* Bloom's Modern Critical Views. Ed. Harold Bloom. New York: Chelsea House Publishers, 2009,
17–35.

West, Carolyn M., ed. *Violence in the Lives of Black Women: Battered, Black,
and Blue.* Philadelphia: Haworth Press, Inc., 2002.

Wright, Richard. "The Ethics of Living Jim Crow: An Autobiographical Sketch."
In *Black Voices: An Anthology of Afro-American Literature,* Ed. Abraham
Chapman. New York: Mentor, 1968. 288–98.

Yellin, Emily. *Our Mothers' War: American Women at Home and at the Front
During World War II.* New York: Free Press, 2004.

Zastrow, Charles and Karen K. Kirst-Ashman. *Behavior and the Social Environment.* Belmont, CA: Brooks/Cole, 2010.

GATHER TOGETHER IN
MY NAME

READING TO WRITE

IT IS difficult for an author to follow up a book that realized phenomenal sales and achieved widespread popularity. The next book is bound to be anticlimactic and a disappointment to some when its predecessor is widely known and widely praised. Such was the task that Maya Angelou faced when she worked for three and a half years on the first of her five followups to the autobiography *I Know Why the Caged Bird Sings*. This time the narrative, titled *Gather Together in My Name*, covers only a three- to four-year time span—the years directly after the end of World War II in 1945—and the time in the author/narrator's life when she was a sixteen- to nineteen-year-old single mother living with her mother and her mother's husband in San Francisco. A book like this which is, in some senses, written as a kind of sequel also presents challenges, for the author and publisher will want it to "work" both with those readers who are familiar with *Caged Bird* and those who read only *Gather Together in My Name*. In considering this book as the primary source of an essay topic, we will try to include both kinds of readers/writers here too—that is, those who know both books and those who know only the second.

You will want to begin by reading the book through carefully, and, if possible, read it at least twice. If the book belongs to you, make use of comments and questions in the margins, and highlight the passages that stand out to you. If the book does not belong to you, jot down some of your thoughts and questions after your first reading; try to formulate a working statement of the theme of the book—that is, what the entire work, including events, characters, settings, and language, seems to be aimed at conveying to the reader. It is also useful to ask who seems to be the audience Angelou has in mind—young and, if so, how young? Black or white or both? Female or male or both? Capturing some of your first impressions of a book, even if they change as you read it again or consult and absorb criticism of the work, can be helpful as you move toward writing your essay. On a second reading, take fuller notes of thoughts and ideas as they come to you. Be sure to note the page numbers of the edition you are using in your notes, as you will need them both to find the passage again easily and to document the sources of your paper later. The more thorough your reading and note taking, the better position you will be in as you begin to formulate and write your paper. Among other things, you will be able to pick out the ideas you feel strongly about or to which you relate, and that kind of involvement with a text can be essential in producing an essay on it.

When considering writing topics that emerge from a text, it is always of interest and benefit to closely consider the title, dedication, and introduction to the book. In this case, as with *I Know Why the Caged Bird Sings,* a prologue serves as the opener, though here it is unidentified as such. *Gather Together in My Name,* first published in 1974, has a title with religious connotations; Angelou has said it is based on "the New Testament injunction for the travailing soul to pray and commune while waiting patiently for deliverance" (O'Neale 33), but it can also be a somewhat different reference to Matthew 18:20—"For where two or three are gathered in my name, there am I among them" (Bible, English Standard Version).

The book itself is anything but religious in content or tone. One of its harshest critics, Selwyn R. Cudjoe, has said that the incidents seem "gathered together in the name of Maya Angelou" (20). Angelou herself has given another nonreligious version of the origin of the title in an interview with Claudia Tate. The title comes, the author said, "from the fact I saw so many adults lying to so many young people," and "I thought for all those parents and non-parents alike who have lied about their past, I will tell it" (154).

The book is dedicated to "my blood brothers"—Bailey Johnson, her literal blood brother, plus "the other real brothers who encouraged me to be bodacious enough to invent my own life daily: James Baldwin; Kwesi

Brew; David Du Bois; Samuel Floyd; John O. Killens; Vagabond King; Leo Maitland; Vusumzi Make; Julian Mayfield; Max Roach"; followed by "a special thanks to my friend Dolly McPherson" (Angelou n.p.; further references to *Gather* will be indicated by just page number). Those familiar with the further volumes in Angelou's six "autobiographical novels" will recognize many of the names as being from her later life in New York City, Egypt, Ghana, and her tours of Europe. Dorothy Randall Tsuruta, interviewing Angelou in 1980, asked her "to share a glimpse of the role" these men "played in her life." Angelou then describes how they helped her raise her son, Guy, and how they were always "at the end of the telephone." She then gives specifics about many of them, from Kwesi Brew, "a Ghanian ambassador and a great poet," who said of Angelou, "she may not be a Ghanian, but she is a sister," to the South African Vusumzi Make, whom the interviewer calls Angelou's "ex-husband" but Angelou more accurately calls her "brother/lover" (106–107).

The book opens in San Francisco, with Angelou, the sixteen-year-old mother, and her baby son at the large boardinghouse home of her mother, Vivian Baxter, and Vivian's husband at the time, "Daddy" Clidell. But we do not learn this until the end of the four-page prologue, after a sweeping and expressive description of, first, the exhilaration of the postwar city immediately after victory in World War II and then the letdown, particularly for many black Americans, of old realities and injustices surfacing once again. The language in the book is immediately slangy and casual: The postwar period "was a 'come as you are' party and 'all y'all come.'" "Hadn't we all joined together to kick the hell out of *der Gruber,* and that fat Italian, and put that little rice-eating Tojo in his place?" (227). These derogatory references to the World War II Axis enemy—Germany's Hitler, Italy's Mussolini, and Japan's Tojo—hint at the temporary nature of the racial truce of the immediate postwar days, but temporarily joy prevails among the sharecroppers who had learned to use "lathes and borers and welding guns," the women who had exchanged "maid's uniforms and mammy-made dresses" for "men's pants and steel helmets," and even the children who had collected paper and tin foil "into balls as big as your head" (227). So high are the wages, and so great the new respect, such as getting "called Mister/Missus at their jobs or by sales clerks," that Angelou right after the war concludes that "race prejudice was dead" and "if war did not include killing, I'd like to see one every year" (228).

Of course it does not last, and two months after V-Day the layoffs and shutdowns begin, some with offers to pay southern workers' tickets back "to the mules they had left tied to the tree on ole Mistah Doo hiccup farm." An apt simile describes the black army veterans who could be seen "hanging on corners like forgotten laundry left on a backyard fence." But none of these people are about to return to what was before the war, and with a couple of descriptive terms—*expanded* and *accordioned*—she says it well: "Their expanded understanding could never again be accordioned into these narrow confines. They were free or at least nearer to freedom than ever before and they would not go back" (228).

What is true of this larger community is also true of the person we turn to next: Angelou herself, the teenaged Marguerite Johnson, husbandless, jobless, with a young son, and living with her mother and stepfather in a boardinghouse that is rapidly losing its boarders. A series of metaphors conveys Angelou's feelings. Her "textured guilt" is biting and gnawing; guilt is her "familiar, my bedmate. . . , my daily companion whose hand I would not hold" (229). This guilt, stemming in large part from those "Christian teaching[s] . . . dinned into my ears in the small town in Arkansas," she carries around "like a raw egg" (229, 230). She finally comes to a resolution—to go out on her own and find a job, child care, and a place to live. Retrospectively, it looks foolhardy, and Angelou generalizes from her examination of her experience in serious, nonslangy language and with two stately sentences: "The mixture of arrogance and insecurity is as volatile as the much-touted alcohol and gasoline. The difference is that with the former there is a long internal burning usually terminating in self-destroying implosion" (231). Thus the prologue of this autobiography sets up our expectations of great difficulty and of great risk in a time of turmoil and the quest for personal identity. Angelou has described this second book not as simply an autobiography but as one that "is trying to do something else" and that is "carrying a fictional character along—the woman who didn't escape" (Weller 14). Elsewhere she has said that it was the most painful of all her books to write but also the best of her first three or four works (Hill 113).

Lyman Hagen titles his chapter on the book "Picking the Way" and describes the work as a travel book (San Francisco to Los Angeles to San Diego to Stamps, then back to San Francisco, to Stockton, and at last to Oakland) with a varied cast, including criminal or suspicious types (pimps, conmen, prostitutes, dealers in stolen goods, and drug addicts).

Hagen also describes the rhythm of this and the next book, *Singin' and Swingin' and Gettin' Merry Like Christmas*, as having "swinging syncopations," in contrast to the "homeyness" of *Caged Bird* and the "thoughtful ballad tones" of *Heart of a Woman* and *All God's Children Need Traveling Shoes*, numbers four and five, respectively, in the series of six (74, 53). As we work our way through the book, we expect to be confronted with the continuing maturation and growth of the main character or at least the slight victory of her once again surviving. *Gather Together in My Name* will not disappoint.

TOPICS AND STRATEGIES
Themes

Gather Together in My Name is set in a variety of places and features a large number of characters of various types. The prologue introduces the societal context in which Angelou places the struggle of Marguerite, her protagonist and herself. Here we will consider why Angelou has structured the book in the way she has. What does she intend to convey and impress on the reader? After you have read the book carefully and developed a sense of the elements that to you seem most distinctive or noteworthy, what do you find recurring? What pulls the work together? Where do we come out at the end? Are the foolhardy risk taking and struggle suggested in the prologue played out in the full text? Is Angelou's expressed intent, not to lie to the young but to tell the truth so often hidden from them, conveyed by the text? If so, how? If you have also read *I Know Why the Caged Bird Sings*, do you see similarities in theme? Differences?

Sample Topics:

1. **Honesty:** Since Angelou has said she wanted to tell the truth about the past, and since she believes most parents and adults do not tell young people the truth, what things in the book lead you to conclude that she is honest? Are there events and actions you would never tell about if it were your own past being related? Are there places where you think she is not totally open and honest? Do you agree with Angelou that it is important that someone tell the truth? She has said in an interview with Larry King that "the artist is always trying to

show the truth of our experience, not necessarily the facts" (290). What do you think is the difference between "truth" and "facts"? Do you agree with her that adults too often do not tell the truth to the young?

2. **Single motherhood:** Angelou's experience and publication of this book predate the most recent women's and feminist movements in the United States, so there was little in the media about women who juggled working with raising a family and especially little (or little that was sympathetic) about young single mothers who were also black. How does Angelou depict this experience—is it all negatively portrayed, or are there bright spots? What does she learn from the experience? Is guilt a common struggle for such women? Is it warranted? Have things changed for single mothers since the time she is describing?

3. **Teachers, positive and negative:** Angelou learns many things from various people in the book, some good, some bad, some the result of direct teaching, some indirect. She also learns from bad examples of behavior as well as good. Does this give you any sense of what the power of teaching is? Are these multiple depictions a big part of her intent to tell the truth? She ends the book in chapter 31 with a rather lengthy description of a man named Troubadour Martin, who, she says, does her a great kindness—he is the one who has cared for her more than anyone else in her short life. (Remember that the end of the book is of prime importance, second only to the beginning of the book in its impression on a reader.) Since what Troubadour Martin does is take her to "a hit joint for addicts" (382) where she watches him shoot up, in what way is this a great kindness? Does his nickname, Troubadour, fit with his role in her life? Does she end the book with this experience because she learns much from it and, if so, what? Is his action an example of an adult telling the truth to a young person?

4. **Locations:** Are there differences in the various places she lives and works? What are they? The chapters of her brief return to Stamps, Arkansas, and Grandmother Henderson, or Momma, occur at the center of the book. What are the positive things about this rural setting? The negative? Is Angelou's exile from

Stamps at the hands of her grandmother a significant turning point for her?

Characters

Family members naturally dominated Angelou's first autobiography, but here in the second, we have a large number of characters who are not family as well. This seems to be supportive of her plan for the book, to have family members appear periodically as reference points or refuges for her, as she makes her way in the world and meets a variety of people struggling through the same process.

Sample Topics:

1. **Mother, Vivian Baxter:** Angelou describes her mother in not solely complimentary language in the prologue to the book and in chapters 18 and 23. Look closely at these descriptions. What things are positive and what negative? Are both mother and daughter working their way out of the past? Is it a second chance for the mother to make up for her abandonment of Angelou as a child by relating to her grandson and giving advice to her daughter? Is the daughter trying not to replicate her mother's irresponsible behavior in the past? In what ways is Vivian helpful to her daughter between her sixteenth and nineteenth years, and in what ways is she not? What behaviors of her mother does Angelou take as positive models for her own life, and what behaviors does she eschew?

2. **Grandmother Henderson, or "Momma":** Angelou's second autobiography in effect contains the obituary of the strong, religious woman who was so important to Angelou in her early life, though she does not die in the period covered by the book. Angelou does not see her grandmother again before her death, which occurs in the next book, *Singin' and Swingin' and Gettin' Merry Like Christmas,* and which she learns of only from an after-the-fact report from her husband. Look closely at chapters 16 and 17 of *Gather Together in My Name,* the portion near the center of the book that relates the story of the young mother and son taking the train back to rural Stamps, Arkansas. What is it that the author first appreciates about the southern location?

What changes her mind about the positive qualities? Is it significant that this change in attitude is spurred by an encounter with
a white sales clerk? What habits has Angelou brought from the
North that do not sit well with the southern whites? Is Momma
right to send Angelou and her son away for their and her protection? Why does Mamma slap Angelou? Does the slap mean the
same thing to the recipient as it means to the giver?

3. **Brother Bailey:** Angelou's brother, too, largely disappears
   from her autobiographies after this book. Here he struggles
   to get out of trouble; finds a woman to love, Eunice; and then
   loses Eunice to illness. Why does Angelou label his next habits—drugs, liquor, religion—"palliatives"? (371). Are the sibling
   roles reversed in this book, as contrasted with *Caged Bird*, with
   Angelou helping Bailey now rather than his helping her? Why
   does Bailey particularly object to his sister getting involved with
   prostitution? Does his opinion have an impact on Angelou at
   this point?

4. **Clyde, or Guy:** Though he is still a baby and then a toddler in
   this book, Angelou's son plays an increasingly important role.
   In what ways does she find him a delight? A bother? Does she
   ever completely forget about him? How much of her confusion
   do you credit to her still being a teenager, barely more than a
   child herself? Do you see anything about the descriptions of
   what happens to the young child here that leads you to predict
   or anticipate the nature of his development in further books?

5. **Curly (Charles):** Her first love, Curly, is attractive, gentle and
   affectionate and expresses an attentiveness to Angelou's son. Yet
   he makes clear from the beginning that he is going to marry
   another woman, something Angelou conveniently blocks from
   her mind while their affair is occurring. When he leaves, she is
   bereft until Bailey advises her to move elsewhere. Is this a positive portrayal of a first love? Does Curly end up being a model to
   Angelou of what a man should be—honest, kind, sensitive, and
   kind to her son?

6. **Johnnie Mae and Beatrice:** Angelou meets these lesbian prostitutes in the bar where she works in San Diego and thoroughly
   describes Sunday dinner at their house, including smoking

marijuana for the first time. Angelou arrives nervous and leaves, as she says, with "two whores and a whorehouse. And I was just eighteen" (270). Is this a believable narrative? Is it part of her claim to be telling the truth to the young? Why do you think Angelou describes this encounter and outcome so thoroughly and lengthily? Does the series of incidents support her statement about feeling morally superior to the prostitutes? Does this behavior agree with your definition of a snob? Does this sequence of events become the lowest point in her narrative since she has to return to Stamps and Grandmother Henderson for fear of being declared an unfit mother?

7. **R.L. Poole:** Working still as a waitress, Angelou, continuing to use marijuana, answers her door one day to find Poole, who asks if she is a dancer. Why not, is Angelou's reaction, and in a humorous sequence in which she attempts to do splits, auditions right there. When he instructs her in tap dance, something in which she is not trained, she falls in love with both the freedom of movement and with Poole, and she delightedly moves into "show business" as his partner. The passages in chapters 21 to 24 describing her introduction to performance begin with a tone of self-deprecating humor. Are there passages you find funny? Why does Angelou make so much fun of herself? When Poole's former partner returns and both Vivian and Bailey are in trouble, the prose becomes more serious. Examine some of these passages. Do they indicate that she is becoming more serious about dance performance? Is Poole one of the more decent men with whom she gets involved? What does he teach her that she can make use of throughout her life?

8. **Big Mary:** Big Mary is babysitter to Guy in her own home while Angelou works as a waitress in Stockton, 80 miles from San Francisco, but the young mother also gets involved with a man named L.D. Tolbrook, who entices her gradually into prostitution. How does he do this? When Angelou is called back to San Francisco to her mother and Bailey's dying wife, Eunice, she leaves Guy with Big Mary, and when Angelou returns to pick him up, both babysitter and son have disappeared. How is this

event a turning point, a moment of realization for the narrator? As a mother? As a maturing adult?

9. **Troubadour Martin:** This character, late in the book, manages to convince Angelou to change her ways by fully revealing to her the realities underpinning his own life. How do her descriptions of the "underworld" change in this final chapter of the book? What would motivate Troubadour Martin to help her in the way he does? Since ending the book with this story and character places great importance on him and his role in the text, is this warranted? Do we feel that this is another crucial turning point in her life? What does it lead us to expect in the subsequent autobiographical volumes Angelou would write?

History and Context

The untitled prologue places the book in the immediate and then longer-term domestic aftermath of World War II. The rest of *Gather Together in My Name,* however, pays little attention to national and international events or context. (Angelou's attempt to enter the military is one exception. Foiled not by the child she has kept hidden but by having attended the California Labor School, considered by the army to be communist, Angelou here anticipates the McCarthyism and communist witch-hunts of the 1950s.) Does this emphasis on the smaller, personal world fit with her depiction of the underground world of shady characters? Does the emphasis also fit with her child being young and dependent throughout the book? Jacqueline Jones has described World War II as a "watershed" for black Africans because of the large numbers who were employed in factories and the creation of the Fair Employment Practices Commission (FEPC). At the same time, Jones states that the opportunities after the war were "meager" (298). Does Angelou's range of employment in this book illustrate the paucity of jobs?

Sample Topics:

1. **Employment:** What racial discrimination does Angelou run into in the book? Why does she open chapter 1 with the example of the telephone company? Does their treatment of her serve as an example of postwar employment opportunities for black women? Why does she so quickly leave the table-busing job she

undertakes later? Judging by the jobs she holds down for a longer time, what are her requirements for a bearable job? Patricia Hill Collins has coined a term *motherwork* to describe "the inseparability of work from motherhood in oppressed communities" (Koyana 2). Is this a useful term to describe what Angelou is trying to convey in her book?

2. **Housing:** Along with the return of race discrimination in hiring, the postwar period also saw great difficulty for urban, northern black Americans in obtaining affordable and decent housing. Is this reality reflected in the book? Where does Angelou end up living, and how does she select the locations? How important is child care in influencing her decisions?

3. **Single motherhood:** Looking at the history of attitudes toward sexuality and single motherhood, Estelle Freedman says that the stigma of the unmarried mother included both black and white women before and during World War II but that after the war, the stigma began to be lifted for young white women, with the concomitant encouragement to "give up" their babies for adoption. In other words, there was great demand among childless couples for white babies but not for black ones (301). Does Angelou's book illustrate the stigma still in place for her as a young black mother? What does she do to hide Guy? Does her judgment of people come from their willingness or unwillingness to accept and appreciate her child?

4. **Nightclub world:** Does Angelou's experience as a dancer and performer illustrate an attitude of the time that black Americans are more acceptable to whites as entertainers than as neighbors or fellow office workers? If so, why do you think this is? Does Angelou indirectly comment on this specific cultural bias?

5. **The North and the South:** At the center of the book is Angelou's and Guy's return to Stamps, Arkansas. How would you describe the contrast between the two places? Has the North changed more than the South? Have any of the changes wrought by the war and its aftermath affected Stamps? What are the accommodations a black person has to make in one or the other, the North and the South?

Philosophy and Ideas

Sample Topics:

1. **Integration and black-white friendships:** Pick out the black-white friendships in the book, beginning with the young woman in the record store. What makes these relationships so difficult at the time, and what makes this particular relationship work? Are there stereotypes of which both participants have to rid themselves? Are single incidents and connections like this important to the overall goal of integration, which will come into greater prominence as a national issue in the 1950s and 1960s?

2. **Child care:** The issue of child care, particularly in relation to the employment of women, has come to the fore in recent years probably because so many more women are working outside the home. Does Angelou's experience decades earlier illustrate some of the difficulties of the issue? Does Angelou express or seem to feel a mother's guilt?

3. **Innocence:** The book concludes with the narrator finding "my innocence. I swore I'd never lose it again" (384). Why does she use that word, and what does she mean by it? Is it the opposite of guilt or something else? In what sense do you see the events of the book as depicting her losing her innocence, and how does she find it again at the end?

Form and Genre

In many ways, this second of Angelou's autobiographical volumes is more novel-like than her first, with its significant amounts of dialogue featuring a range of verbal and conversational styles and its strategic arrangement of events to give the work a structure and sequencing that does not seem to be strictly chronological. Mary Jane Lupton has pointed out that what distinguishes Angelou's "autobiographical method" from "more conventional autobiographical forms" is her "denial of closure" together, in this volume, with a fragmentary or episodic structure, "reflections of the kind of chaos found in actual living." The episodes, Lupton says, are like "bus rides" or "dance movements" but with no progress or achievement being realized. Instead, the narrator "circles in place, at the edge of the dance floor, whereas in the following three [now four] volumes she is in the air, like a bird or a jet, soaring to Europe, Africa, Germany, and back to

Africa" (*Singin'*, 2; *Maya* . . . 78, 79). We still have the first-person narrator, but that narrator has changed, naturally, with age, and self-deprecating humor infuses the text. There are also fewer references to and appropriations of African American folk materials, except jazz and the blues. The community and its life, as represented by church services, picnics, and group gatherings to listen to the radio, has disappeared, to be replaced by mostly competitive individuals relating only briefly to one another. This, of course, also fits with the different kind of world Angelou is living in as a teenager, as contrasted with the child in Arkansas and St. Louis.

With the question of ethics and autobiography—the ways in which a writer can wittingly or unwittingly hurt and damage those close to her/him—Angelou, with this volume, said she had read passages about drugs and prostitution to her mother and brother and son and gave them the say as to whether those sections of the manuscript should be included. "Each accepted" what the author had written. "Her family's encouragement made it possible for her to represent a young black woman's struggle [to] tell the truth, even when the truth could possibly cause harm to herself and others" (Lupton, *Maya* . . . 77). To her friend Dolly McPherson (to whom *Gather* is dedicated, along with "blood" and "real" brothers), Angelou revealed that she left out "a lot of unkindness" expressed by her mother in all the books (139).

Sample Topics:

1. **Structure:** The book has thirty-one chapters, and while there are parts of the work in which a particular story extends over two or three chapters (Johnnie Mae and Beatrice; R.L. Poole and Angelou's introduction to performing), mostly the chapters relate separate, independent episodes occurring in different places. Do you find this episodic structure effective? Ineffective? Somewhere in between? How effective is Lupton's metaphor of circling on the edge of the dance floor in figuratively describing this structure? If Angelou is going in circles at the edge of the floor in this book, where do you expect her to be in the next ones? What does the dance floor represent in this particular metaphor?

2. **Narrator:** How would you characterize the style of the first-person ("I") narrator in this book? Has the narrator changed

from *Caged Bird*? Does the way the narrator introduces herself in the prologue ("I was seventeen, very old, embarrassingly young, with a son of two months, and I still lived with my mother and stepfather," 229) lead you to expect ambiguities and contradictions?

3. **Jazz and blues:** Lupton says that "like certain kinds of twentieth-century African American music, especially jazz, *Gather Together in My Name* has a musical structure in which several melodies are played simultaneously by different instruments" (*Maya . . .* 79). Do you detect any of this jazz-influenced structure in the book? Can you expand this comparison by picking out some of the instruments and melodies? Would this approach, as a basis for the structure, explain the seeming disjointed and episodic nature of the narrative? How does the jazz image compare with the circling image Lupton also uses?

4. **Ethics and censorship:** Those who wish to censor Angelou's first two autobiographies especially object in this book to her depictions of illegal activities, particularly prostitution and drug use. Do you think Angelou makes clear her condemnation of these activities, or can she be accused of "moral relativism," that is, conveying the belief that moral values of right and wrong depend on time and culture? What emerges in the work as her notion of what is wrong and what is right? Would you be in favor of keeping this book out of the hands of junior high or middle school students? Of high school students? Why or why not? Does her articulated aim to tell the truth to the young inevitably lead to material which some will want to censor?

Language, Symbols, and Imagery

The narrator's language in this book achieves considerable range, from slangy and even risqué to serious and formal. Annie Gottlieb has described the sense one has of Angelou's developing style—she has "the born writer's senses nourished on black church singing and preaching, soft mother talk and salty street talk, and on literature" (129). Similes and metaphors are more sparsely placed than in the previous book, but when they are used, they are particularly descriptive and apt, such as the metaphor "Her teeth were all the same size, a small white picket fence semi-circled in her mouth" (233) or the double simile and metaphor of "self-pity in its early stage is as snug as a feather mattress. Only when it hardens does it become uncomfortable" (241). Imagery, or impressions perceived by the senses, is prevalent, such as her rich description of skin colors in the Creole restaurant before she introduces Curly, her first love. "Butter-colored, honey-brown, lemon- and olive-skinned. Chocolate and plum-blue, peaches-and-cream. Cream. Nutmeg. Cinnamon. I wondered why my people described our colors in terms of something good to eat" (238). Some actions become symbolic, such as Momma's slap to the narrator's face before she exiles her from Stamps, which represents the strict discipline of the segregated and religious life Momma will always accept and Angelou will grow to reject. Objects also take on symbolic import in the work, such as clothing, which Angelou uses to register attitudes about promiscuity, money, and independence.

Sample Topics:

1. **Simile and metaphor:** What are some of the similes and metaphors you find particularly effective? What makes them so resonant and well chosen? Does Angelou employ these modes of language often? Too often? Can a text be too rich for a reader if figurative language is used extensively?

2. **Slang and colloquial speech:** Are you surprised or shocked at some of terms and descriptions Angelou uses? Why is she so blunt with her language about prostitution and drugs, for example? Is this part of her aim to "tell the truth" to the young? Would such language and depictions have been more shocking at the time Angelou published the book than they are today?

3. **Dialogue:** Pick out examples of different people talking to one another. How does Angelou display their characteristics and differences? What does their language reveal about them? Consult other autobiographies. Do these other works use as much dialogue as Angelou does? Why does she use so much dialogue here?

4. **Allusions:** Allusions are references, typically literary, historical, cultural, or popular in nature. Mary Jane Lupton points out some allusions Angelou might be making in the book—Troubadour Martin's tour of his world, which suggests the descent into the underworld, a common literary device reaching

back to Homer's *The Odyssey*. Troubadour's name also suggests the musician-poets of the Middle Ages. In addition, some critics have seen the mother-daughter relationship as being based on the Greek myth of Persephone (*Maya* . . . 92). Look up some of these allusions and see if you think Angelou might have had them in mind or might be suggesting them.

Compare and Contrast Essays

Writing on topics that look at two or more characters, settings, or ideas, describing what are seen as similarities (comparison) and as differences (contrast), and sometimes making a judgment of which is better than the other and justifying it can be a strong and rewarding approach to an essay. It may be confusing to use the word *comparison* in both describing a simile or metaphor and as it is being used here. With metaphor or simile, the comparison is between two things one would normally not put into the same category, such as a girl compared to a fox. In the latter, the comparison is between things in the same category, such as a girl compared to a boy. In collecting material for a comparison and/or contrast essay, it is probably a good idea to list all the ways one could compare the two elements being considered and then begin to place those observations into categories to refine your approach.

Sample Topics:

1. **Men and relationships:** Angelou describes several relationships with various men in the book, both romantic partners and people with whom she works. How do these men compare? Is it possible to construct Angelou's virtual "ideal man" from the various men? What would be the most important characteristics to her of such a man and what the least important?

2. **Mothering styles:** Prominent in this book are the similarities and differences between the ways Vivian Baxter raises her children and the way the narrator tries to raise her son. Are there some good and some bad qualities in the approach of each? Are there differences due to their being representative of different generations? Is one mothering style better than the other?

3. **Food:** There are many references to food in this book—preparing it, consuming it, finding comfort and communion in it. How do

the foods compare? How important is food in our lives? Our culture? Is food a key to descriptions of different cultures? Are there definable differences between black and white culture, as reflected in the rituals and realities of food?

4. **Jobs:** Angelou holds many jobs in this book and describes the livelihood of many other people, some legitimate, such as child care, cooking, and dancing and singing, and some not so, such as prostitution and selling stolen goods. How do these jobs differ in growth and fulfillment to the employee? In positive contributions to society? In sustainability—that is jobs with stability and staying power?

Bibliography and Online Resources for *Gather Together in My Name*

Angelou, Maya. *Gather Together in My Name*. In *The Collected Autobiographies of Maya Angelou*. New York: Modern Library, 2004. 223–384.

Cudjoe, Selwyn R. "Maya Angelou and the Autobiographical Statement." In *Black Women Writers 1950–1980*. Ed. Mari Evans. New York: Anchor Books/Doubleday, 1984.

Freedman, Estelle B. "The History of the Family and the History of Sexuality." In Eric Foner, Ed. *African American History Post World War II*. Philadelphia: Temple University Press, 1997. 285–310.

Gottlieb, Annie. "The Serious Business of Survival: *Gather Together in My Name*." In *Readings on Maya Angelou*. Ed. Mary E. Williams. San Diego: Greenhaven Press, 1997. 129–31.

Hagen, Lyman B. *Heart of a Woman, Mind of a Writer, and Soul of a Poet: A Critical Analysis of the Writings of Maya Angelou*. Lanham, Md.: University Press of America, 1997.

Hill, Esther. "Maya Angelou: Resolving the Past, Embracing the Future." In *Conversations with Maya Angelou*. Ed. Jeffrey M. Elliot. Jackson and London: University Press of Mississippi, 1989. 109–14.

Jones, Jacqueline. "Shifting Paradigms of Black Women's Work in the Urban North and West: World War II to the Present." In Kenneth Kusmer and Joe William Trotter. *African American Urban History Since World War II*. Chicago and London: University of Chicago Press, 2009. 295–315.

King, Larry, with Pat Piper. "Maya Angelou: Poet." *Future Talk: Conversations about Tomorrow with Today's Most Provocative Personalities*. New York: HarperCollins, 1998. 290–94.

Koyana, Siphokazi. "The Heart of the Matter: Motherhood and Marriage in the Autobiographies of Maya Angelou." *Black Scholar.* Summer 2002. Vol. 32, Issue 2, 35–45. Page numbers here are to the EBSCOhost online printout version, 1–14.

Lupton, Mary Jane. "Singing the Black Mother: Maya Angelou and Autobiographical Continuity." *Black American Literature Forum* 24:2 (1990): 257–76. Page numbers here are to the EBSCOhost online printout version, 1–15.

———. *Maya Angelou: A Critical Companion.* Westport, Conn., and London: Greenwood Press, 1998.

McPherson, Dolly. *Order Out of Chaos: The Autobiographical Works of Maya Angelou.* New York: Peter Lang. 1990.

O'Neale, Sondra. "Reconstruction of the Composite Self: New Images of Black Women in Maya Angelou's Continuing Autobiography." In *Black Women Writers (1950–1980): A Critical Evaluation.* Ed. Mari Evans. Garden City, N.Y.: Doubleday, 1984. 25–36.

Randall-Tsuruta, Dorothy. "An Interview with Maya Angelou." In *Conversations with Maya Angelou.* Ed. Jeffrey M. Elliot. Jackson and London: University Press of Mississippi, 1989. 102–08.

Tate, Claudia. "Maya Angelou." In *Conversations with Maya Angelou.* Ed. Jeffrey M. Elliot. Jackson and London: University Press of Mississippi, 1989. 146–56.

Weller, Sheila. "Work in Progress: Maya Angelou." In *Conversations with Maya Angelou.* Ed. Jeffrey M. Elliot. Jackson and London: University Press of Mississippi, 1989. 10–17.

SINGIN' AND SWINGIN' AND GETTIN' MERRY LIKE CHRISTMAS

READING TO WRITE

THE PUBLICATION of Maya Angelou's third volume of autobiography, in 1976, covering five years in the author's early twenties and her breaking into the performing world, signaled another first, since most autobiographical works up to that point were written in one volume and led to a definitive resolution and ending. However as Mary Jane Lupton has pointed out, Angelou is particularly unlikely to describe her life or anything else with definite closure ("Singing" ... 2). The title of the third volume sounds joyful, *Singin' and Swingin' and Gettin' Merry Like Christmas,* but upon reading it, one finds out that the title contains some of the same ambiguity as *I Know Why the Caged Bird Sings,* for the book relates many of the conflicts present in the narrator's life. Angelou faces the discrepancy between her preconceived notions of marriage and domesticity and the reality of life with her first husband, Tosh Angelos. Another conflict centers on Angelou's negative images of white people and how her attitudes influence her interactions with the white world, as she and the other characters inhabit an increasingly interracial world. The central conflict, however, of this third book in her autobiographical series hovers around the demands she feels as a mother of a growing son, the pressure of needing to work, then, ultimately, the appeal of performance and the travel that goes with it.

Though we saw some of the mothering/working conflict in the previous book, *Gather Together in My Name*, as well, in that autobiography, her son, Clyde, was too young to articulate fully his loneliness and frustration at his mother frequently leaving him. In *Singin'*, however, he is old enough to speak and write her letters dripping with these emotions. The boy also experiences psychosomatic reactions in the form of persistent rashes and skin problems seemingly caused by her long absence touring with the opera *Porgy and Bess* in Europe. Angelou has said that the title of this third book was a reference to rent parties of the 1920s, when people who did not have enough money to pay the rent threw a party that lasted from nine o'clock Saturday night until early Sunday evening, including church attendance Sunday morning (Tate 154–55). So here we have, in a sense, another "laughing to keep from crying" title, or singing and getting merry in order to both hide from but also cope with difficulties such as the mother/son relationship and the concerns and problems it engenders.

As always when reading a literary work in preparation for writing an essay, it is a good idea to read the book twice, the first time mostly for enjoyment and appreciation and the second time for a more detailed consideration of the work and one's reactions to and questions about it. Additional readings also present the opportunity for the recording of notes, questions, and observations. Be sure to note page numbers when you take notes, and be sure to put quotation marks around any passages you copy exactly, all things that will help you in preparing citations in your final paper. Deciding on a topic for your paper, particularly if it is relatively short, three to five pages, will mean that you will likely start with a rather big idea but then will want to narrow it down to a focused topic you can say something significant about in the amount of space afforded you. As an illustration of this process, here are two passages of *Singin'* in which two themes of the book collide—the narrator's, or Angelou's, dedication to raising her son and her increasing involvement in performance, dancing, and singing.

The first passage is in chapter 16. Here Angelou has traveled from San Francisco to New York City for an audition, telling Clyde that she will be back within a few weeks. When she learns that she has gotten the part for which she auditioned, she also learns that she has a chance for another role, replacing one of the dancer/singers in *Porgy and Bess* in their State Department tour of Europe and North Africa. If she commits to the engagement, what she really wants to do, she will go directly to Montreal the next day and not get back to San Francisco for months or years. An apt simile expresses her confusion: "My mind turned over and over like a flipped coin: Paris, then Clyde's motherless birthday party, Rome and my son's evening prayers said to Fluke [his imaginary playmate], Madrid and Clyde struggling alone with his schoolwork" (Angelou 511; subsequent references to this text will be given by just page numbers). She calls home to where her mother and her mother's two housemates are taking care of Clyde. They encourage her to "go for it," with folksy adages of advice, such as her mother's "'treat everybody right, remember life is a two-way street. You might meet the same people on your way down that you met going up'" (512).

Angelou's conversation with her son, Clyde (he later picks the name Guy, so they will be used interchangeably), is another matter, one that leaves her in tears. She resorts to a technique she "loathed," talking to him as though he was a small child "with faulty English." Clyde soon poses the question he most wants answered—when was she coming home? She equivocates, not next week, she tells him, but "soon . . . very soon." The paragraph ends with a short sentence that says much about Clyde's sense of rejection and even anger: "He hung up first" (512). It is at this point that Angelou states directly what a reader familiar with her first autobiography, *Caged Bird*, might already be thinking. "The past revisited. My mother had left me with my grandmother for years and I knew the pain of parting. My mother, like me, had had her motivations, her needs. I did not relish visiting the same anguish on my son, and she, years later, had told me how painful our separation was to her." Then she states her reasons—or excuses—and makes a resolution: "But I had to work and I would be good. I would make it up to my son and one day would take him to all the places I was going to see" (512). Angelou's use of the word *visiting* in "visiting the same anguish on my son," suggests she also had in mind the Old Testament passage that in some translations reads, "the sins of the father visited upon the children." Not only is she feeling personal guilt, but she is likely feeling a kind of religious guilt or recognition attached to her religious upbringing by her Grandmother Henderson back in Stamps, Arkansas.

The next passage we will consider is in a chapter further on, 25, close to the end of the book and profiling her return to San Francisco after considerable time away on tour. At this point, with plenty of experiences, successes, suitors, countries, and time for reflection under her belt, she admits for the first time that her guilt is not just over leaving Clyde so long; it is for her enjoying herself so much. She had soothed the guilt by saying she had to work, and it was "the good-mother thing to leave my son at home." Now, however, she recognizes that she "was reveling in the freedom," her escape from the chatter of a small child, from having to fix breakfast, or come home early, or hide a hangover. "The truth was," she concludes, "I had used the aloneness, loving it" (598–99). Those familiar with Angelou's first autobiography, with its thorough and graphic depictions of her rape as an eight-year-old, will recognize here, too, the painfully honest Angelou. Here she admits something not exceptional, as the rape was, but a common feeling sometimes shared by many parents, a feeling not often acknowledged.

Taking this conflict between being a parent and being an individual with personal and professional interests as a starting point for a paper topic might lead one to narrow it to a discussion of Angelou's admission to herself that she has actually enjoyed being away from her child for an extended period of time. This thesis could give rise to a few key questions. What has led her to this honesty? Is it evident to a reader that she tremendously enjoys the European-African tour even before she admits it openly? Does the admission help her in any way to a deeper understanding of herself? Of mothering, especially good mothering? Of Clyde? Lyman Hagen, who has written the only monograph on all of Angelou's work up to the time of his book's publication, thinks that this book is less interesting and weighty than its predecessors, largely because it is less introspective (92). Is that one of the things that makes this passage about her true feelings stand out—that it is more introspective than much of the book? (Hagen also describes much of the last part of the book, the chronicle of the tour, as merely show business anecdotes [92, 95].)

In taking up the topic of marriage as well as working and mothering, Siphokazi Koyana has summarized well the significance of Angelou's depictions here in relation to larger historical and personal issues. Angelou challenges "the prevailing notions of maternity" by studying her own experience, particularly "the feasibility of a domesticated motherhood for working-class black women, the supremacy of the nuclear family structure," and the "idealization of marriage." By challenging myths prevalent at the time of her writing *Singin'*, she shows her own struggle for "a self-empowering identity" and becomes "an inspiration for women (black or white)" (9).

TOPICS AND STRATEGIES
Themes

Many possible themes that can be discussed will likely occur to you as you read the book, especially so if you read it twice. Remember that a theme is not a refined topic for a paper. Like the other elements of the book that are considered in this discussion—character, history and context, language, and imagery—the following will give you a place to start in defining your paper topic and thesis. Some of the questions posed will help you think more about your own reading of the text and about the organization and content of your essay.

Sample Topics:

1. **Mothering:** Three generations of mothers from one family appear in this book—Angelou; her mother, Vivian Baxter; and Angelou's father's mother, Annie Henderson, the last only in the report of her death and in the author's short paean to her at the end of chapter 5, a tribute echoing Shakespeare's *Hamlet* in its reference to death as an "undiscovered country." How would you compare and contrast these three women in their mothering roles? Is it part of the natural flow of time and of the generations to have Angelou's grandmother essentially disappear at this point in her life? Is Angelou's learning from her mother more conscious and deliberate than her learning from the grandmother who raised her? Does the relationship of Angelou and her mother illustrate the power of forgiveness?

2. **Show business:** We learn a great deal about what it takes to be a performer in this book; we learn as Angelou describes her own education in this respect. At first, she is surprised that the singers in the opera *Porgy and Bess* can be so moving and touching in their performances and then walk offstage and transform from the character they were playing back to their real lives and identities. Is this something a performer has to learn, to easily inhabit and then abandon the roles played? She interestingly

describes the individual sounds of the singers warming up and their moving into their roles as the performance approaches. Have you experienced anything like this—a part in a play or a concert? What happens, what must the performer do, if it is a performance repeated more than a couple of times?

3. **Love and marriage:** What is Angelou's dream of marriage? Is it connected to media, particularly the movies? Is it realistic in any way? Do you think that if she did attain this vision, it would be satisfying to her, from what you have learned of her in the book? Does she fall in love too easily? Does love during the teenage years have more to do with images of self and others than with real people and emotions? Angelou describes her marriage to Tosh Angelos as giving up more and more of her "territory." What does this mean in her case? How does she handle it when it becomes too frustrating for her? Is it a complaint you have heard elsewhere? Did the feminist movement help to change this for women?

4. **Names and naming:** In this book, both Angelou and her son pick names for themselves. Marguerite Johnson, or Ritie, becomes Maya Angelou, a combination of her brother, Bailey's, childhood name for her, Maya, as in "maya sister," and a slightly different version of her first husband's last name, Angelou instead of Angelos. Clyde becomes Guy. They have different reasons, it appears, to assume new names. Angelou needs a good show business name, and Clyde attempts to assume greater control over his identity and individuality. What is the significance for each of them in choosing a name? Is naming an important process? To individuals? Groups? Does changing a name in some way change a person or group? Is a name more meaningful when chosen by the person or group named rather than someone else? (Think, for example, of black or African American, which replaced what was seen as the increasingly distasteful or disrespectful "Negro" or "colored.")

5. **Blacks and whites:** This book records a lot of the attitudes that many black people, including Angelou, automatically ascribe to white people before they know them. Lyman Hagen says that there are more than fifty such instances in *Gather* (92). Find some of these passages and look at how Angelou handles them.

First, why does she include them? Second, is her mind always changed after she comes to know someone, or is the expectation sometimes confirmed? Do some of the items surprise you? Are some reflective of the time in which the book is set, that is, were they true when she wrote the book but not true today?

6. **Loneliness:** The book opens with a blues song about loneliness and then describes the way music helps Angelou through the loneliest times. In the latter part of the book, in recounting her European and African travel, she repeatedly describes sessions of loneliness, especially a longing to see her son. How does she deal with these feelings? Does she mature and learn throughout the book? Does the ending offer a kind of resolution to this problem of loneliness?

Character

In her earlier autobiographies, especially the first, chronicling her childhood and youth, family members and relatives play the most prominent roles. In this book, the family, as an entity, becomes increasingly distant, except for Clyde—at the end of the book, the two of them are in Hawaii with no other family members nearby. Men and sex are naturally more prominent for someone in her early twenties than in the younger years recounted in the earlier books. Angelou's friendships are also of a different kind when, in the second half the book, she has entered the show business world. As more and more people of a greater variety of status, occupation, and ambitions appear, one thing holds true throughout all the autobiographies: Angelou is very adept at sketching a character's looks, behavior, and nature. In preparing a character study as an essay topic, it is good to ask whether Angelou pushes us into certain judgments about people through her descriptions of them and exactly how she achieves this with her language.

Sample Topics:

1. **Clyde/Guy:** The presence of Angelou's son—named Clyde by his mother at the beginning of the book but picking the name Guy for himself at the end—is threaded throughout as a kind of leitmotif, or repeated theme. He grows considerably during the five years the book covers, from inventing imaginary friends

and loving guns and other weapons to expressing antimilitarist sentiments in school after acquiring a kitten to quell his own attraction to violence. He suffers from his mother's long absence in Europe and North Africa and is a changed person, listless and with skin problems, when she returns. Does his name change connect with or reflect some of this suffering he goes through? How does he react to her return? Does taking him with her to her next job in Hawaii serve as a positive step in their healing process? How do we know? (Look especially at the final chapter and words of the book.)

2. **Louise Cox:** Angelou describes this record store owner and then employer as her first adult white friend, and the relatively long first chapter of *Singin'* relates the long process Angelou undergoes before she feels confident and comfortable with Louise. Why would the author open the book with this character, who rather quickly disappears, and this experience? Why is Louise's pronunciation of Marguerite's name ("Marg-you-reet") so important to Angelou? What other characteristics and actions does Louise demonstrate that bring the two young women closer?

3. **Ivonne Broadnax:** Angelou's closest black friend, during the first part of the book especially, Ivonne is the person she turns to for advice and support and to whose house she moves when she has no other place to go. What is the difference between taking help from a friend rather than from one's mother? Do you agree with Ivonne's advice, as when she tells Angelou to take the record shop job Louise has offered her, but "watch her like a hawk" (398)? Angelou suggests that one of the reasons she turns to Ivonne is that this friend has lost the romantic ideas of love and marriage, which Angelou herself considers her own "lifelong affliction" (396). How does this make Ivonne a helpful friend to have? How does Angelou make use of Ivonne's lack of romanticism?

4. **Tosh Angelos:** A white sailor of Greek heritage, Angelos first surprises the narrator in the record shop by his knowledge and love of black music. Against her mother's disapproval of her dating a white man, Angelou begins dreaming of this kind man as a father for her son and soon considers and accepts his pro-

posal of marriage. Angelou's brother, Bailey, who does not make as extensive an appearance in this third book as in the earliest ones, approves of the match, and for a while the marriage seems to be a good one. What external and internal forces and feelings break up this first of Angelou's marriages? To what extent are the main problems the traditional roles of wife and mother in society at the time? To what extent is difference in religious attitudes to blame? How big a role does the interracial nature of the marriage play, directly or indirectly?

5. **Vivian Baxter:** Angelou's mother appears many times in the book, primarily in representing both a literal and figurative home for Angelou and her son when both are in the United States and for the son when his mother is out of the country. The narrator is not always complimentary in what she says about her mother, but she is learning to be more appreciative and objective as an adult than she was as a child and teenager. How do you see Vivian Baxter's actions toward daughter and grandson? What are some of her faults, according to the daughter? What is her attitude toward white men, such as Tosh Angelos and the playwright George Hitchcock, both of whom come home with Angelou? Is the attitude based more on class and dress than on skin color?

6. **Yanko Varda:** This artist and his partying friends become faithful groupies to Angelou at her nightclub and then opera performances, even meeting the *Porgy and Bess* troupe's train when it arrives in Paris. Does he represent many other people who play small roles in the book or who are not mentioned? Does her relationship to these people show an increasing comfort level with whites?

7. **Julian, the purser, and the doctor:** These three men, the first from Yugoslavia and the other two from the ship that takes the opera troupe from Athens, Greece, to Alexandria, Egypt, and back, are two would-be lovers and one real lover of our narrator. Why do you think she includes so much about them? Is her narration of Julian's inept stalking of her essentially humorous, or does it also show some sympathy for the man? The two men on the ship represent kindness, in the purser, and good looks, in the doctor. Is it significant that Angelou has sexual relations

with the latter but not the former? Are they both after the same thing, basically, marriage to a U.S. citizen in order to obtain citizenship? Does her appeal as an American give Angelou any new ideas about or appreciation of her country?

8. **The *Porgy and Bess* troupe:** We have many descriptions of the looks and the actions of many members of this troupe. How do their offstage actions match their onstage roles? What difference does it make that the cast is all black? To which people does Angelou feel most close? From whom does she learn the most?

History and Context

Angelou does not mention historical events directly in this third volume of her autobiography, but there are background elements that situate her experiences in the cultural context of the 1950s. When she gets the call from Clyde/Guy's school asking her to come in on account of the comments her son has made about the military (chapter 12), she recalls her attempt to join the army, foiled not by the pregnancy and child she hid but by her attendance at age fourteen and fifteen of a labor school which was on the House Un-American Activities Committee list. Yes, he got these opinions at home, she tells the principal and teacher, justifiably fearful that even this much revelation could get her blacklisted in the entertainment industry. As we have noted, Angelou begins this book with a blues song and devotes the first chapter and many other places in the book to a discussion of black music and musicians. Martin Halliwell, in his study of the 1950s, says that it was black music that ushered in the new visibility of African American culture (141), a shift that reflected a necessary step toward the intensification of the civil rights movement that would soon follow. Much of Angelou's book is spent on her tour of Europe and North Africa with the *Porgy and Bess* performers and crew. Though she does not mention it as historically significant, this was part of an innovative and largely successful effort of the U.S. State Department to bring the most positive aspects of American culture to other countries to counter the negative American images that often prevailed abroad. This particular tour, made possible by the State Department Emergency Fund, sought to reach the less prosperous countries of eastern Europe, the Middle East, and Africa (Prevots 2829).

Sample Topics:

1. **Black music:** Gather together what you know and what you can find out about the musicians mentioned in chapter 1 especially, but also elsewhere, such as chapter 25, where the opera company parties with Lionel Hampton and his band in Tel Aviv. (Angelou says that normally a jazz group would have nothing to do with an opera group and vice versa, but things are different when out of the country.) Listen to as many works as you can and compare your notes with what Angelou says about them. Are these names and songs that are familiar to you, or are they new? Can you see or hear ways in which this 1950s music led to later music, even up to today? Do you think that music has a role in leading the way in sociopolitical movements such as the civil rights movement?

2. **Cultural touring:** The State Department–sponsored tour of *Porgy and Bess* to Eastern Europe, the Middle East, and North Africa had as its goal increased understanding and appreciation of the United States in those regions. Why would the State Department have chosen *Porgy and Bess*? A black troupe? Is there evidence in Angelou's narration that the goals are met, that is, that the Americans are better appreciated and understood after their visits to the various cities? Be sure to include offstage encounters in your thinking as well as the performances of the opera. Does Angelou emphasize enough the opera itself, or is she too occupied in the book with the activities beyond the performances?

3. **What is left out:** There were several significant events in African American history that occurred during the years Angelou covers in the book, 1949 to 1955, events she does not mention. The color line in American professional sports was broken and weakened in several ways, with baseball star Jackie Robinson named most valuable player in the National League. Althea Gibson became the first black individual to compete in the U.S. Lawn Tennis Association Nationals at Forest Hills and at Wimbledon in England. Four black basketball players signed contracts to play in the National Basketball Association (NBA). Artists and authors gained prominence as well, with poet Gwen-

dolyn Brooks awarded the Pulitzer Prize for *Annie Allen,* Ralph Ellison receiving a National Book Award for *Invisible Man,* and James Baldwin's *Go Tell It on the Mountain* being nominated for that award. The U.S. Supreme Court made rulings about segregation, including the important 1954 *Brown v. Board of Education,* desegregating the public schools and overturning the legal basis for segregation dating from *Plessy v. Ferguson* in 1896. Finally, two events involving individuals looked backward and forward in race relations. Lynchings did not disappear, but they diminished significantly, despite the well-publicized death in Mississippi of fourteen-year-old Emmett Till from Chicago, evidently for flirting with a white woman clerk. This case would become the basis for Baldwin's powerful play, *Blues for Mister Charlie.* The funeral display of Till's mutilated body and the publication of the pictures in *Jet* magazine brought the horrors of lynching to the forefront and led to national protest. In that same year, 1955, Rosa Parks sat down in the white section of an Alabama bus, leading to the Montgomery bus boycott and the rise to increasing prominence of Martin Luther King Jr. (Finkelman 256–57).

Why do you think these and other historical events are left out of this volume of Angelou's autobiography? Is the omission a way of showing that she only slowly becomes politicized? Is her lack of involvement with the larger world typical for her age group, the early twenties, at this time?

Philosophy and Ideas

Angelou is not particularly introspective or engaged in philosophical or abstract notions during this period in her life. Nevertheless, there are a couple of key, central ideas that are approached either indirectly or directly. The first is a continuation of a struggle she deals with in her earlier autobiographical volumes as well—race relations, particularly in the United States and between blacks and whites, though she narrates some incidents in Europe that also indirectly address this thought. The other related idea she does address directly is victimization and its impact on the victim.

1. **Integration and black-white friendships:** Angelou's friendship with the young woman in the record store, mentioned in *Gather Together in My Name*, is discussed extensively in the first chapter of *Singin'*. What makes this relationship so difficult for Angelou? What are the suspicions she must overcome to relate normally to Louise? Are those suspicions well founded or exaggerated? Are there stereotypes of which she must rid herself? Are single incidents and connections, like the one between Angelou and Louise, important to the overall goal of integration, which will come into much more prominence as a national issue in the next books? Are there additional incidents throughout the book that also illustrate the difficulty of black-white friendships? In what ways are the biases and expectations of whites in Europe different from those in the United States?

2. **The safety of victimhood:** When Angelou, in chapter 9 of *Singin'*, is treated by singer Jorie and her friends from the Purple Onion as an equal who "could do whatever they could do," she describes herself as having to give up old habits of lashing out, being haughty, or "withdrawing into righteous indignation." Then she describes the enervating effect that being repeatedly kept from opportunities can have on a person—"one can use the rejection as an excuse to cease all efforts" and to feel superior at the same time (461). Does this description ring true for you in relation to your own experiences or someone else's? What does Angelou do to get beyond this feeling, and is there a model or lesson in her recognizing and handling this situation?

Form and Genre

The thirty chapters of *Singin'*, with no preface as in the previous two books, divide themselves rather neatly into fifteen chapters leading up to Angelou's departure for Europe and Africa and fifteen dedicated to her touring with *Porgy and Bess*. The two longest chapters, 22 and 23, are found in the second part and cover Yugoslavia, Greece, and the ship to North Africa, including several of Angelou's romantic involvements with men. At the beginning of the book, Angelou acknowledges the help of the Bellagio Study and Conference Center in Italy and the Rockefeller Foundation. (For a good description of writing and eating at this elaborate center, see Angelou's *Hallelujah! The Welcome Table* 113–16.) One almost gets the feeling that she adapted her writing here to her surroundings among other professional researchers and writers and maybe took too much advice too willingly. The voice adopted for the book seems to be more standard than the image-filled, emotional *Caged Bird* or the slangy, freewheeling *Gather Together*. This is particularly true of *Singin's* two longest chapters, which read like set pieces, designed for the maximum humorous effect.

In the first part, there is some attempt to introduce the intensity of emotion and inward struggle, particularly with Angelou's first marriage, to Tosh Angelos. Her increasing dissatisfaction with the marriage is said to be part of their differences on religion and attached to her worry that her son is growing up godless. She describes church shopping and a "threshing floor" conversion experience, much like that of James Baldwin in *Go Tell It on the Mountain*. The religious overtones seem to disappear in the second part of the book, however, almost as though they were referenced as a means of explaining the breakup of what seems otherwise to be a satisfying marriage.

While the first part of the book seems more forced and calculated, the second part moves along inexorably like a flood or like all travel in foreign lands: image following upon image, impression upon impression, experience upon experience, experiment upon experiment. Evidently, Angelou began her devotion to writing during this first European tour, in the form of long letters to her mother back in San Francisco (and via her mother to her son). Perhaps she kept copies of those letters or made copies of them to use in writing *Singin'*. It is said that Vivian Baxter took the letters out after the book was published and was impressed at how accurately her daughter had remembered events (Rich 80); more likely, Angelou somehow had letters to which she could refer, and this is why the descriptions of the trip are so detailed.

In relation to autobiography as a literary form, the third volume adds new difficulties and complexities to Angelou's approach to relating her story. First, the author is becoming a known and praised performer, and it is increasingly hard to describe this without sounding self-aggrandizing. Angelou perhaps consciously counterbalances any implied egotism with the extensive offstage situations and encounters she includes and the jocular ways in which they are described. Second, the people she is with are also, at least some of them, known to a wider audience and might have objections to her depictions. Checking passages with her family, as she did previously, is not a workable plan with acquaintances and friends outside the family, and the result often seems to be a kind of toned-down prose more dedicated to exterior or surface impressions. Mary Jane Lupton has described the "plot" of this book as setting up opposing "incidents and attitudes," including the prominent pattern of "affirmation and denial" (*Maya* 101). This back-and-forth movement some readers may find realistic, especially when Angelou deals with motherhood and its conflict with career. Others may become impatient with it, however, thinking it overdone. It is inevitable that anyone reading more than one of Angelou's autobiographical books is going to find some of the same themes repeated, which prompts the question, Have the new forms the issues have taken on here created any new understandings or resolutions? If not, what is the value of an additional volume of autobiography?

1. **"Part one" and "part two":** Which of the two sections, the first fifteen chapters, on breaking into show business, or the second fifteen, dedicated to the performing and traveling, do you find more engaging? Why? Does the theme of motherhood-career conflict adequately hold the two parts together, or do you see any other themes that lend unity to the whole?
2. **Travel as unifying principle:** Is it possible to see the book as a dual travel narrative, with the protagonist/narrator traveling ever farther abroad while she also travels deeper and deeper into herself, her feelings, motivations, frustrations, and resolutions? If so, what are the understandings the narrator comes to by the end of the book that she did not have at the beginning? Of herself? Of others?

Language, Symbols, and Imagery

Singin' is a more straightforward book in its language than the previous two, with somewhat sparser figurative language, including the use of simile and symbol. In many ways, the reduced use of simile, especially, as compared with the earlier autobiographies, makes the occasional appearance of the literary device stand out all the more. The title itself includes a simile in the "like Christmas," and chapter 1 opens with first the lines from a blues song and then a beautiful extended metaphor on the meaning of music to a lonely woman. Mary Jane Lupton, in her book *Maya Angelou: A Critical Companion,* finds the use of repetition in this book a prominent stylistic device and mentions the passage where Angelou notes how she is repeating her mother's actions in leaving her child and where Angelou seeks out help and consolation from older men, perhaps to make up for her sense of abandonment from her father.

1. **Similes in conversion experience:** Look closely at the figurative comparisons Angelou uses in chapter 4 describing her experience at the Evening Star Baptist Church. Is she making fun of the service and her participation in it with comparisons such as her feet "slithering and snapping like two turtles shot with electricity" and the "Amens" and "Yes, Lords" bouncing around the room "like the balls in a cartoon sing-along"? What does the description leave you thinking about this period in her life?

2. **Language in the death of Momma/Grandmother Henderson:** At the end of chapter 5, her husband tells Angelou about the death of her grandmother in Arkansas while Angelou has been very sick. Notice how the language changes in this short passage. What is the intent and impact of that switch to a more formal structure and language?

3. **Dialogue:** We have noted previously that most autobiography contains little dialogue and that this is one of the ways Angelou's books differ from traditional autobiography to become more like fiction. Pick a section of the book with plenty of dialogue, and ask some questions about it, including, "How could Angelou actually remember what everyone said in this situation?" and "Does each person speak in a different way?" How do the various modes of language Angelou employs, from more formal to slang inflected, reflect the variation in the characters presented and their individual modes of speaking?

Bibliography and Online Resources for *Singin' and Swingin' and Gettin' Merry Like Christmas*

Angelou, Maya. *Singin' and Swingin' and Gettin' Merry Like Christmas.* In *The Collected Autobiographies of Maya Angelou.* New York: Modern Library, 2004. 385–617.

Davis, Curt. "Maya Angelou: And Still She Rises." In *Conversations with Maya Angelou.* Ed. Jeffrey M. Elliot. Jackson and London: University Press of Mississippi, 1989. 68–76.

Finkelman, Paul et al, eds. *Encyclopedia of African American History, 1896 to the Present.* Volume V. New York: Oxford University Press, 2009.

Hagen, Lyman B. *Heart of a Woman, Mind of a Writer, and Soul of a Poet: A Critical Analysis of the Writings of Maya Angelou.* Lanham, Md.: University Press of America, 1997.

Halliwell, Martin. *American Culture in the 1950s.* Edinburgh: Edinburgh University Press, 2007.

Koyana, Siphokazi. "The Heart of the Matter: Motherhood and Marriage in the Autobiographies of Maya Angelou." *Black Scholar.* Summer 2002. Vol. 32, Issue 2, 35–45. Page numbers here are to the EBSCOhost online printout version, 1–14.

Lupton, Mary Jane. "Singing the Black Mother: Maya Angelou and Autobiographical Continuity" *Black American Literature Forum* 24:2 (1990): 257–76. Page numbers here will be to the EBSCOhost online printout version, 1–15.

Prevots, Naima. *Dance for Export: Cultural Diplomacy and the Cold War.* Middletown, Conn.: Wesleyan University Press, 1999.

Rich, Judith. "Westways Women: Life Is for Living." In *Conversations with Maya Angelou.* Ed. Jeffrey M. Elliot. Jackson and London: University Press of Mississippi, 1989. 77–85.

Tate, Claudia. "Maya Angelou." In *Conversations with Maya Angelou.* Ed. Jeffrey M. Elliot. Jackson and London: University Press of Mississippi, 1989. 146–56.

THE HEART OF A WOMAN

READING TO WRITE

THOSE WHO have read Maya Angelou's three serial autobiographies leading up to *The Heart of a Woman*, her fourth, will find many ideas and elements carried over from one to another, all chronologically following the author's life and all displaying learning and growth. But there are differences among the works, and Angelou is careful to make it possible for each of the autobiographies to stand alone, even though they explore many similar themes. *The Heart of a Woman*, published in 1981 and covering the historically significant years of 1955–1962—significant especially for African Americans—finds this prolific chronicler of her life at a more mature stage. No longer the child of *I Know Why the Caged Bird Sings*, the earliest and best known of these books, nor the teenage single mother finding her way through the drugs and prostitution of *Gather Together in My Name*, nor the struggling dancer, singer, and actress of *Singin' and Swingin' and Gettin' Merry Like Christmas*, Angelou is, by the time covered in *Heart*, an increasingly well-known writer and performer and innovative civil rights worker, making friends of the powerful and maintaining her gutsy "can do" approach to life. She is also no longer the mother of an infant son, nor a toddler, nor an elementary school student but of a teenager who is showing increasing independence and impatience, too, with his mother's many moves, her many men, and her overprotectiveness.

While moving through time, the book also travels ever east to three significant cities or countries, from San Francisco, where Angelou's mother, Vivian Baxter, lives, to New York City and then to Cairo, Egypt, with some time spent in London in between. The "ancient spiritual" epigraph to the book's long, untitled prologue—"The ole ark's a-moverin', a-moverin', a moverin', the ole ark's a-moverin' along"— captures and suggests this sense of motion, movement, and progress. The careful reader, perhaps on the recommended second reading, will wonder about the book's title and dedication and may formulate some ideas of how they fit the book itself. Just as her first autobiography took its title from a Paul Laurence Dunbar poem about a caged bird, so does this fourth book take its title from a poem including a bird and a cage, this one lesser known than Dunbar's and by a woman, Georgia Douglas Johnson. "The Heart of a Woman," in the Johnson poem, "goes forth with the dawn / As a lone bird" and wings and roams until nightfall, when it "falls back" and, in desperation, "enters some alien cage," trying to forget dreams of stars while it "breaks, breaks, breaks on the sheltering bars." Is Angelou suggesting the new freedom she feels moving cross-country from her mother to New York City and finding her place in the Harlem Writers Guild? Working for Martin Luther King Jr.'s Southern Christian Leadership Conference? Is she hinting at the alien entrapment she feels in her never legalized "marriage" to Vusumzi Make, a South African liberationist? Or do the words of the poem suggest that she goes from initially thinking of the foreignness of Egypt as a delight to eventually feeling it to be something of a cage? Does the book end with "break, break, break" or with a new morning and a new lone flight? The dedication of the book suggests a new step. First, it is dedicated to her grandson, so readers who have been following her son Clyde/Guy feel that his story, not finished here, has some positive outcomes in the next generation. Next, she sends a thank you to fourteen "sister/friends whose love encourages me to spell my name: WOMAN" (Angelou n.p.; further references to the book will be given by page number only). Previous books in her series had been dedicated to family and to brothers; here we sense a new identification on Angelou's part with her role as a woman, an identification that is spelled out in the book itself.

If a reader assigned a paper chose to write on the continuing struggles of Angelou in raising her son, with the son now in his teens, there are many possible ways to narrow that general topic down to something about which one can make significant comments and analysis in five to ten pages. One possibility is to look closely at a passage in which Angelou, with her typical honesty, briefly reflects on Guy's growing sexuality and attraction to his mother, a stunning figure who is, after all, only sixteen years older than he is. The passage is found in chapter 9, in the middle of Angelou having dinner with Vus Make for the first time. She begins with a statement of universality: "The sensuality between parents and children often is so intense that only the age-old control by society prevents the rise of sexuality" (743). Then she starts to zero in on her own situation, first indicating increased "strain" when the parent is single and the child is of the opposite sex. How does one demonstrate love in this situation, she asks, "without stirring in the young and innocent mind the idea of sexuality?" Too many parents, she then suggests, solve the dilemma by withdrawing physical contact, which does not, by implication, seem to her a positive solution, since it problematically leaves "the children yearning and befuddled with ideas of unworthiness." Then Angelou moves directly to her own case with a short sentence using a cliché in its figurative comparison. The paragraph reads: "Guy and I had spent years skating the thin ice" (743).

Then Angelou moves immediately to an illustrative example, a California memory of some years earlier, when Guy was twelve, and the two came home from a summer swimming party and he "startled" her by saying: "'You know, Mom. Everyone talks about Marilyn Monroe's body. But we were watching today and all the guys said you had a prettier shape than Marilyn Monroe.'" Angelou reacts to this statement in noting that "if I began to figure in his sexual fantasies he would be scarred" for life. So Angelou then describes how she went through her clothing, taking out all "the provocative dresses" to give to the Salvation Army, in favor of "the staid outfits which were more motherly." She also "never again bought a form-fitting dress or a blouse with a plunging neckline" (743–44).

To analyze this passage, one possibility is to use a Freudian approach, that is, apply a theory of human behavior promulgated by Sigmund Freud early in the twentieth century and suggesting that our unconscious minds influence our conscious acts and feelings. One description Freud gave was of the Oedipus complex, named after the Greek king who unwittingly kills his father and marries his mother in a Sophocles drama called *Oedipus Rex.* In Freud's conception of the Oedipus complex, the early love of the male child for his mother can escalate into sexual desire with a corresponding jealousy and desire to kill the father. In Angelou's passage, it is significant that she brings this memory up in the middle of entertaining a new man in her life, a man she intends to marry, breaking off her engagement to another man. Angelou notes that this new love interest, after dinner, has unwittingly taken "Guy's chair." So it is with trepidation that she awaits Vus's private talk with Guy and with great relief that she witnesses both males coming out of Guy's room smiling and happy. If anything were to clinch her sudden switch of partners, it is undoubtedly the feeling that having a father figure around will be potentially helpful to them all.

Mary Jane Lupton, in her book *Maya Angelou: A Critical Companion,* does a short Freudian analysis of *Heart* and then goes on to give a more recent "Psychological/Feminist Reading," which, she explains, puts the woman at the center rather than assuming she is subject to a husband, father, or other man. In this kind of analysis, one might relate this passage to Angelou's other thoughts about being a woman, going back to her abandonment by her parents and the rape that occurs in *I Know Why the Caged Bird Sings.* Lupton believes *Heart* offers "a wealth of woman-centered insights," including perhaps another possible topic for an essay—does Angelou show a suppressed attraction to women? "A psychological feminist," Lupton says, "would help Angelou deal with her conflicting attitudes towards lesbianism, suggesting a greater openness toward the likelihood that she consciously or unconsciously desires women more than she is willing to admit" (135–37).

TOPICS AND STRATEGIES
Themes

Many possible themes will likely occur to you as you read the book carefully, if at all possible, twice. Remember that a theme is not a refined topic for a paper. Like the other elements of the book that will be considered—character, history and context, language, and imagery—the following will give you a place to start in defining your paper topic and thesis. Some of the questions posed will help you think more about your own reading of the text and about what you would like to say in your essay.

Sample Topics:

1. **Sexuality of a teenaged son:** We have looked at one passage above where Angelou directly discusses Guy's developing sexuality especially in relation to his mother. Do you find other passages that directly or indirectly deal with him in relation to sex? Do you think that Angelou handles these situations in positive, effective ways, or do you see flaws in her reasoning and behavior? Are there elements in American history and American culture that make this issue even more explosive for a young black man than it would be for a white man? (Look, for example, at Angelou's discussion in chapter 2, in the paragraph beginning: "The black mother perceives destruction at every door. . . .")

2. **Sexuality of the mother:** Angelou is very open about her own sexual needs, principles, and satisfaction. Find some of the passages that reflect and express her sentiments in regard to sexuality. Angelou says that she finds strong intellectual ability and learning sexually appealing. Is this played out in her relationship with Vus Make, particularly in her frequent repetition of his being *fat*—a word with negative connotations, when she could have used a more neutral word such as *heavy* or *big*? In other words, can sexual appeal be other than physical? Do you think Angelou's own openness about her own sexuality has a positive or negative influence on Guy? Does marriage, even her not legally recognized "marriage" with Vus Make, change her actions? Are the affairs of the husband more justified than the affairs of the wife? In her mind? In yours?

3. **Sexuality and leadership:** Look at the sensual appeal Angelou finds in Martin Luther King Jr. and Malcolm X, especially the latter. Does it make some sense that sexual appeal is part of the power of a speaker or leader? (Some have even analyzed the effectiveness of Adolf Hitler's speeches with this in mind.)

4. **Writing:** Angelou moves to New York City in *The Heart of a Woman* in part to find new opportunities for her talents as a performer but also to work on her newfound interest in writing. She does not start at the bottom, with a beginner's group or course of some kind, but rather with the Harlem Writers Guild, with many of the participants established, published

writers. Why do you think she spends so much time in chapter 2 describing her fear of reading for the group, her horror and embarrassment at their criticism, and her struggle to continue? Do only other writers know what writers go through?

5. **Samplings of the African continent:** Look at the passages in chapters 15 and 19 describing Angelou's and Guy's arrivals in Cairo, Egypt, and Accra, Ghana. What are her expectations? What is she most surprised at? What is she most shocked at? Pleased with? How does she use physical description of settings to convey her amazement? In the case of Cairo, after she has been there awhile, how do her ideas about the place change? Does a first-time visitor to a place see, notice, and detect things that people who have been there for a while do not? How does her experience abroad make her look at her home country, the United States, differently?

6. **Women's roles:** In chapter 10, Angelou first describes her dreams of Africa activated by her romance with Vus. She then goes on to recount her activities and Vus's responses when she returns to New York City to rent and furnish an apartment for them and then her constant extreme cleaning and cooking, never to his satisfaction, as he continues his "liberation" activities. Do these experiences symbolize and summarize the changes women went through in the civil rights movement, leading to the women's movement that followed? How are the South African man's expectations of a wife different and how the same as expectations would be in an American man at the same time?

7. **Jobs:** Angelou repeatedly jumps into jobs she has no experience doing—from acting to initiating a fundraising cabaret to running an office to editing and writing. What enables her to embrace new situations and challenges with such confidence? How does she go about mastering something new, for example, the editing job in Cairo, in chapter 16? Does "putting on a good front"—that is, looking confident and competent—help her both get and perform the jobs? Thinking of the time of which she is writing, the early 1960s, what are the relationships between men and women on the job and the attitudes of men toward women

working? Does Angelou appear to be much happier when she is working at something new and difficult rather than playing the role of the "ideal housewife"?

Character

Except for her son, Guy, many of the primary people in the previous books in Angelou's serial autobiography do not appear in this one. Some are no longer living, such as Grandmother Henderson/Momma, who raised Angelou and who was a key figure in the first book in the series. Some family members are still living but fall into the background, such as Angelou's brother, Bailey Johnson, and her mother, Vivian Baxter, who only appears here in chapter 1 at a thoroughly described hotel farewell between mother and daughter and in chapter 14 as a distraught divorcee who finds a new dependence on her daughter, rather than vice versa, which surprises them both. Instead, many new characters are introduced in the new locations of New York City, London, Cairo, and Accra, many of them people already famous during the time Angelou is covering, others who would become famous and whose names one might now recognize. In the following topic suggestions, some of the characters will be grouped into categories, and some will be examined individually, basically in the approximate order in which they appear in *The Heart of a Woman*.

Sample Topics:

1. **Billie Holiday:** Angelou's long, untitled, and unnumbered introductory chapter to *Heart* includes an extensive and unexpurgated section on the famous jazz singer, who stayed several days with the narrator and her son only months before Holiday's death. Angelou tolerates "Lady Day's" language and her criticism but definitely thinks the singer has gone too far when she yells obscenities at Guy. Guy, in turn, grows angry at his mother for letting the woman yell at him. Look up information on Billie Holiday and her life and death, her talent, and her character, and then ask why Angelou chooses to begin this book with this woman. Is it to provide a contrast to the way she sees her own life or hopes it will be? Is it a kind of warning that talent and fame can mislead a person into carelessness about things that might be more important, such as health

and relationships? Or is it, as Cherron Barnwell suggests, to assume "the self-image of a female blues singer whose stature equals Lady Day's" (143)?

2. **The Harlem Writers Guild:** Angelou is introduced to the idea of serious writing, of moving to New York City, and of joining the guild by one of its co-founders, author John Killens, whom she met when he was in California to read the screenplay of his first novel, *Youngblood* (1954), about a black Georgia family in the early twentieth century. (His second novel, *And Then We Heard the Thunder,* from 1962, would be nominated for the Pulitzer Prize.) At the meeting at which Angelou reads her play, described in chapter 2, other published writers are present and offer their critiques: Sarah Wright, John Henrik Clarke, Paule Marshall. What does Angelou learn from this gathering? From their discussion of a political issue of the time, fair play for Cuba, during the gathering? From her discussions with various people, including Killens, after the evening? What does the reader learn about Angelou from this chapter?

3. **Godfrey Cambridge:** Stage, screen, and television actor Cambridge became a good friend and collaborator with Angelou on the Cabaret for Freedom fundraiser for Martin Luther King Jr.'s Southern Christian Leadership Conference. He was also a fellow actor in the Broadway production of Jean Genet's *The Blacks* that Angelou was part of. Though she clearly wishes to have a romantic relationship with Cambridge, it never gets to that point. Why?

4. **Martin Luther King Jr., Bayard Rustin, Ralph Abernathy, and SCLC staff and speakers:** Angelou and Cambridge go to hear King speak in a Harlem church, and he is preceded by other speakers such as Abernathy. Inspired to plan their fundraising cabaret, Angelou goes to discuss the project with SCLC, and eventually she is hired to run the Harlem office of the organization, which is when she meets King personally (chapters 4 to 6). How do other information and descriptions of these now historical figures compare and/or contrast to Angelou's depictions of them? Do her descriptions bring them to life in ways a history book cannot?

5. **Vusumzi Make:** This South African freedom fighter during the time of apartheid comes to New York and sweeps Angelou off her feet. She breaks off her engagement and imminent marriage to another man in order to go with Make to London, back to New York City, then to Cairo, Egypt (chapters 8 to 18), which makes him a key character throughout the central section of the book. What is it about this man that makes her want to be, as she says, the handkerchief wiping up his sweat when he speaks? What are Make's faults and strengths? When does she begin to have doubts about the relationship? How do Make's concepts of what a woman and a wife should be clash with Angelou's self-image? What does the reader learn about the lives of freedom fighters in exile from their countries? Why are the sources of Make's money never clear in the book?

6. **Freedom fighter wives:** In London, Angelou meets some of the other wives attached to exiled freedom fighters from various countries and attends social events with them (chapter 10). How does she describe these people briefly? What characteristics does she home in on in order to capture a character or a look? When the other women begin telling their stories and showing their scars, Angelou tells the stories of Harriet Tubman and Sojourner Truth and quotes Truth's speech with the refrain "an' ain't I a woman?" What connections does Angelou see between liberation movements elsewhere in the world and the history of slavery in the United States? What connections do you see? One of the wives, after a few drinks, surprises Angelou by saying that there is "more to life than being a diligent maid with a permanent pussy." How does this description come all too true for Angelou back in New York City?

7. **Women and men in Cairo:** Chapters 17 and 18 describe various activities and events in the Egyptian city, some that occur among people in a similar situation to the Makes and others from the diplomatic corps of various other countries. How does Angelou identify with the women? Do the other men make assumptions much like Vus Make's about the roles of husbands and wives? Are there exceptions?

History and Context

The Heart of a Woman contains many historical allusions, or references, a departure from Angelou's previous work, *Singin' and Swingin' and Gettin' Merry Like Christmas,* in which many events of the time that are significant to African Americans are not referenced. At the beginning of *Heart,* Angelou almost seems to be making up for this by listing several historical and cultural events: tennis player Althea Gibson winning the U.S. Open women's singles championship; President Dwight D. Eisenhower sending federal troops to Little Rock, Arkansas, to integrate the public schools; the innovative popularity of Jack Kerouac's book *On the Road.* These cultural allusions provide a frame of reference for the earliest of her and Guy's experiences recorded in *Heart.* First, they live beatnik style on a houseboat in Sausalito with several unnamed fellow Beats, which gives Angelou a "respite from racial tensions" and Guy "an opportunity to be around whites who did not" either exoticize or ignore him (624). Then they live as the only blacks in a white community and, after trouble with Guy's school, move to a racially mixed part of the city.

Of interest historically are the events and movements during their time in New York City and Cairo, from 1955 to 1962—Rosa Parks refusing to give up her bus seat in Montgomery, Alabama, leading to the bus boycott and elevating Martin Luther King Jr. to a leadership position; the rise of the Nation of Islam and leader Elijah Muhammad; the tensions between the second in command of the "black Muslims," Malcolm X, and King's newly established SCLC; increasing African independence and the murder of the imprisoned Patrice Lumumba, freedom fighter and then first prime minister of the newly independent Republic of the Congo, in 1960.

Sample Topics:

1. **The Beats:** Look up some information about a group of poets and other writers, such as Jack Kerouac, called the Beats. They lived primarily in San Francisco and rejected the materialism of American culture, arguing for freedom of drug use and sexual experimentation. Does Angelou's rather brief description of her "houseboat days," including her Afro, her bare feet, and her clothing express any attitude that is reflective of the movement

and its proponents? What makes her want to "move on"? Does placing her Beat phase early in the autobiography, but quickly moving on, suggest that this segment of her life marked a kind of transition to greater maturity?

2. **Whites in the civil rights movement:** Review the roles whites played in the civil rights movement of the 1960s. In chapter 4, when Angelou first goes to the SCLC offices to speak of her and Godfrey Cambridge's planned Cabaret for Freedom, she ends up talking with two white men, and, later, running the SCLC office (chapters 6 to 8), she is upset by the hiring of additional whites. Does she ever get accustomed to working with or for whites in "the Movement"? Is her attitude typical, do you think, for a southern black of her generation? When a white woman comes to her in tears after a performance of *The Blacks* (chapter 12), Angelou bluntly refuses to be her friend, a reminder of a scene in *The Autobiography of Malcolm X*, when a white woman asks, after one of Malcolm's speeches, what she can do to help and he curtly says, "Nothing." Were whites helpful in making progress? Did it make a difference if whites were in leadership positions or followers and supporters?

3. **Organizing a demonstration:** Chapter 11, the longest in the book by far, describes Angelou's learning experience with a group she and others have originated, the Cultural Association for Women of African Heritage. They plan a simple demonstration, which turns into a mob, at the United Nations General Assembly when U.S. ambassador Adlai Stevenson is set to announce the death of Patrice Lumumba. What does she learn from this experience? What does she learn from Malcolm X, when two organizers seek him out for support? Does Angelou make use of this experience and learning in other events in the book?

4. **South African apartheid:** While Angelou is involved with the South African freedom fighter Vusumzi Make, and they are living in New York City, she begins to get phone calls talking of his infidelity and culminating in a fake call from a hospital emergency room claiming that her son, Guy, is there. Make tells her that it is a South African police tactic for intimidating exiles

like him. Look up information on apartheid and see if you can find anything to support Make's claim, including descriptions of other ways the police made life difficult for exiles.

5. **Br'er Rabbit and the briar patch:** In chapter 16, when Angelou takes on the job of assistant editor at the *Arab Observer* in Cairo, she ends the description of her first day of work with a bit of southern black folk material, a story of Br'er Rabbit. What is the origin of these stories (sometimes called "Uncle Remus Stories"), which elevate the rabbit to clever victory over larger, more powerful opponents? Why did these stories get passed on in the African American community? What effect did they have? Why does Angelou reference these stories here?

Philosophy and Ideas

Some of the central ideas explored in *The Heart of a Woman* are extensions of similar discussions found in the previous volumes of this serial autobiography. Some of the philosophical strands Angelou explores develop as a result of the new experiences she describes in this volume. We will concentrate on the latter, but keep in mind that such topics as violence and psychology, from chapter 3 of *Caged Bird*, or love and marriage, from chapter 5 of *Singin'*, are also relevant to this book. In this fourth volume, it seems as though Angelou is making significant progress in working toward a personal philosophy suited to her background, goals, talents, and experiences. The work is set during a time of ferment, debate, demonstration, and riot in American life, perhaps the necessary ingredients of national progress. Understandably, that ferment leads to a general climate of inner searching, debate, and change.

Sample Topics:

1. **Nonviolent civil disobedience versus "by any means necessary":** Martin Luther King Jr.'s carefully articulated argument for peaceful demonstrations in order to protest and change discriminatory laws or practices is increasingly in conflict during this period with Malcolm X's refusal to eschew force, power, or violence to achieve freedom. Which side does Angelou lean toward in the book, or is she more practical, thinking "all kinds are needed" in the battle? Does she change as the book

progresses? Does the rage she often feels (Lyman Hagen calls it not "repressed" but a healthier "suppressed rage" [160]) suggest she could easily resort to violence? Or do the negative experiences she has faced with resisting and striking back suggest to her that her Grandmother Henderson's passive endurance is a kind of resistance too? Are there appropriate times for a show of force, such as when she curbs gang violence against Guy by displaying a borrowed pistol to a gang member? Do both tactics benefit from Vivian Baxter's advice, in chapter 1, never to show fear?

2. **Integration versus separation:** King's and Malcolm's philosophies also differ in their goals—King fighting for integration and Malcolm X subscribing to the Nation of Islam principle that all whites are "the devil" and the only salvation is in separation. (Keep in mind that *integration* does not mean "assimilation" and *separation* does not mean "segregation." Ideally, *integration* will mean a back-and-forth relationship of two equal parties, whereas *assimilation* would mean a smaller or less empowered group of individuals being absorbed into the dominant one. *Separation* is the self-chosen drawing away of one group from another, and *segregation* is division forced on another group by the dominant one.) Do you think Angelou takes a position on these various goals? Do her comments seem more favorable to King or Malcolm X? How are these various terms and the social realities they express reflected in Angelou's writing?

3. **Writers and activism:** Writers such as Angelou's friend James Baldwin express a conflict between becoming activists in important movements of their time, like the civil rights movement, and sticking to their writing. In a sense, they feel guilty if they are not doing something more than writing but then are not able to devote as much time to their creative work if they become too active. This was the case with Baldwin, who became a form of spokesperson for black America for a time. Do you sense some of this conflict in Angelou, too, as in chapter 3, when she resolves to get out of show business ("I would never again work to make people smile inanely and would take on the responsibility of making them think") but then is asked

to sing at the famed Apollo Theater and takes the gig? How does she seem to resolve this conflict over time, or does she simply escape it through marriage?

4. **Genet's *The Blacks:*** When Angelou first reads and then acts as the White Queen in this play that posits a reverse in the power dynamic between black and white, she disagrees vehemently with the thought that blacks moving into power positions over whites would act as unjustly as whites do. Does she change her mind about this, or does she think there is a heritage of justice among blacks that would keep them from simply duplicating the past? What are some of the elements of that heritage, according to Angelou?

Form and Genre

The kind of autobiography Angelou writes starts to change as she meets, befriends, and includes many more people who are well known, individuals about whom other descriptions can be found. With these inclusions, one could argue that she tones down her language and censors any criticism or negative impression she might otherwise have recorded (Lyman Hagen describes this book and the next as being written in "thoughtful ballad tones" [53]). There are fewer extremely short chapters, with twenty-one chapters in total, counting the prologue. The shortest chapter is five pages, the longest twenty-five, and the average about twelve. This structure lends a tone of seriousness to the book, reflective of her resolution to stop making people "smile inanely" and to start making them think. The longest chapter, eleven, appears about halfway through and concerns the Cultural Association for Women of African Heritage and their organizing of the U.N. protest at the time of Patrice Lumumba's murder. Not only does the chapter struggle with the many contemporaneous issues swirling around demonstrations and riots, but it also provides a kind of emphasis on and transition to both Africa and Angelou's involvement with women. Also, as Angelou's readers had possibly come to expect, there is a lack of closure in the final chapter. Rather, the book ends seemingly with a lead-in to the next entry in the series. Still, one of Angelou's primary ongoing themes, motherhood, is granted some form of conclusion. *The Heart of a Woman* ends with Guy moving to the University of Ghana, after he makes a speech to Angelou about being a wonderful mother but not being needed any more since he is a grown man. Angelou's final line, "I'll be able to eat the whole breast of a roast chicken by myself" (879), suggests, as Mary Jane Lupton has said, the "recurring motif," or thematic image, of family chicken dinners in the entire series of autobiographies ("Singing . . ." 11). Elsewhere, Lupton has added that "the breast represents both the nurturing aspect of the mother as well as a weaning of herself from Guy's demands" (*Maya Angelou . . .* 131).

Sample Topics:

1. **Mothering and the independent adult:** What do you find to be Angelou's culminating description of motherhood—its pains, joys, worries, and rewards? Does her experience sitting at the bedside of the badly injured Guy after his car accident provide both Angelou and the reader a means of reviewing and summing up this strong recurring theme in her books?

2. **Descriptions of the famous:** Compare and contrast the descriptions Angelou makes of some famous people, such as Martin Luther King Jr. or Malcolm X, to the descriptions you find in a history textbook, biography, or other standard reference work. Do you think she is rather careful in what she says because the person is well known?

3. **Travel:** Opening with "the old ark's a-moverin" and ending with a new life in Ghana, West Africa, this is a book about Angelou's moving and traveling. Do you see this as a figurative motif as well, as Mary Jane Lupton says, "a voyage into the self" (*Maya . . .* 119)? What are some of the stars that guide her in that voyage, some of the resting places? What are some of the obstacles and some of the crossroads and turning points?

Language, Symbols, and Imagery

Corresponding with the toned-down, more mature tone and nature of the book as compared to the previous ones, Angelou's reliance on devices common to the novel, such as exciting plotlines and crisp and often humorous dialogue, also lessens in *Heart,* as does her use of the simile and metaphor. There is little to no dialect, though she attempts to match a person's language to his or her character. Carol Neubauer has pointed out that, in some scenes, Angelou has tried to use fictionalization "to create a sense of history larger than the story," combining "the re-creation of credible dialogue with historical references that go beyond her individual life" (3–4).

Sample Topics:

1. **Physical impression of Malcolm X:** In chapter 11, when Angelou first meets black Muslim leader Malcolm X, her language is extreme in describing his effect on her—"his aura was too bright and his masculine force affected me physically. . . . Up close he was a great red arch through which one could pass to eternity. His hair was the color of burning embers and his eyes pierced" (779). Look closely at this description and note how Angelou uses metaphor and simile; hyperbole, or exaggeration; stumbling speech on her part and articulate statement on his. Contrast this passage to his media appearance. How do the descriptions collectively convey her impression of this man?

2. **Appearance at the Apollo:** Chapter 3 contains a rather long description of how Angelou departs from the usual musical fare for a performer at the Apollo Theater in Harlem, including the singing of an African "call and response" song that requires audience participation. Look closely at how Angelou writes this narrative, from her portrayal of a doubtful theater manager becoming a convinced one to the description of the song itself and its theme, which seems to be making a point about a change in African Americans' relationship to Africa. Is this an effective way to make a point? Does Angelou's telling of the story echo the event itself, involving the reader in a response too?

3. **SCLC speeches:** Chapter 4 includes descriptions of several speakers, leading up to Martin Luther King Jr. How does Angelou convey the differences in the speakers' tones, style, language, appearance, and relation to the audience?

Comparison and Contrast Essays

Sample Topics:

1. **Black women and white women:** In an interview eliciting her views of the women's movement, Angelou once said that, though

"all the struggles are one" between black and white women, still the battle arenas are "different because of our histories" (Paterson 115–16). Explore this statement in terms of other things you have read by women, black and white. What might she mean by different arenas? How are the histories different? Are there also ways they are not different, either in the arenas or their histories? Has the women's movement helped or hindered the cooperation and understanding among black women and white women?

2. **Thomas Allen and Vusumzi Make:** Angelou experiences the attitudes and expectations of an American bail bondsman, Thomas Allen, and a South African freedom fighter, Vus Make. She is engaged to marry Allen but breaks it off to go away with Make. Compare and contrast these two men as individuals and in their relationships with her. Which characteristics are individual and which societal, which American and which South African? What is the appeal of Make to make her take such drastic action on short acquaintance? How long does her relationship to Make last? Might marriage to Allen have lasted longer since her expectations of him were not as high as what she hopes to derive from her relationship with Make?

3. **American women and other women:** In London and Cairo, Angelou is acquainted with many other women from African countries, and in chapter 10 she reports on an extensive gathering where many speak, including Angelou, who offers a long comment on women in black American history, such as Sojourner Truth and Harriet Tubman. Compare and contrast these women from different continents. How are they alike? How are they different?

Bibliography and Online Resources for *The Heart of a Woman*

Angelou, Maya. *The Heart of a Woman*. In *The Collected Autobiographies of Maya Angelou*. New York: Modern Library, 2004. 619–879.

Barnwell, Cherron A. "Singin' de Blues, Writing Black Female Survival in *I Know Why the Caged Bird Sings*." In *Maya Angelou*. Bloom's Modern Critical Views. Ed. Harold Bloom. New York: Chelsea House Publishers, 2009. 133–46.

Hagen, Lyman B. *Heart of a Woman, Mind of a Writer, and Soul of a Poet: A Critical Analysis of the Writings of Maya Angelou*. Lanham, Md.: University Press of America, 1997.

Lupton, Mary Jane. *Maya Angelou: A Critical Companion*. Westport, Conn., and London: Greenwood Press, 1998.

———. "Singing the Black Mother: Maya Angelou and Autobiographical Continuity." *Black American Literature Forum* 24:2 (1990): 257–76. Page numbers in the text are to the EBSCOhost online printout version, 1–14.

Neubauer, Carol E. "Displacement and Autobiographical Style in Maya Angelou's 'The Heart of a Woman.'" In *Maya Angelou*. Bloom's BioCritiques. Ed. Harold Bloom. New York City: Chelsea House Publishers, 2002, 85–100. (Page numbers used in the text here correspond to the EBSCOhost online version, 1–6.)

Paterson, Judith. "Interview: Maya Angelou." In *Conversations with Maya Angelou*. Ed. Jeffrey M. Elliot. Jackson and London: University Press of Mississippi, 1989. 115–24.

ALL GOD'S CHILDREN NEED TRAVELING SHOES

READING TO WRITE

A S RELATED by the fifth book in Maya Angelou's autobiographical series, *All God's Children Need Traveling Shoes*, the author's life has undergone additional changes. Her age and her continent of residence have changed by the time covered by the book, 1963 to 1966. She is now in her thirties, and the son she bore as a teenager and raised as a single mother has declared his independence as he enters college, giving her an "empty nest" feeling of both freedom and loneliness. He attends the University of Ghana in the city of Accra, where Angelou also lives during these four years. *Traveling Shoes* also differs because the author's developing prose-writing skills come to fruition here. Such changes in both content and form make the work a good source of intriguing writing topics, second only to the first book in the series, *I Know Why the Caged Bird Sings*.

From critics and reviewers, this fifth book has received both harsh criticism and praise. Some readers think it moves too slowly in its storyline and is too pedantic or leading in its tone, while others, such as Eugenia Collier, find it to be "the apex toward which the other autobiographies have pointed" (qtd. in Lupton 139). The strong preferences for or criticisms of this book seem to be dictated by its introspective qualities; much more than the other volumes in the series, this one weighs, considers, concludes, and searches for articulate answers to significant questions, especially about identity. The book is, in a sense, the story of Angelou's "recovering her independence and spiritual solitude after giving too much of herself in a failed marriage" (Barnwell 144). Also, as James Robert Saunders has noted, the book "at times . . . suggests a certain mysticism" (13). It may be that this tendency toward introspection is somewhat unexpected in an autobiography, but Angelou has always been a writer breaking new ground rather than repeatedly planting the same seeds in the same places.

As always, it is good to read the book at least twice, once for a general overview of its content and style and then an additional review for looking more closely at how Angelou achieves her effects. As always, it is a good idea to highlight and write comments on the pages throughout both readings if you own the book you are using; if you do not own it, use a notebook to write down these thoughts and ideas, indicating in each case the page number and specific passage to which you are referring.

A few things spring immediately to attention in this book, particularly if one is familiar with the other Angelou autobiographies. It is one of the shortest books in Angelou's autobiographical series. In addition, one formal and stylistic departure is immediately noticeable: There are no chapter headings in *Traveling Shoes*, just extra line spaces at repeated points in the text. This gives the feeling of a more unified, thematic book, rather than the series of anecdotes or set pieces that can stand alone as chronologically arranged short stories, a pattern that we have become familiar with in the previous books. Also, we are led to expect what the unifying theme of the book will be from the word *traveling* in the title; from the book's dedication, "to . . . all the fallen ones who were passionately and earnestly looking for a home"; and from the epigraph, which takes up a full page, is set all in capital letters, and is taken from the refrain of a well-known spiritual: "SWING LOW, SWEET CHARIOT, COMING FOR TO CARRY ME HOME" (Angelou n.p.; further references to the book will be given by page numbers in the text). What is the idealized concept of home, we immediately wonder, especially for an African American who has suffered discrimination at "home" in the United States and who is living abroad, especially in Africa, long considered the "real home" or place of origin for this group of individuals. Questions and deliberations about notions of home permeate this book and arrive at a form of answer or resolution by the conclusion. Is it dangerous for blacks from the diaspora to go back to Africa expecting to be made whole, Angelou was asked in 1987, and she answered that it was good for the discoveries made, that "somehow you are made more strong." You find out that you are an American, but you find out that you are also an African, Angelou said (Kay 199).

The search for home is not a new theme for Angelou to explore in her autobiographical series, yet here it is approached with new resonance and complexity. This is evident in closely examining a particular passage that deals with a stage in her search for home. This section appears about a third of the way through the book (943–47), when the "small boy" Angelou and her housemates have hired and supported for school announces "Auntie, there are some people to see you," and she finds the yard "filled with people dressed in rich cloth and gold" (943). They turn out to be Kojo's large family—parents, brothers and sisters, uncles and aunts, grandparents, and great grandparents—come to "bring the thanks" in the form of crate after crate of "garden eggs" or eggplant, "onions, plantain, pineapples, cassava, yam, coco yam, mango, paw paw," and snails in ice (945). The surprise experience sets Angelou to thinking about the "nameless orphans of Africa who had been shunted around the world," and she finds herself envying the Africans their "centuries of continuity," that despite bondage, exploitation, and colonization, they have achieved the continuity of land and family (946).

Could people of African descent from elsewhere ever "really return to Africa"? She is hit with the realization that it cannot be done, then encases her feeling in horrifyingly violent and painful similes: "We wore skeletons of old despair like necklaces, heralding our arrival, and we were branded with cynicism." Black Americans might become doctors, lawyers, and teachers; they might laugh and dance and start families, but under "glorious costumes . . . we carried the badge of a barbarous history sewn to our dark skins" (947). Black Americans, she suggests, are forced to forever carry denigrating identification labels, like the badges Jews were forced by the Nazis to wear during World War II. The label and stigmatization for the African American remains despite changes in status, education, and achievement, the legacy of a nation that made race and skin color synonymous with slavery. Thus, in *Traveling Shoes,* Angelou manages to describe one side of her experience in Africa, giving her an understanding of the ways she differs from the Africans and moving her closer to defining and achieving her own sense of home.

The question is continued in an interesting and somewhat more positive way in her description of a reception she attends for President Tubman of Liberia, the west coast African state created in 1847 by 3,000 slaves returned to Africa. Angelou is asked to sing "Swing Low, Sweet Chariot," and the Liberians ardently join in. She knows they are not singing out of religious zeal, "so for what chariot were they calling and what home could they possibly miss?" Are they not "back home" in Africa in their native land and country? It is through these musings that Angelou realizes that there is a power that comes to African Americans from their history and their suffering, a power that comes out in distinctive tones in music, in "velvet and wistful sounds which were capable of reaching the ear and heart with an undeniable message of pain" (1,031–32). These are not compensations for the struggles faced, but they are things of beauty and significance grown out of the pain. These realizations echo the words of the historian Herbert Aptheker who wrote that what he calls the "superiority" of certain groups—African Americans, Jews, women—comes not from the pain and suffering itself but from the struggle against oppression (167, 174).

TOPICS AND STRATEGIES
Themes

A central theme running through and informing *All God's Children Need Traveling Shoes* is the search for a home. Here we will look at the possibilities of writing not about that entire theme and the entire book but about some components of that larger theme that would be suitable for an essay topic. This focus enables the essay writer to examine a shorter portion of the text more fully and completely and makes it possible to say something significant in the space of a shorter critical essay. In writing about one of the following topic suggestions, remember in the final paper to frame the discussion with a few sentences about the overall theme as well.

Sample Topics:

1. **The "Revolutionist Returnees":** Angelou uses this phrase to describe the group of black expatriate friends she develops at the beginning of her stay in Ghana. The group includes a man who is fleeing from the FBI and CIA in the United States, a union organizer, some teachers, a plumber, and a doctor. They gather to criticize the United States and praise Ghana and, as Angelou writes, feel that they "had come home," ignoring any problems in their new place of residence in favor of a necessary illusion. Angelou compares her feeling at this stage to that of a young girl falling in love, with the love unrequited. Is this a common feeling among newcomers to a place? Is it exaggerated in people who have suffered in their previous "homes"? How does she depict the lack of interest Ghanaians have in black Americans? How does she get over it?

2. **A new understanding of rejection:** Confronted by a rude sales clerk who looks just like Angelou herself, the author forms an automatic and hostile response, before realizing that there might have been many times in the past when she reacted to a white sales clerk as though that person was motivated by racism rather than just being an unpleasant individual in general or a person having a bad day. Look at the passage containing this exchange and the insight Angelou takes away from the experience. Could this only happen in a country where the clerk looks like Angelou herself? Angelou says that this experience "temporarily sobered my intoxication with Africa" (914). Is this an important stage to go through in really learning about another country or another people?

3. **Hair as metaphor:** Angelou is already wearing an Afro—untreated, unstraightened hair and a 1960s sign of black liberation and militancy in the United States. In Ghana, however, she has her hair done Ghanaian style, a process she describes humorously for its pain—jerking, pulling, and tugging—and for the woman hairdresser, ironically named Comfort, who jokes, tricks, advises, and laughs as she inflicts the hurt. When finally Angelou looks in the mirror, she is "relieved" that she looks like other Ghanaian women. Why is hair such a powerful symbol of

identity or political position? Think of other ways in which this is also true, particularly in the 1960s, when long hair or a crew cut seemingly identified a position on war—dove or hawk—and a trend that gave rise to the musical *Hair*. Consider also Chris Rock's 2009 documentary exposé called *Good Hair*, a film in which Angelou appears as an example of a carryover from the 1960s who has gone back to straightening and weaving her own "crowning glory."

4. **The importance of ritual:** Angelou is invited first to an "out-dooring," the first rite of passage for a Ghanaian baby, at eight days of age, and then a thanksgiving feast, or *durbar* (933–35). She thinks she can "get a glimpse of Africa's ancient tribal soul" (923). Examine her descriptions of these events and the ways they are contrasted with other experiences in Ghana (for example, the conclusion of the *durbar* dancing is followed immediately in her book by a dance accompanied by an orchestra). What kind of understanding of ritual does she come to? Is ritual the same thing as tradition? What is the importance and what is the power of ritual in human life? How does it connect to the idea of home?

5. **Homesickness and food:** The Revolutionist Returnees, that is, the black Americans in Ghana, gather for a sausage patty feast after a box arrives from the United States. Despite the bad memories from which they are escaping, the smell and taste bring a surge of homesickness, something they are loath to admit. What is it about taste and smell that can bring back memories of place? Is this admission of homesickness a step in Angelou's growth as charted in the book? Why is the party followed by a serious discussion of James Baldwin, W.E.B. Du Bois (who was also in Ghana and very sick), and Martin Luther King Jr. and plans to stage a demonstration in Ghana to support King's March on Washington? Does food have the power of identification with others or with a cause? Does it often have a connection with ritual?

Character

Supportive to Angelou's new independence from mothering and from her dependence on others such as her mother, there is less emphasis here on other people whose actions and language play a large role. Many shorter encounters and brief acquaintances, each rather symbolic, take place and position, and become part of Angelou's digestive process in taking in Ghana. Some of these will be discussed in the section "Language, Symbols, and Imagery" on page 153. Some important historical figures who are also characters in this book, particularly W.E.B. DuBois; his wife, Shirley Graham Du Bois; and Malcolm X, will be considered in the section "History and Context" on page 147.

Sample Topics:

1. **Julian Mayfield and the Revolutionist Returnees:** Author, director, and playwright Julian Mayfield is the hub around which the expatriates circle in Accra, and he serves as a kind of translator between the Africans and the Americans. From 1961 to 1965, he was a writer in the office of Ghanaian president Kwame Nkrumah; edited the *African Review,* a political and economic journal; and helped to establish the first international branch of the Organization of Afro-American Unity. He returned to the United States in 1967. Angelou dedicates this book to Mayfield ("Julian") and Malcolm X ("Malcolm"). How do Mayfield's contacts, knowledge, and generosity help Angelou? What does she learn from him? How does he counter the image Angelou paints of other Americans living in West Africa?

2. **Efua Sutherland:** Head of the National Theatre of Ghana and introduced to Angelou by Mayfield, Sutherland helps Angelou get a job at the Institute of African Studies. What does Angelou learn from this first of her African "sisters" and friends?

3. **Kojo:** Angelou becomes a kind of mother and teacher to this young man who helps her at the cottage residence she shares with two other expatriate women, Alice and Vicki. How does Angelou's mothering of Kojo take the place of the nurturing she once extended to her now-grown son, Guy? How does Kojo's family differ from those she has known? How are they the same?

4. **Sheikhali from Mali:** Angelou introduces this towering man in the setting in which she first sees him—a dance floor—and, speculating on the differences of males and men and females and women, she defines him as a real man. He is "exotic, generous

and physically satisfying," she notes, but the two lovers find the "translation" between them difficult (941), especially in relation to his insistent proposal that she become "one of" his wives. Is she ever tempted to enter into this marriage? If not, why not? How does this character enable Angelou to explore the differing expectations of men and women in Africa and the United States?

5. **Kwesi Brew:** Poet and Ghanaian minister of protocol, Brew, is, along with Julian Mayfield, one of the two "real brothers" to whom Angelou dedicates her second book in the series, *Gather Together in My Name*. Brew speaks extensively about "mother Africa" and the sanctity of mothers and mothering and leaves Angelou speechless when he asks her how black Americans can have invented a curse word suggesting sexual relations with one's mother. What does Angelou learn from Brew, especially about language and the use of language?

History and Context

The time covered by the book, from 1963 to 1966, was a tragic and tumultuous one in the United States. The first year, 1963, saw the publication of James Baldwin's *The Fire Next Time*, which set the nation talking about black-white relations and issues. Martin Luther King Jr. was arrested in Birmingham, Alabama, and wrote his famous "Letter from Birmingham Jail." NAACP field secretary Medgar Evers was assassinated in Jackson, Mississippi, and four African American children were killed in a church bombing of the Sixteenth Street Baptist Church in Birmingham. King gave his "I Have a Dream" speech at the Reflecting Pool in Washington, D.C., during the summer March on Washington. President John F. Kennedy was assassinated in Dallas in November, and in Ghana, the ninety-five-year-old W.E.B. Du Bois died, simultaneous with the March on Washington. The next year continued the tragedy in the deaths of three civil rights workers in Philadelphia, Mississippi, and race riots throughout the United States. That year also saw a form of progress and change in the passage of the Civil Rights Act, in King's receipt of the Nobel Peace Prize, and in Malcolm X breaking with the Nation of Islam to found the Organization of Afro-American Unity. Hearing of these events from Ghana, Angelou has a powerful perspective on them, offering a kind of double vision. Particularly in regard to Du Bois and Malcolm X, she is privileged to know firsthand of their thinking and legacies.

Sample Topics:

1. **Writers and activists:** Read one of the works mentioned above—Baldwin's *The Fire Next Time*, King's "Letter from Birmingham Jail" or the "I Have a Dream" speech—and try to detect any thoughts Angelou picked up from them, and through them, of the ferment of the times. Do these written pieces play a role in her decision to go back to the United States?

2. **Malcolm X breaking with the Nation of Islam:** The encounters and conversations between Angelou and Malcolm X described in the book take place after he has, through his *hajj* or pilgrimage to Mecca, moved from his antiwhite, nonintegrationist phase to believing in the possibility of cooperation across race lines. (Look at Alex Haley's *The Autobiography of Malcolm X*, published at the end of the year Malcolm was killed, for a thorough description of his life and death.) What can you conclude about the leader's statements to Angelou about his current state of mind, for example, in his scolding her for her hostility toward Shirley Graham Du Bois?

3. **Martin Luther King Jr. vs. Malcolm X:** At one point in *Traveling Shoes*, just before the March on Washington and the news that W.E.B. Du Bois is dead, the expatriates discuss what is going on in the United States and make fun of King's peaceful demonstrations: "King leading a march. Who is he going to pray to this time, the statue of Abe Lincoln?" and "Give us our freedom again, please suh" (982). Read the history of the conflict in the early 1960s between King as a leader and the "by any means necessary" Malcolm X. The Oxford *Encyclopedia of African American History: 1896 to the Present* would be a good source. What kinds of people supported each of the leaders, respectively? Why do these expatriates lean so much away from King's principles of nonviolent civil disobedience? What stance does Angelou take at this time?

4. **W.E.B. Du Bois:** As Angelou and her friends take part in a sympathy demonstration for the March on Washington, they learn of the death of Du Bois, and Angelou writes eloquently of what the man's leadership had meant throughout the twentieth century: "to many of us, he was the first American Negro intellectual" (985). Consult assessments of Du Bois's contributions and compare them to what Angelou says. Why would it be important for black Americans, especially someone like Angelou, to have an intellectual figure with whom to identify? Why did Du Bois live the last years of his long life and die in Ghana? What is Angelou's frustration with Du Bois's widow, Shirley Graham Du Bois, and how does Malcolm X talk her out of it?

Philosophy and Ideas

Many questions, issues, and topics that inform and surface in Angelou's previous books in her autobiographical series come to a form of culmination in the fifth book. The ongoing question of identity in relation to one's family, one's children, one's race, and one's country develops new dimensions from the international and more introspective and mature perspective Angelou is afforded. Mothering moves from her concentration on one son to the sense of the word in larger contexts, such as in Mother Africa. The differences between the sexes and sex roles are studied with more deliberation, and the growing sympathies of the women's movement begin to align more closely with Angelou's thinking about topics such as lesbianism and marriage. The possible growth and understanding of others' pain that can come from dealing with early childhood trauma, such as Angelou's rape at age eight in *Caged Bird*, is demonstrated here. The frustration the narrator feels in that first book in the series with her Grandmother Henderson's enduring stoicism and the ongoing debates about the effectiveness of pacifism versus violence and of integration rather than division find political expression in the 1960s in the nonviolent civil disobedience of Martin Luther King Jr. and the "conversion" experience of Malcolm X. These currents of thought, ideology, and change can give rise to a powerful essay about the ways Angelou's work intersects with history and reality.

Sample Topics:

1. **African American identity:** Look at the ways Angelou comes to her realization that she is indeed African American, that is, equally African and American. What are the traits she finds common to both? What are the things she finds mutually exclusive? How do the realities and influence of American history—slavery, pain, suffering, and discrimination—lead to some positive traits? Can such a dual identity be both positive and negative? How?

2. **Mothering in a worldwide context:** Siphokazi Koyana has pointed out that "the significance of motherhood is a unifying element in Angelou's five [now six] volumes" and that these books "attempt to reveal the multiple and dynamic interconnections between households—home and family—and the larger political economy" (n1; 1). In what ways is the *all* in the title of the book significant in the progression Angelou makes through stages of mothering? Look at some of the strong mother figures Angelou describes in the book, particularly when she travels alone to the west coast of the country and encounters and stays with villagers. Look also at poet Kwesi Brew's statements about the power of motherhood, the differences between Ghana and the United States in valuing motherhood, and the meaning of Mother Africa. In her article "Singing the Black Mother: Maya Angelou and Autobiographical Continuity," Mary Jane Lupton suggests that the ending of the book depicts Angelou giving her son, Guy, to Mother Africa. On a literal level, he is staying in Ghana to complete his university degree, while she returns to America, but on a more figurative level, Lupton says, "Guy has become . . . a 'young lord' of Africa, given back to the Mother Continent freely, not lost, like so many other children, in midpassage or in slavery" (12). How does Angelou articulate the connections suggested here between her singular mothering experience and the experience of living in Africa? You might find helpful essays and speeches in an anthology like Niara Sudarkasa's *The Strength of Our Mothers: African and African American Women and Families,* published by Africa World Press in Trenton, New Jersey, in 1996. Among other possibly

applicable things, Sudarkasa, an anthropologist, says that, in African families, stability lies more in lineage than in marriage (xxi).

3. **African sex roles:** How does the African value placed on motherhood jibe with the practice of having multiple wives? What does a man like Sheikhali from Mali expect of his wives? What are the differing roles of the various wives? What role does he anticipate that Angelou as one of his wives would play? What kinds of resolutions does Angelou come to in this book about her relationships to men and to marriage? Is some of the same questioning of traditional sex roles going on during these years in the seeds of the women's movement, particularly in the United States?

4. **Strength and creativity from struggle against oppression:** Angelou becomes somewhat reconciled to her people's history of slavery and discrimination by recognizing the beauty and might of the spirituals. Do you find other examples in the book of the ways in which she sees strength coming out of her people's struggles?

5. **Nonviolent civil disobedience and moral superiority:** The elements of Martin Luther King Jr.'s peaceful campaign for change included 1) determining what laws are in agreement with "God's laws," 2) peacefully disobeying unjust laws en masse, and 3) taking the punishment for the disobedience, essentially filling the jails. By this means, he said, the rule of law is upheld, but the unjust law is eventually changed while the protester does not lower himself or herself to the same actions and moral level of the oppressor. Angelou describes here and in *The Heart of a Woman*, the previous book in the series, acting in Jean Genet's *The Blacks*, a play that presents a differing point of view, positing the belief that if power relations are reversed, that is, if blacks are put in power over whites, or women over men, that the newly empowered would act just as badly and cruelly as their predecessors. *The Blacks* seems to be more popular with white Americans and Europeans than with blacks, and touring with the play, Angelou has many encounters and discussions with such viewers. Can you find evidence in *Traveling Shoes* that Angelou struggles with

the two positions represented by King and Genet, without fully resolving them? How would you resolve them?

Form and Genre

Traveling Shoes departs from Angelou's previous division of her autobiographies into numbered chapters in favor of a continuous text with extra line spaces to indicate breaks, an organizational and structural choice that lends the book a greater sense of thematic unity. There are forty-two such divisions in the book, all relatively short, with the longest, only seven pages, devoted to her trip to the west coast of Ghana and her thoughts about the sites of initial enslavement and then shipping of her people from Africa. We have also mentioned that the introspection and thoughtfulness of this book, as contrasted to the almost nonstop action of the others, appeals to some readers more than others, has been both criticized and praised, and can be seen as different from the traditional expectations readers brought to autobiography as a genre in the last half of the twentieth century. What Angelou's work does hark back to, in some senses, is that early form of the autobiography in black literature, the slave narrative, which George Kent has called "a journey through chaos" emphasizing survival, freedom, protest, and work ethic. Mary Burgher even more relevantly lauds the slave narrative as describing mothers who "instilled in their sons positive survival skills, aided in their development of self-awareness and created among the younger slaves, the group-mindedness and interdependence that even today are the mainstay of Black families" (110). Certainly Angelou makes rich use of the themes Joanne M. Braxton says characterize autobiographies by black American women: family, nurturing and rearing of children, and a "quest for self-sufficiency, self-reliance, personal dignity, and self-definition" (184), though it should be added that Angelou is groundbreaking when it comes to the exploration of these themes in the twentieth century, motifs and subjects that have now become characteristic of the works of other black female authors as well.

Sample Topics:

1. **No chapter divisions:** If you have read one or more of the other Angelou autobiographies, how do you compare/contrast the ramifications of working in a chapterless format as opposed to a traditionally divided work? If you have not read other Angelou

autobiographies, how did you respond to the absence of chapters here? Does this method make the book seem to be more unified or composed of separate, discrete incidents? Are there other things in its arrangement that made this book readable or less readable to you?

2. **Autobiography—courageous or self-serving?:** Some have commented that writing and publishing autobiography is a courageous act, while others have thought it egotistical or self-serving. How do you regard autobiography? Would you ever consider writing about your life and publishing it? Would you be tempted to alter the truth or embellish the facts in any way? Would that make your narrative more or less interesting to a reader?

3. **Autobiography and memoir:** In recent years, writers, publishers, and readers have become more accustomed to memoirs rather than full-blown autobiographies, with a memoir covering a shorter period, not a whole lifetime, and often covering one primary subject, such as drug addiction. Even more recently, it has become common to check up on a memoirist's accuracy— did he or she exaggerate, invent, or leave out material that would logically be included in order to make the book unified? How does this book compare to memoirs you have read? Why do readers seem to find memoir fascinating?

Language, Symbols, and Imagery

Angelou's book can be viewed as the culmination of her prose-writing skills, an assertion that is supported in looking at the devices she uses to convey her central points and observations. More than the previous installments in the autobiographical series, this book contains more parallel structures with repetition; more expanded metaphors and similes than the previous clipped, clever ones; more carefully constructed paragraphs and juxtapositions; and more deliberate creating of significant symbols. Considering this expansion of Angelou's voice and writerly sophistication can be the basis for a strong essay.

Sample Topics:

1. **Descriptions, imagery, and metaphor:** When Angelou and her son, Guy, arrive in Accra, Ghana, they are astounded and

delighted. Immediately, in the first paragraph, Angelou seduces the reader with the sensual delight of the place, encasing her language in parallel structures—like the breezes of a West African night "licking," "sweeping," and "disappearing" (890). Mother and son are entranced by the acceptance of their skin color, by the other swirls of color they see, and by the sounds of the airport. They laugh and laugh. Then Angelou recaps the ending of *The Heart of a Woman,* the previous book in the series, recounting Guy's frightening, serious accident and his long recovery, her vigils at the hospital, and the process of reviewing their lives together. Here she tends to use metaphor, or figurative comparisons—the months stretching out like a fat man after dinner, Guy in his "prison of plaster" (890). Choose a passage in the book that you find particularly effective and analyze the way Angelou combines imagery and metaphor to show how this passage fits and furthers the themes of the book.

2. **The flag:** In the march to the American embassy in Accra, the protesters jeer at black and white soldiers raising the American flag. But then Angelou writes a long, thoughtful passage, in which she realizes that this is her only flag and that the flag's symbolism has meaning to her and to her people. The passage ends with "It lifted us up with its promise and broke our hearts with its denial" (987). Does it seem strange that the symbol of the flag seems to have been taken over by prowar, anti-immigration forces to the right of the political spectrum rather than by those believing in peace, justice, fairness, and dissent, some who have been led at times to such extreme measures as burning the symbol of the flag?

3. **Car keys:** When Angelou drives into the countryside in western Ghana, she is mistaken for an African of the Bambara tribe, and she surrenders her car keys to someone in the village who says he will fetch her suitcase. Is this a turning point for Angelou's understanding of Africa? Is surrendering oneself to the country the only way to learn it? Why would car keys be a potent symbol of what she is going through?

4. **The unclaimed body:** Angelou is astounded one day when the usually very composed Efua appears at her door, distraught over

a small, second-page news story about a body that has gone unclaimed for two days. "Africa is breaking," she says (1035). Why is an unclaimed body she knows nothing of so significant to this woman? When Angelou reflects on Efua's statements and grief, she contrasts it to the millions of unclaimed bodies throughout the history of slavery and segregation. Look at this comparison and try to determine why this event is an important stage in Angelou's development in this book

5. **Rain and water:** When the death of W.E.B. Du Bois is announced to the protesters who have come through a torrential downpour, the African marchers say they should have told the crowd, since "a driving rain always followed the death of a great soul." When Angelou asks if this is because God is weeping, she is quickly corrected—no, it was the way the spirits came to wash and fetch that soul (986). Many natural elements, such as rain, fire, and sunshine, are thought to be symbolic, but it is possible to recognize them also as symbols of their opposite—too much of an essential or good thing, such as rain, can destroy crops and cause flooding. How is this passage significant in Angelou's understanding of African life?

6. **Sentence structure:** One of the techniques Angelou uses often in the book to give her prose weight and memorability is parallelism in sentences, sometimes with a word or phrase repetition, sometimes through the parallelism of parts and forms of speech. A passage near the end of the book serves as a good illustration: "the women wept and I wept. . . . There was much to cry for, much to mourn, but in my heart I felt exalted knowing there was much to celebrate" (1050). Another technique to emphasize a sentence is to make it periodic, that is, to retain key elements of its basic structure, such as an independent clause or part of that clause, until just before the period. Note how the following sentence uses a dependent clause before the independent clause to put emphasis on the latter: "Although separated from our languages, our families and customs, we had dared to continue to live" (1050–51). Pick out a passage you find effective and analyze the structure of the sentences.

Bibliography and Online Resources for *All God's Children Need Traveling Shoes*

Angelou, Maya. *All God's Children Need Traveling Shoes.* In *The Collected Autobiographies of Maya Angelou.* New York: Modern Library, 2004. 881–1051.

Aptheker, Herbert. "Afro-American Superiority: A Neglected Theme in the Literature." In *Black Life and Culture in the United States.* Ed. R. I. Goldstein. New York: Thomas Y. Crowell, 1971. 165–79.

Barnwell, Cherron A. "Singin' de Blues, Writing Black Female Survival." In *Maya Angelou.* Bloom's Modern Critical Views. Ed. Harold Bloom New York: Chelsea House Publishers, 2009. 133–46.

Braxton, Joanne M. *Black Women Writing Autobiography.* Philadelphia: Temple University Press, 1974.

Burgher, Mary. "Images of Self and Race in the Autobiographies of Black Women." In *Sturdy Black Bridges: Visions of Black Women in Literature.* Ed. Roseann P. Bell et al. New York: Anchor Books, 1979. 107–22.

Kay, Jackie. "The Maya Character." In *Conversations with Maya Angelou.* Ed. Jeffrey M. Elliot. Jackson and London: University Press of Mississippi, 1989. 194–200.

Kent, George E. "Maya Angelou's *I Know Why the Caged Bird Sings* and Black Autobiographical Tradition." *Kansas Quarterly,* 7:3 (1974): 72–78. Reprinted in *I Know Why the Caged Bird Sings.* Bloom's Modern Critical Interpretations. Ed. Harold Bloom. Philadelphia: Chelsea House Publishers, 1998. 15–24.

Koyana, Siphokazi. "The heart of the Matter: Motherhood and Marriage in the Autobiographies of Maya Angelou." *Black Scholar.* Summer 2002. Vol. 32, Issue 2, 35–45. Page numbers in the text are to the EBSCOhost online printout version, 1–14.

Lupton, Mary Jane. *Maya Angelou: A Critical Companion.* Westport, Conn., and London: Greenwood Press, 1998.

———. "Singing the Black Mother: Maya Angelou and Autobiographical Continuity." *Black American Literature Forum* 24:2 (1990): 257–76. Page numbers in the text are to the EBSCOhost online printout version, 1–14.

Saunders, James Robert. "Breaking Out of the Cage." In *Maya Angelou.* Bloom's Modern Critical Views. Ed. Harold Bloom New York: Chelsea House Publishers, 2009. 3–15.

Sudarkasa, Niara. *The Strength of Our Mothers: African and African American Women and Families.* Trenton, N.J.: Africa World Press, 1996.

A SONG FLUNG UP TO HEAVEN

READING TO WRITE

A SONG FLUNG Up to Heaven, the sixth and final installment in Angelou's autobiographical series, did not appear until 2002, or sixteen years after the previous one. It takes Angelou's life story up to the time of her writing *Caged Bird,* the first book in the series, in other words, covering 1966 to 1969.

The final book is the shortest of the six, though is not short on violent national events to which Angelou was close and familiar. It is framed by the assassinations of Malcolm X in 1965 and Martin Luther King Jr. in 1968, with the Watts riots in Los Angeles situated in between. Yet even one of Angelou's most astute and devoted critics has called the book "perfunctory" and without passion (Lupton 85), with another unimpressed critic describing it as having "writing that is bad to God-awful," that it is "a tell-all that tells nothing in empty phrases and sweeping generalities," and that "something is being flung up to heaven all right, but it isn't a song" (Coleman). Of course there are those who praise the book, even seeing it as a good way to end the series, with more summary rather than new or lively material and writing. John McWhorter takes a slightly different and more helpful stance. He is critical of all six Angelou books when he reads them as autobiography, suggesting there is not enough self-revelation and too much presentation of only the positive, including in one way that especially bothers him: Angelou has her primary "characters" speak in standard English and her narrative voice is always "cleaned up" with a bigger word where a smaller one might do. McWhorter, however, seemingly experiences an epiphany when he stops reading the books as autobiography and begins to approach them as something that was more common and necessary during the times of which Angelou writes. "The subject of Maya Angelou's memoirs is finally not herself at all. The subject is African American life." With this understanding, the sixth book in the series becomes "a celebration and a defense of black American people as a whole," giving it "a meaning and a value" (6). Cherron Barnwell comes to much the same conclusion, saying "autobiography, for Angelou, serves . . . to teach survival and invoke the sense of transcendence of blues reality. It lifts her spirit and her autobiography lifts ours. . . . Angelou patterns her six-volume autobiographical series into a canon of life-sustaining songs which situate her firmly in the black literary and cultural canon of black survival." She is "a blues priestess who auctions her pains for the survival of her community" (144). Eleanor Traylor also suggests as an overall purpose for the series something that is not (or was not at the time Angelou was writing) usual for autobiographies. She calls them "narratives of liberational identity" that "interrogate the cultural text of the American dream." And Traylor then lists the five eventually liberating experiences the books move through: "assault, descent, navigation, development of a critical consciousness, and the recovery of a voice" (99, 103).

It bears repeating that a reader about to write an essay about a particular aspect of *A Song Flung Up to Heaven* should, if possible, read the book at least twice and take notes with page numbers while reading (unless you own the book and can highlight and comment on passages right on its pages). As an example of the close reading that is necessary in developing effective essay-writing strategies, look more closely at an element of the book that Mary Jane Lupton has said is often missed by reviewers and critics who pay too much attention to the way it is written or to the violent events. This book is "more about sexuality than politics," Lupton says (87–88). Many of the passages about sexuality are in reference to a man Angelou just calls "the African," but Lupton hypothesizes he is Nana Nketsia, "first African vice-chancellor of the University of Ghana and the tribal chief of the Ahanta people" (88), a man who appears also in the previous book, *All God's Children Need Traveling Shoes*. When Angelou, while singing in Hawaii, begins losing audience to Della Reese, who is singing down the street, she decides to go back to Los Angeles, but on her last night, she dances instead of singing and receives a standing ovation. In one of her more lyrical passages in the book, she writes, "I danced for the African I had loved and lost in Africa. I danced for bad judgments and good fortune. For moonlight lying like rich white silk on the sand before the great pyramids in Egypt and for the sound of ceremonial fonton-fron drums waking the morning air in Takoradi" (Angelou 1084; further references to this book will be indicated by page number only). Here Angelou displays the use of repetition in the two instances of "I danced"; parallel structure and opposing sense in "bad judgments and good fortune"; evocative and alliterative figurative comparison in the simile "like rich white silk"; allusion to foreign places and objects both known and unknown with the pyramids and Takoradi; and the use of imagery of both sight and sound in the moonlight and the drums, with an apt metaphor—the drums are "waking the morning air"—for the final coming of the dawn. The reader anticipates hearing more about this African who produces such powerful memories in the narrator. The reader is not disappointed, for the man enters the narrative through a phone call from New York and then arrives in California in chapter 12. "My great love and my greatest fear," Angelou dubs him, the man "I felt had taken the heart out of my body and worn it boldly on his shoulder like an epaulette," a double-edged image of dedication and mauling. That combination is soon confirmed, for he is as "loud, bombastic and autocratic" as ever, and though Angelou reports that her "body was in a state of utter bliss," she is displeased with his need "to be waited upon as if he were an invalid," especially when he uses what she considers to be an old-fashioned word carried over from slavery: *fetch*. This is an often tempestuous, passionate relationship, in which he roars at her, and she screams back (1,108), but he charms everyone. Others whisper to her how lucky she is. After an unspecified time, they have a final argument about a Rock Hudson/Doris Day movie—why can't we be like that, wonders the African (1,107–11).

A large portion of the outsized position the African takes in this book comes in later chapters, in New York City, after Angelou and the woman who becomes her good friend and biographer, Dolly McPherson, discover that this man has been seeing them both, on the two coasts, telling each that the other is just a helpful "old woman" he knows. First comes the humorously dramatic scene when McPherson appears at the door after Angelou has thoughtfully invited this presumed old woman to come before the beginning of a big party, in case she has to leave early. After their realization and shock at the African having duped them, Angelou ends chapter 17 with a double entendre: "We had both been had by the same man. In more ways than one" (1124). Later, in chapter 26, the African calls Angelou to set up a party for him and his United Nations associates, and Maya and Dolly plan their revenge. The scene is dominated with sexual suggestions made through metaphor, with various references to tongues, eating, and swallowing, and ends with their chagrin at the way the African handles their little surprise—by making them feel unworthy of the trickery they have imposed on him. "'Well, sister,'" the chapter ends with Angelou speaking first, "'we couldn't swallow the big cat easily. He seems to have stuck in our throats.' She said, 'Yes, I know'" (1145).

TOPICS AND STRATEGIES
Themes

A theme is not a topic for an essay; it is a framing idea designed to suggest questions and observations that might lead to a suitable topic. We will begin with one possible thematic thread we have already examined—sexuality—and then move on to other suitable possibilities.

Sample Topics:

1. **The language of sexuality:** At the end of chapter 25, Angelou makes a rather extended comment on the language of attraction between two people and then concludes with saying that she is "slow-witted" in this area, unable to speak or understand this special tongue. Thinking of the African and personages in this book, or of the depictions of her loves and affairs in the other five autobiographical volumes, does this seem to be the case? Is she joking with the reader here? Trying to hide something? Or why would she include this?

2. **Defending James Baldwin against Eldridge Cleaver:** In her first book, *Caged Bird*, Angelou, as a young teenager, gets pregnant after she instigates a one-night stand with a neighbor boy in order to see if she might be a lesbian. In her second book, *Gather Together*, she is invited by a lesbian couple to Sunday

dinner and ends up becoming the "madam" in a prostitution scheme using them. In this book, she writes extensively of her friendship with James Baldwin, who is either gay or bisexual. She is upset with a recent attack on Baldwin made by Eldridge Cleaver in his book *Soul on Ice,* answered with a Baldwin essay, "No Name in the Street." Angelou does not mention either publication here but becomes angry that Baldwin is still on good terms and plans to work with Cleaver. Look up these writings and some of the controversy swirling around them at the time of which Angelou writes. Why would she be so upset at the anti-gay attack if Baldwin is not gay himself? Since she is presumably writing the text in the early 2000s, should she have taken into account some of the ways the issue of homosexuality has changed in almost forty years? Could she have been more open in her discussion of Cleaver?

Character

Sample Topics:

1. **Name-dropping:** Critics have pointed out, and it is pretty evident to a reader, that Angelou does a lot of what can be called name-dropping, or referring to famous people she knows, and she seems to do more of it in this book than in the others in the series. Do an Internet search of some of the names she "drops" and see if you detect any patterns. Why would she or anyone do this?

2. **Family:** As would seem appropriate for a book that sums up her life and experiences through the late 1960s, Angelou brings in her closest family members, each accompanied by a short description or associated action that has characterized the person throughout the series of autobiographies. Her mother, Vivian Baxter, is the most beautiful woman Angelou has ever known, and she always has a circle of admiring men around and some brusque and sometimes racy, but always true and accurate, words of wisdom to share. Grandmother Henderson offers similar insight, only using the language of her time and place. Bailey, Angelou's brother, is portrayed as short and beautiful and her source of guidance and protection; he melds with James Baldwin after the first part of the book, also a short, beautiful,

and powerful guide and friend. Guy, Angelou's son, once again ending up in the hospital, in this book in San Francisco, is still a worry and still asserting his independence. Two "husbands" are mentioned—the African and Vusumzi Make. Both "married" her with informal agreements, and they share aristocratic, authoritative natures. Her first and legal husband, Tosh Angelos, has entirely disappeared from the books, except, ironically, in her adopted surname, Angelou. Also absent are her father, her maternal grandparents, and her uncle Willie in Arkansas. Is this the way it is with life, that family becomes less and less important as other relationships take over? Is it quite natural, then, that the family members get reduced to summarizing taglines in this final work in the series?

3. **Dolly McPherson:** Though or perhaps because they first meet under unusual circumstances as common mistresses to the same man on two coasts, Angelou and McPherson become good friends. What are the qualities that draw the two together? Look at McPherson's book on Angelou, *Order Out of Chaos*, and see if you find evidence of their friendship in this critical reading. Is it a good idea for someone so close to a writer to become her biographer? Some reviewers have opined that the most interesting thing in this book is the lengthy chapter 7, called "An Addendum: A Conversation with Maya Angelou" (131–62). Here McPherson manages to elicit some discussion not duplicated in the multiplicity of other interviews of Angelou, including discussions of the ethical questions in writing about real people and the issues of selectivity and the relations of the reported events to what actually happened. "I've never wanted to hurt anybody. So many of the people are still alive," Angelou says and then describes trying to find incidents that are "dramatic without being melodramatic or maudlin." To the criticism that she "novelizes" the events she relates, she responds that she sees the incidents as "drama . . . in the theatrical sense . . . so that each event I write about has a beginning, a middle, and an end" (139–40). Does close friendship with Angelou enable McPherson to ask more probing questions than a stranger would ask?

History and Context

Two of the individuals who might have been included in the section "Characters" will appear here instead: Malcolm X and Martin Luther King Jr. The descriptions of these two people and others in *Song* are not as full and engaging here as they have been in previous books, so, if possible, a reader wanting to write on one of these historical figures should consult the fourth book, *The Heart of a Woman*, for King, and the fifth book, *All God's Children Need Traveling Shoes*, for Malcolm X. A possible way for a twenty-first-century reader of Angelou to elicit a sense of the tumultuous time she is writing of here, 1966 to 1969, would be to consult news magazines of the period—*Time, Life, Newsweek, U.S. News and World Report*—and page through the articles and pictures. In February 1965, Malcolm X was killed by the black Muslims from whom he had recently split to form the Organization of Afro-American Unity. Speaking in the Audubon Ballroom in New York City, with his wife and young children and hundreds of supporters present, he was shot. The Watts neighborhood of Los Angeles erupted in violence and rioting in August that year, the first urban area of many to go up in flames. It caused thirty-four deaths, 1,032 injuries, and $35 million in damage. There were advances as well as setbacks between the time of Watts and the assassination of Martin Luther King Jr. in April 1968. Thurgood Marshall became the first black associate justice on the U.S. Supreme Court; Constance Baker Motley became the first African American woman federal judge; Carl Stokes became the first black mayor of a major American city, Cleveland, Ohio; and the Supreme Court unanimously nullified antimiscegenation laws in fifteen states.

Sample Topics:

1. **Death of Malcolm X:** Angelou is a close friend of Malcolm X and is taking a break in California, after returning from Ghana and before working for him in New York, at the time of his assassination. Is it her closeness to the man, and admiration for him, that lead her to expect that the black community will explode in anger at his death? What does she glean from the realization that his death means little to other people, including her mother? By looking at news reports from the time of his death, try to assess what the consensus of opinion, black or white, was

while he was living. How do you explain the popularity of a man like this after his death rather than before? Check the five volumes of the *Encyclopedia of African American History: 1896 to the Present* (New York: Oxford University Press, 2009) for articles, with bibliographies, about Malcolm X; his wife, Betty Shabazz; the Nation of Islam; and Malcolm X's fledgling group at the time of his death, the Organization of Afro-American Unity. Volume 5 contains a complete index (273–517), and there you will also find a helpful "Thematic Outline of Entries" (229–43) and a chronology of events by year from 1896 to 2009.

2. **Prelude to the Watts riot:** Chapter 8 opens in Los Angeles and ends in the prelude to self-destructive violence. Angelou has moved to the city, found an apartment near the Watts section, and found a job going door to door questioning women about their use of household products. What does she learn from talking to women and from her observations about the events that lead up to the riots? Is this an effective chapter, in a sense contrasting the American Dream with the inequality and injustice still visited on some members of the black community?

3. **Watts riot description:** Chapter 9, on the riots Angelou walks to see, is the book's longest. Lupton finds Angelou uninvolved and unattached in her descriptions, especially in her use of passive voice, as in "vans were filled and driven away" (the passive voice means there is no actor in the sentence but rather things acted upon), and in her own inactivity, as in "I stood on the corner" (85). Does Angelou display her attitude toward the events and the people by the way she describes them? Was hers a common middle-class black attitude at the time?

4. **Death of Martin Luther King Jr.:** At the time of Malcolm X's death, Angelou is seemingly planning on dedicating her life to working for the man and his new organization. At the time of King's death, on her fortieth birthday in 1968, she has been convinced by King to work for him for a short time recruiting congregations to support the upcoming Poor People's March on Washington, D.C. Does the difference in attachment to the men and their methods say something about Angelou? About her identification with movements and politically active people of

the time? Or since this is written in retrospect from thirty years later, might she be playing up her involvement with Malcolm X and playing down involvement with King? If so, why would she do this?

Philosophy and Ideas

Sample Topics:

1. **"The son always kills the father":** When Angelou reports her discussion with Baldwin about Eldridge Cleaver in chapter 24 (see the section "Themes" for additional discussion of this episode), she has Baldwin explain his friendly relations with Cleaver with reference to "killing his father," by whom he means the writer Richard Wright, who was stung by the young Baldwin's essays "Everybody's Protest Novel" and "Alas, Poor Richard." This observation seems to disagree with a 1984 interview with Julius Lester for the *New York Times,* in which Baldwin says, "I reject in toto" the analogy between him and Wright, on the one hand, and Cleaver and Baldwin on the other. Read more about this controversy as well as the relevant Baldwin essays. Why would Angelou introduce this conversation, whether it occurred or not, at this point in her book? Is she trying to demonstrate for a twenty-first-century reader her familiarity with black literary history? Her closeness to Baldwin? Her sympathy for gays?

2. **Laughing to keep from crying:** In chapter 7, Angelou writes that "dancing songs," blues, gospel, and love songs are all based on dealing with "the burden of . . . color and . . . race memory" (1081). Do you see this idea of a methodology used to deal with pain and suffering elsewhere in the book? Does it motivate other characters, such as Angelou's mother? Does it seem that this method of getting through suffering is different from the stoicism Grandmother Henderson displays in *Caged Bird,* or does religion become her way of confronting and accepting personal pain? Is the role dancing plays in Angelou's life comparable?

3. **Human and black survival:** The final words in the final chapter of this book, and thus the final words in the series of six

books, wax lyrical about the creation and survival of human beings, who were, after all, "born to forever crawl in swamps" but who somehow stood erect and have stayed standing through the intervening millennia of war and peace. Then Angelou goes back to the beginning of the first book and the Easter morning recitation she opens with there: "'What you looking at me for? I didn't come to stay.'" Does this make an appropriate, effective conclusion to the series of autobiographies? By coming full circle, bringing her life up to the point of writing the first words of the first book, does she give the series a kind of coherent shape and theme? Does this conclusion contrast with her opening of the book, on the Pan-Am flight from Ghana, which seems to be racially centered? In other words, do you think it is significant that Angelou does not put the emphasis on race in her conclusion but rather is inclusive of all human beings?

Form and Genre

In the previous books in the autobiographical series, Angelou is careful to make each book stand alone as well as work as part of a developing, ongoing series. In other words, she tries to make sure that a reader unfamiliar with any of the other five books will find the volume in hand meaningful and coherent. In this final, book, which summarizes Angelou's life experiences up to that point, she seems to be less concerned about the books' various interrelations, writing a conclusion that will probably be meaningful only to those who have read the other books in the series. With this in mind, we notice from the prefatory materials that the book is dedicated to grandchildren and "my entire family wherever and whoever you are" and that she thanks "my living teachers," seven "reverends" who do not appear anywhere else in the series, so are probably people she knew after the time periods covered by the books. Finally, chapter 1 opens with an epigraph that suggests the paradox of themes of the previous books: moving and home, "[t]he old ark's a-movering . . . and I'm going home." With no formal preface, the book then moves through thirty-three chapters, all but one (the previously noted chapter 9) very short, one to six pages each. Exploring and theorizing about Angelou's structural choices can lead to insightful and memorable essays.

Sample Topics:

1. **Structure of the book:** Look at what is covered in the thirty-three chapters of the book, and see if you detect any patterns or clustering around place or a specific activity or character. Does the book divide into sections or seem to have a climax and a denouement or conclusion such as a drama would often have? Some of the previous books in the series, including the well-known first one, *Caged Bird,* seem to be made up of a succession of anecdotes with mild morals at the end, and this final book seems to hark back to that pattern. Chapter 11 stands as a strong example, when Angelou and others go in a car with Phil, who describes himself as "a lying nigger" who could be "ornery, too" (1,105) and who stops on the railroad tracks with a train coming. Their narrow escape ends with a moralizing gesture: "believe people when they tell you who they are" (1,107). None of these characters is mentioned before or after this incident. Do you see other chapters that seem to follow or reflect this pattern? Or is this sloppy or ineffective writing on the part of the author?

2. **Is the book written under pressure?:** There are some chapters that seem unconcluded or unresolved, where Angelou's point in relating the incident is not readily apparent, for example, in chapter 20, about finding an apartment in New York City and people giving her furniture. Lupton feels that the book as a whole was written "under pressure," maybe from Random House, Angelou's publisher, or maybe from Angelou herself, wanting closure. Do you feel this sense in the book, that she is in a hurry to get it done and behind her? By the time of this book's publication, 2002, Angelou is a famous national figure, especially after her poem written for and read at President Bill Clinton's inauguration. Might she be too busy to spend adequate time on this book or not anxious to write more about her prefame life? (One reviewer, in the Sunday *Times* of London, lamented that this volume was all about "me, me, me—the song [Maya Angelou] is merrily flinging up to heaven is that of a shameful egotist. We can only hope that God feels grateful.")

3. **The genre of autobiography:** Angelou broke new ground in her adaptations of the genre of autobiography. It is perhaps unfair

to look at this particular volume in that light, but overall, what do you see as innovative, gutsy, or influential in Angelou's series of works? Do you agree with John McWhorter, cited earlier in this chapter, that "the subject of Maya Angelou's memoirs is finally not herself at all. The subject is African American life," and the value of the books is in their "celebration and . . . defense of black American people as a whole" (6)?

Language, Symbols, and Imagery

Sample Topics:

1. **Similes and metaphors:** Angelou's use of figurative language is not as prominent in this book as in some of the previous ones, particularly the first, *Caged Bird.* Is this an indicator of hurried or disinterested writing? Of a change in her concerns as an individual and writer? Find some places where she uses similes or metaphors, and evaluate their effectiveness, for example, at the beginning of chapter 16, where she compares human beings to plants, or the beginning of chapter 30, where she attempts to describe her feeling after the death of Martin Luther King Jr.

2. **Sound:** Some of the strongest imagery—that is, words that appeal to the senses—in this book are sound images, for example, in chapter 1, the sounds of Idlewild Airport in New York City, in contrast to the African airports to which she has become accustomed over the previous four years. Find examples of sound imagery and evaluate their effectiveness. Does the use of sound imagery bring a reader closer to an experience than just visual imagery would?

3. **Smell:** In her description of the five days of rioting in Watts in chapter 9, Angelou begins and ends with the sense of smell. Look closely at how she does this, approaching from a distance and getting ever nearer. Is this effective? Can you think of other literary examples that use imagery of smell to such an extent?

4. **Synesthesia:** When imagery mixes the senses, such as hearing color or smelling pain, this is called synesthesia. An example would be in chapter 9, when Angelou says, "the sirens were in my nose, and smoke packed my ears like cotton" (1,094). Do

you find this effective in describing the riot? Do you find other examples in the book? When would you use synesthesia in your descriptions?

Compare and Contrast Essays

Sample Topics:

1. **The poetic response to crisis:** In chapter 9, in describing the Watts riots, Angelou resorts to the use of free verse poetry, written at the kitchen table after seeing both the riots and the television coverage of the riots. Can you see the contrasting presence of the eyewitness reports and the television coverage in the poem? What is Angelou's critique of journalism in this chapter? This poem is reminiscent of one by W.E.B. Du Bois, "A Litany at Atlanta," written hurriedly on the train after he witnessed the 1906 riots in that southern city. Read the Du Bois poem and compare/contrast the two. Do you think Angelou had Du Bois's poem in mind when she felt inspired to write hers? Is creating a poem or a prose record a kind of instinctive response to a crisis for anyone who writes?

2. **The book compared to others in the series:** If you have read any of the other six books in Angelou's autobiographical series, compare and contrast one of the other books to this one, both in form and in content. Do the styles differ in order to cover different periods and places in national and international life? In order to cover the different stages of life she has gone through? What conscious changes has Angelou adopted later in the series as her autobiographical sequence grows?

3. **Comparison to other black women's autobiographies:** An early extant autobiography was a "told to" narrative by the slave Linda Brent, or Harriet Jacobs, published as *Incidents in the Life of a Slave Girl.* Joanne Braxton, in her book from 1987, *Black Women Writing Autobiography: A Tradition Within a Tradition,* says she had hundreds of autobiographies by black women to choose from, but she picked *The Diaries of Charlotte Forten Grimke; Crusader for Justice: Ida B. Wells;* Zora Neale Hurston's *Dust Tracks on a Road;* and Era Bell Thomson's *American Daughter,* before looking closely at Angelou's *Caged*

Bird as an example of the modern. A reader wanting to compare and contrast one or more of Angelou's autobiographies has a wealth of more recent examples to choose from as well: Anne Moody's *Coming of Age in Mississippi;* politician Shirley Chisholm's *Unbought and Unbossed;* poet Audre Lorde's *Zami: A New Spelling of My Name;* poet Nikki Giovanni's *Gemini;* Marita Golden's *Don't Play in the Sun;* and autobiographies by a large number of entertainers, including Lena Horne, Eartha Kitt, Diahann Caroll, and Whoopi Goldberg. Taking any one of these or other autobiographies by African American women, compare and contrast to one of Angelou's, both as to writing style and content.

Bibliography and Online Resources for *A Song Flung Up to Heaven*

Angelou, Maya. *A Song Flung Up to Heaven.* In *The Collected Autobiographies of Maya Angelou.* New York: Modern Library, 2004. 1059–167.

Barnwell, Cherron A. "Singin' de Blues, Writing Black Female Survival in *I Know Why the Caged Bird Sings.*" In *Maya Angelou.* Bloom's Modern Critical Views. Ed. Harold Bloom. New York: Chelsea House Publishers, 2009. 133–46.

Braxton, Joanne M. *Black Women Writing Autobiography: A Tradition Within a Tradition.* Philadelphia: Temple University Press, 1989.

Coleman, Wanda. Rev. of *A Song Flung Up to Heaven* by Maya Angelou. *Los Angeles Times,* 14 September 2002, n.p. available.

Du Bois, W.E.B. "A Litany at Atlanta." In *Black Voices: An Anthology of Afro-American Literature.* Ed. Abraham Chapman. New York: Mentor/Penguin, 1968. 360–63.

Finkelman, Paul, ed. *Encyclopedia of African American History: 1896 to the Present.* New York: Oxford, 2009.

Lester, Julius. "James Baldwin—Reflections of a Maverick." *New York Times.* 27 May 1984, Section 7, Page 1, Column 1.

Lupton, Mary Jane. "'Spinning in a Whirlwind': Sexuality in Maya Angelou's Sixth Autobiography." In *Maya Angelou.* Bloom's Modern Critical Views. Ed. Harold Bloom. New York: Chelsea House Publishers, 2009. 85–90.

McPherson, Dolly A. *Order Out of Chaos: The Autobiographical Works of Maya Angelou.* New York: Peter Lang, 1990. Volume I of the Studies in African and African-American Culture, James L. Hill, general editor.

McWhorter, John. "Saint Maya." *The New Republic.* 20 May, 2002. Volume 226, Issue 19. 35–41. Page numbers here are to the EBSCOhost online printout version, 1–8.

Traylor, Eleanor W. "Maya Angelou Writing Life, Inventing Literary Genre." In *Maya Angelou.* Bloom's Modern Critical Views. Ed. Harold Bloom. New York: Chelsea House Publishers, 2009. 91–105.

POETRY

READING TO WRITE

MAYA ANGELOU has produced a sizeable body of poetry known for its accessibility and lyricism (she even worked for Hallmark to write for cards, collectibles, and other products). Critic Harold Bloom states that "her poetry has a large public, but very little critical esteem. It is, in every sense, 'popular poetry,' and makes no formal or cognitive demands upon the reader." He also notes that she is "best at ballads, the most traditional kind of popular poetry" (1–2). (A ballad is narrative verse, intended to be sung or danced to. Lyman Hagen points out that many of the poems in Angelou's first book were originally songs [122].) Given the popular nature of her poetic work, probably the best approach to take as a reader writing an essay on some aspect of her poetry would be to pick out the poems one personally finds interesting or helpful or, alternatively, take one of her ceremonial poems, written and read for auspicious occasions such as President Clinton's inauguration, the fiftieth anniversary of the United Nations, or the Million Man March. With the last three poems, there is critical commentary to consult and include. With the rest of her work, the poems not written to commemorate a specific occasion, one possible approach to generating a strong essay would be to find connections to the autobiographies, for Angelou's poetry, in a sense, "distills the emotions and experiences of her lifetime . . . to a remarkably small compilation of verses" (Thomas 67). Many of her poetry collections were published just after the release of one of her serial autobiographies, so it would seem that she customarily has alternated between those two forms in her writing career.

Five volumes of Angelou's poems are handily reprinted in *The Complete Collected Poems* of Maya Angelou, published by Random House in 1994. Thirty-eight of the included poems are from *Just Give Me a Cool Drink of Water 'fore I Diiie,* first published in 1971, just after the publication of Angelou's first autobiography, *I Know Why the Caged Bird Sings.* Another thirty-six come from *Oh Pray My Wings Are Gonna Fit Me Well,* from 1975; *And Still I Rise,* published in 1978, is represented by thirty-two of her poems, with a couple of them among her best known—"Phenomenal Woman" and "Still I Rise." There are twenty-eight from the 1983 book, *Shaker, Why Don't You Sing?,* and thirty-two poems from *I Shall Not Be Moved,* published in 1990. Finally, the text of the poem she wrote and read for President Bill Clinton's inauguration on January 20, 1993, "On the Pulse of Morning," is included in that collection. Of poetry, Angelou has said, "From the time I was 7½ until I was almost 13, I didn't talk. I was persuaded to talk by a woman who knew I loved and memorized poetry. She said, 'Poetry is music written for the human voice. Until you read it (aloud) you will never love it'" (Toppman 142). This is the way Maya Angelou explains the origins of her love of poetry. In the 1983 interview she went on to note:

> Now, poetry was my friend, the thing I would call up when I was lonely or scared—Poe or Dunbar or Countee Cullen or Langston Hughes or Kipling—and she was taking my friend away. So when I was about 12, I went under the house and started to speak poetry. Until I felt it over my tongue, through my teeth and across my lips, I would never love it. That has influenced the way I hear poetry when I'm writing it; I write for the voice, not the eye (Toppman 142).

That she writes "for the voice, not the eye" suggests to the reader that, for Angelou, poetry is more of a public genre best suited for recitation and performance. In light of this, consulting audio recordings of Angelou reciting her poetry would be an ideal way of approaching the poems. Listening to some of Angelou's own readings allows listeners to get a sense of the rhythms, patterns, and sounds she relies on. There are many descriptions of performances of her work. One presentation described by Greg Hitt took place in a muggy, loud Mount Zion church after the rousing choir and a lot of *amens:*

She talks for a few minutes, painting unsettling images of nighttime and tears, before moving into *Still I Rise,* her historical indictment of racism.

"You may write me down in history, with your bitter twisted lies," she says.

"You may trod me in the very dirt, but still, like dust, I'll rise. Does my sassiness upset you? Why are you beset with gloom, because I walk like I've got oil wells pumping in my living room."

She delivers the last line with an unexpected sense of hope, laughing and strutting and pumping her arms to give life to the image.

The crowd responds with laughter and applause (212).

Hitt also describes her reciting "Weekend Glory," "about a working woman who tried to fit a party and church into the same weekend," and reports that "it is poetry—at least it was published as such—but coming out of Miss Angelou's mouth it sounds more prosaic, more like she's giving somebody a piece of her mind" (209–10).

Another possible approach to discussing and illuminating Angelou's poetry is listening to gospel music, spirituals, or the sermons and the speeches of Martin Luther King Jr. to get a sense of the early and enduring oral influences on Angelou's poetry. "I loved the songs" of church, she has said, and "I also loved the sermons. . . . The music of the sermons inspired me then and still does today" (Elliot 87). Angelou's poems are mostly short, the exception being the works written for ceremonial occasions. Lyman Hagen points out that 40 percent of the 135 poems in the Bantam collected edition are less than fifteen lines, and the lines themselves are also short, made up usually of two to four beats to the measure (119). (Beats are accented syllables, and a measure is made up of one accented syllable and one or more unaccented syllables.) Angelou has often explained the special "black rhythms" she uses, as, for instance, in "Harlem Hopscotch," the final poem in *Give Me:* "Now, hopscotch, anywhere it's done," she says, "is da-da-da, da-da-da, da-da-da. But in Harlem, . . . there are other counter-rhythms that are going on, so that the kids stamp, 'Dadadatadatadatam.' See?" In this Bill Moyers interview she then quotes the poem (27) and uses it as an illustration of the process of writing poetry—"I try to enchant myself. . . . I try to find the natural rhythm of the piece. . . . If the muse is being stingy, I work on the rhythm of the piece. If I'm writing about an autumn day, I work on the rhythm. There's a flow to it. Then I try to make the content fit" (Blum 41).

Reading through an entire book of her poetry, you will note that the title of the book will be significant and that the poems are sometimes grouped in subheadings. Such is the case with her first collection, *Just Give Me a Cool Drink of Water 'fore I Diiie* (nominated for the Pulitzer Prize). Angelou agreed with an interviewer who found the overall theme of the author's work to be "the refusal of the human spirit to be hardened," and then she explained this particular title:

> I believe we are still so innocent. The species is still so innocent that a person who is apt to be murdered believes that the murderer, just before he puts the final wrench on his throat, will have enough compassion to give him one sweet cup of water. If I didn't believe that, I wouldn't get up in the morning (Weller 15).

This book is divided into two parts, the first titled "Where Love Is a Scream of Anguish" and the second "Just Before the World Ends." Both those divisions suggest that the poems will not be predominantly joyful in tone, mood, or subject matter, but they also suggest difference, that the topics of the first section will be more personal and those of the second more public. The title of Angelou's second book of poetry, *Oh, Pray My Wings Are Gonna Fit Me Well*, she described as coming from a nineteenth-century spiritual:

> *Oh, pray my wings are gonna fit me well.*
> *I'm a lay down this heavy load.*
> *I tried them on at the gates of hell.*
> *I'm a lay down this heavy load.*

Then she added: "I planned to put all the things bothering me—my heavy load—in that book, and let them pass" (Tate 155). This book she divides into five untitled parts, which seem loosely to emphasize losing love, then love lost, then Africa, then people in trouble, and, finally, a more historical and forward-looking perspective. The poem that Angelou, in 1975, called her "favorite," "Song for the Old Ones," is in this section. She describes this poem as being so important, because young black revolutionaries had decided that Uncle Toms are to be laughed at and ridiculed, and I feel just the opposite. We often don't realize how those people who were scratching when they didn't itch, laughing when they weren't tickled, and saying, 'Yassuh, you sho' is right, I sho' is stupid' ... [that] they did that so they could make a little money, so they could pay for somebody to go to school, to get some shoes. So that poem is for them. A lot of my work is for them, because I know they were successful, because if they hadn't been successful I wouldn't be here to talk about it (Blum 44–45).

Angelou has also explained some of her other titles. *Now Sheba Sings the Song* is "a play on the Song of Solomon. We never heard Sheba's song" (Forna 164). It is dedicated to "all my brown, black, beige, yellow, red and white sisters. The book is an attempt to herald the various kinds of beauty of women, some plain, some young, and of all colors" (Sookia 190). *Now Sheba* is a collaboration with artist Tom Feelings. "He contributed dozens of elegant sepia drawings of black women." Angelou wrote the text, a poem that "celebrates the spirit of black women, [a] ... tribute to the strength, dignity, sexuality and beauty of black women." Angelou has commented that "'It's a book that says something that needs to be said. And to say it through the black experience, as all my books do, is something that is needed, too'" (Crane 173). *Shaker, Why Don't You Sing?* is "from a John Henry song" (Rich 129). And *I Shall Not Be Moved* (1990), made up of "new love poems and praise poems" (Hagen 118), is clearly from the civil rights marching song based on an old hymn, "We Shall Not Be Moved."

Perhaps the best introduction to Angelou's poetry is an analysis of one of her best-known works, the ceremonial poem "On the Pulse of Morning," written for President Bill Clinton's inauguration. It is revealing, first, to consider the historical context of this reading. Only one poet had read his or her work previously at a presidential inauguration, and that was more than thirty years earlier, at the inauguration of President John F. Kennedy in 1961, when the elderly Robert Frost worked his way to the podium in bright, cold January sun and found that he could not make out the words he had written for the occasion on its brilliant reflective paper. So instead he raised his white-haired head and recited from memory another of his poems, "The Gift Outright." "The land was ours before we were the land's," it begins, and continues to speak of how "we" possessed the continent of North America before it possessed us and that the culminating "deed of gift" was "many deeds of war." Angelou, a black woman from Arkansas, Bill Clinton's home state, took it upon herself to write a poem that would subtly and kindly raise some contradictory questions about the "we" and the "ours" of the poem Frost recited—were the "founders" of the country all "England's" as Frost wrote? And did these "colonials" "possess" the land or take it, steal it?

At the same time, as she gently probed these questions, Angelou needed to write a poem appropriate to 1993 and, if possible, inspirational to Americans of all backgrounds. The poem also needed to be, if at all possible, a poem from which a listener could gather much at first hearing. Immediately, the "pulse" and "morning" of the title suggest something living and new, fresh and full of possibility (Angelou 269–73; subsequent references to this book will be given by page number in the text). In her first line of the poem, she lists the three figurative, symbolic images: "A Rock. A River. A Tree," and the first stanza then suggests prehistory—the mastodon, the dinosaur—with warnings of their extinction as distant as the "dried tokens" left "on our planet floor." The rest of the poem is then divided roughly into the progression of images listed in the first line, each one depending on the previous, and the whole accumulating meaning as the images are explored. The rock suggests a firm place to stand but, the poem warns, not a hiding place and not a rock to be used as a weapon. "The Rock cries out to us today, / You may stand upon me, / But do not hide your face," with suggestions of Plymouth Rock but also the Declaration of Independence and the Constitution perhaps, those solid principles designed to bring the country into the future, not hide in the past.

The river, next, "sings a beautiful song," provides a place of rest from "thrusting" and "armed struggles for profit." Though "collars of waste" and "currents of debris" litter the shore and the stream itself, "[y]et today I call you to my riverside, / If you will study war no more," an allusion to the old spiritual from the American Civil War. The river harks back to a time "before cynicism was a bloody scar across your brow" and a time "when you yet knew you still knew nothing." Angelou suggests some of her primary critiques of the present day here—that Americans are too careless of the environment, have become distrustful and disbelieving, and too conceited and self-satisfied when it comes to their achievements and power. Then she begins one of her Whitman-like rhymed lists in this poem, beginning with races—"the Asian, the Hispanic, the Jew. / The African, the Native American, the Sioux," continuing with religions and nationalities—"the Catholic, the Muslim, the French, the Greek, / The Irish, the Rabbi, the Priest, the Sheik." Next comes sexual orientation, occupation, and economic status—"The Gay, the Straight, the Preacher, / The privileged, the homeless, the Teacher." All of these, she says, yearn to "respond to / The singing River and the wise Rock," and, moving to and incorporating the third symbol, "They all hear / The speaking of the Tree." The history becomes more specific in the next section, and some of the listed groups, especially Native Americans and blacks, are attached to their American histories. The Cherokee Nation was "forced on bloody feet"—an allusion to the Trail of Tears, the forced march between 1831 and 1838 of this Indian nation and others from the South to reservations in Oklahoma under the Indian Removal Act of 1830. The "Ashanti, the Yoruba, the Kru," African tribes, were "bought, / Sold, stolen, arriving on a nightmare," referring to slavery and the Middle Passage, the transporting of slaves to the New World, journeys that claimed almost 2 million African lives.

In transition to the forward-looking, final section of the poem, Angelou sums up what has come before: "I am that Tree planted by the River, / Which will not be moved. / I, the Rock, I, the River, I, the Tree, / I am yours—your passages have been paid," which seems to be an allusion to the many immigrants who arrived on American shores from many countries over a long period of time and who are still arriving today. We then move into the "day breaking," with the need for all to "Give birth again / To the dream." "Here, on the pulse of this fine day, / You may have the courage / To look up and out and upon me, / The Rock, the River, the Tree, your country." The last stanza of the poem, its last lines, are straightforward and simple, even using a variant of the latter word.

> Here, on the pulse of this new day,
> You may have the grace to look up and out
> And into your sister's eyes,
> And into your brother's face,
> Your country,

And say simply
Very simply
With hope—
Good morning.

The final line and its double-entendre meaning—both a customary greeting for the new day and an adjective describing this day—seem to be intentionally anticlimactic, not taking anything away from the other events of the inauguration but helping us look at our lives and our land anew. "Good morning" almost assumes that status of ritual here, not just habit. We hope for good; we contribute to the good. That is Angelou's wish for her 1990s audience.

An interesting potential writing topic might be to look at all the poetry associated with U.S. presidential inaugurations, beginning with Frost and Angelou. Bill Clinton included a poet and poem at his second inauguration in 1997 as well, Miller Williams and his "Of History and Hope." George W. Bush dropped that option in his two inaugurals, but then President Barack Obama opted for an inaugural reading with another black woman poet, Elizabeth Alexander, whose poem "Praise Song for the Day" is modeled after the African "praise song" for the most ordinary daily things and activities. This poem has some echoes of and builds on the Angelou poem, particularly in the sense of making Angelou's lists active. Here we have not just a list of occupations but people in action in those occupations, not groups of newcomers to these shores but what those groups did, picking cotton, building railroads, stitching garments. Try to define the theme of each of these inaugural poems. If you were to have the privilege of writing and reading a poem for an inauguration, what would you aim for as a theme? What would you want your listeners to walk away thinking or asking? How would you attempt to include Americans of all kinds?

TOPICS AND STRATEGIES
Themes

Many have noticed the range of topics Angelou covers in her poetry. Lyman Hagen says in a chapter of his Angelou book called "Poetry: Something About Everything": "[F]rom the excitement of love to outrage over racial injustice, from the pride of blackness and African heritage to suffered slurs" (118); and as Carol Neubauer says, Angelou includes "personal poems about the nature of love, loneliness, and family as well as poems about human communal strength in the midst of humiliation and threats to freedom" (136–37). Sandra Cookson, reviewing *The Complete Collected Poems of Maya Angelou,* notes that although the pieces "celebrate black people" and "bear witness to the trials of black people in this country," they do not "exclude whites," but in "their robust embrace of life" they are "truly 'celebratory'" (1). The following suggested poems are just a few of Angelou's verse creations that might illustrate an essay on one of these key themes.

Sample Topics:

1. **The excitement of love:** Angelou ambiguously dedicates the collected edition of her poems "to the great love of my life" (n.p.) without specific reference. Could she mean one of the men she has loved? Her son? Her poetry and writing? Her country? There are few poems about love unadulterated with fear of loss, of incompleteness. A short one from her first book called "Sounds Like Pearls" (26), however, takes up the subject. "Remembrance" (127), dedicated to her second legal husband, Paul, is another example. What are the sexual suggestions in this poem? "Where We Belong, A Duet" (128–29) places the love at the end. What does the speaker go through before finding this "true love"?

2. **The pain of loneliness:** Her first book of poems opens with "They Went Home" (7)—all the men who praised, liked the speaker, nevertheless went home to their wives. What does it say to open a book with this poem? Also in that book is a poem called "Remembering" (14), peopled with ghosts and painful recollections. Does this poem express any hope? Is it unusual for Angelou? In a poem called "The Telephone" (64), Angelou evokes frustrated, repeated loneliness, with a bit of a shocking ending. Is this a good example of how an ordinary thing can be made meaningful or symbolic in a poem? Other possibilities to illustrate this theme: "Now Long Ago" (68), "Greyday" (69), and "Senses of Insecurity" (73). "A Kind of Love, Some Say" (125) is also about the pain of love, here attached to, it seems, physical

abuse. Does this poem make sense for what you know or can find out about domestic abuse victims? The eight-line rhymed poem "The Traveler" (157) seems to be Angelou herself speaking, given the place that repeated travel has in her autobiographies. Is the form of the poem effective?

3. **The importance of family:** Angelou's "Alone" (74–75), with echoes of Langston Hughes, does not specifically mention family but certainly confirms everyone's need for a support network. Does "Chicken-Licken" (97) make the same point from a negative perspective, in other words, things that can happen to a person without a support network? "John J." (106) is also negative about family relationships in its depiction of what happens to an unwanted black child. What are the problems of his situation for this boy? If you know Angelou's *I Know Why the Caged Bird Sings*, do his problems bear any relationship to hers as a child? Also related to Angelou's first autobiography is the poem "Willie" (150–51), about her disabled uncle in the grandmother's home in which Angelou and her brother, Bailey, grew up in Stamps, Arkansas. How is Willie treated in the poem? How does he manage to endure? "Kin" (158–59) is for Angelou's brother, Bailey. What are the positive things taken from their relationship? What are the difficulties the brother has gone through? What has been the brother's lifelong influence on Angelou, especially in the lines "You left me to force strangers / Into brother molds . . . "? "Call Letters: Mrs. V. B." (174) is undoubtedly about Angelou's mother, Vivian Baxter. From the activities and relationships suggested in the stanzas, and the conclusion of each, what do you take to be her mother's character in Angelou's eyes?

4. **Enduring slurs and racial injustice:** In "America" (85–86), what are the promises of the United States, and what are the realities suggested in this poem? Is its form (rhymed couplets with two beats to the line) effective? What do you make of the ending? "Request" (83) is short and tough in its look at the "bastard" country, even using a clever euphemism for a common curse, in "mother user." What is the tone of this poem? Does it express any hope? "The Lesson" (140) tries to explain the seeming death wish of the drug abuser by saying he/she

loves "to live." Does this make any sense? "One More Round" (155–56) follows the form of the work song, with its rhythmic repeated refrain, and is, appropriately enough, about physical labor. What is the difference between working and slaving? Is the form of this poem effective, especially read aloud? "These Yet to Be United States" (241) is a contemporary picture of white America. What are some of the references or allusions? Is there any hope expressed in this poem?

5. **Pride in blackness and African heritage:** "Africa" (84) suggests the history of the continent; what are the stages in that history expressed in the poem? What would correlate with the final stanza? In "For Us, Who Dare Not Dare," the grammar of the repeated pattern—"be me," "swim me," "swing me," "taste me"—is unusual in being followed in each case by a noun, as in "taste me fruit." What do you think is Angelou's intent here? How do all of these things fit with the last two lines? How does the title relate to the poem? "Elegy" (115) is "For Harriet Tubman & Frederick Douglass." Find out something about these two nineteenth-century blacks, and ask how the poem relates to their lives and legacy. Angelou's classic poem of victorious pride and endurance even through discrimination and suffering is the title poem, "Still I Rise" (163–64), of her third book of poetry. What kind of pain is endured? How? The second and fourth lines of the first seven four-line stanzas are rhymed, and then the pattern changes, with increasing repetition of the phrase "I rise." Is this effective? Why or why not? "Ain't That Bad" (165–66) is full of references to famous black people. What kind of range of occupations and achievements do those names cover? Why would Angelou use slang and black vernacular English in this poem?

6. **Communal strength in the midst of threat:** Angelou's famous and popular poem "Phenomenal Woman" (130–31) has been an inspiration to countless women, young and old. Do you think a large part of its influence is because of its acceptance of and pride in physical features which might not fit the current ideal? Is it a good antidote for the images of women in the media? "Through the Inner City to the Suburbs" (144–45) is written

from the point of view of the suburbanite passing through the inner city behind a train window. What are the characteristics of the inner city residents? The suburban residents? Why would there be such a difference?

Character

The narrator or speaker in a poem is not necessarily the voice of the poet, but, rather, a poet feels free to speak in other voices, whose identity and nature can be deciphered from the poem itself.

Sample Topics:

1. **"When I Think about Myself"**: Who is the speaker here? Is the lack of standard English a clue? Is it the same speaker for all three stanzas? What can Angelou convey with this speaker that she might not be able to do in her own voice?

2. **"Letter to an Aspiring Junkie"**: What makes this a letter rather than a speech? What does the language tell us about the speaker? Considering the content of the poem and the title, what do you take to be the theme? Why would Angelou choose to write in this voice?

3. **"The Pusher"**: Full of street slang and allusions to the 1960s—Malcolm X, Martin Luther King Jr.—who is the speaker here? What is the point of the poem? This poem might be compared and contrasted to black author Gwendolyn Brooks's well-known short poem "We Real Cool."

4. **"Prisoner"**: Why would Angelou want to write a poem from this point of view? The language here is not slangy or obscene but very straightforward speech in standard American English. What does this say about the prisoner? What is suggested by the refrain, that is, the three lines that follow each of the three stanzas?

5. **"Times-Square-Shoeshine-Composition"**: Who is the speaker? What is unusual about the way his speech is depicted? Does it make a difference to read this poem aloud? Why would Angelou pick this topic and speaker?

6. **"Pickin Em Up and Layin Em Down"**: Who is the speaker here? What is common to the four examples of situations in

which the man departs? Is this a poem that demands reading aloud? Is the repetition effective?

7. **"Little Girl Speakings"**: How successful is Angelou in taking on the voice of a little girl? What do the little girl's "speakings" tell us about what she feels and thinks? Is Angelou making a larger point about family and early security with this poem?

History and Context

Some of Angelou's allusions, or references to things outside the poem, might be to history, some to cultural matters, past or current. The interplay of history and poetry, as channeled through Angelou's voice, is one possible topic to pursue.

Sample Topics:

1. **"Miss Scarlett, Mr. Rhett and Other Latter-Day Saints"**: What are the allusions in the title? How does Angelou develop and follow through with these allusions? What is the meaning of "saint" here? Does this seem to be sacrilegious? Unusually sarcastic?

2. **"Southeast Arkanasia"**: With references to "Eli Whitney's gin," and seemingly to the Great Depression years, this is a poem nevertheless about slavery and its aftereffects. Does it raise these issues effectively? Who is the "you" of the poem? Does the lingering guilt ever disappear? If we are talking about the twentieth century by the end of the poem, what might Angelou mean by the continuation of the guilt? What would she mean by "repair of groans"?

3. **"To a Freedom Fighter"**: Angelou was attached for a while to a South African freedom fighter, Vus Make. Does this poem reflect the South African battle against apartheid? Could it also be a freedom fighter in the United States or elsewhere? The language here is formal and stately, with some words you may not know without looking them up. Why is it written in this way?

4. **"Riot: 60's"**: Angelou was actually there when the Watts suburb of Los Angeles exploded in five days of rioting in 1965. She tells about it in her final autobiography in the series of six, *A Song Flung Up to Heaven*. In fact, some of the images used here

are similar to her descriptions there. Look at the book and compare/contrast to this poetic description. Check some newspaper reports of the riots. Was Watts the beginning of a series of riots in other major cities? How does she convey this in the poem? What are the possible meanings of the line "Lighting: a hundred Watts . . . "? What other things from the news reports do you find in the poem?

Philosophy and Ideas

Many of the ideas and philosophies expressed indirectly in Angelou's poetry are very similar to the ideas and philosophy of her series of autobiographies.

Sample Topics:

1. **"The Calling of Names"**: This poem traces the history of the terms by which black people or African Americans have been called. Though it does not specifically say it, the progression and the last lines suggest that a term chosen by the minority group itself, rather than by the majority group, is much more meaningful and valued. Why would this be the case? What do you make of the center of the poem, the references to the "Jew" and the "Bouquet of Roses"? Can you think of other examples of terminology that make a big difference to a group, such as women?

2. **"On Working White Liberals"**: This is a militant poem about cooperation between the races, with the title a double entendre on "working"—is it an adjective as in "working man," or is it a verbal, with white liberals as the object, the things "being worked," suggesting "worked over"? Since it does not seem to use a speaker other than Angelou herself, this would seem to be her "Malcolm X, Black Muslim, by any means necessary" stage. How does this poem relate to stages in the roles of whites in the civil rights movement? To the speeches of Malcolm X?

3. **"Sepia Fashion Show"**: This is one of few poems in which Angelou expresses disdain for the black middle class. How does she do this in terms of a fashion show? What is the problem the speaker has physically with the models besides their "nasty manners"? How does class difference play out in black history in, for

example, the differences between the National Association for the Advancement of Colored People and the Student Nonviolent Coordinating Committee during the civil rights movement?

4. **"Lord, in My Heart":** This is an Old Testament versus New Testament poem—"an eye for an eye" against "turn the other cheek." What conclusion does the poem draw? Find out who Countee Cullen is and what he wrote, and suggest why Angelou dedicates this poem to him.

5. **"Take Time Out":** This poem goes through several versions of or potential directions for young people—as hippies, veterans, druggies. Is the main point of the title and the last stanza taking responsibility for the problems we see around us, particularly with the young? What is it that has caused the problems, according to the poem? What is the main component of a solution?

6. **"Family Affairs":** Angelou has repeatedly said, when asked about feminism, that black women and white women share a cause, but their ways to the goals of the cause will be different. How is this a poem about that difference? Why does the black woman need to "wait a / While" according to the poem? "Our Grandmothers" (253–56), one of the longest poems Angelou has written, also delineates the difference by tracing the history of black women in the United States. What are the elements of her history? What is the effect of the repeated phrase "I shall not be moved"?

7. **"The Last Decision":** What are the experiences that cause this speaker to make the decision to die? Does this necessarily mean suicide or, given the age of the speaker particularly, might it just mean "letting go"?

8. **"Human Family":** What are the kinds of diversity extolled in the poem? Much of this poem could be called "delight in diversity," but the repeated last lines make a larger point. What is it? Do you agree?

Form and Genre

Angelou favors ballad-friendly rhythm and rhyme schemes, departing frequently from the patterns that seem to be established in a poem. She also uses free verse often, that is, verse that has no patterned rhythm and rhyme scheme. Since she has said that she looks for the "natural" rhythm in what she wants to say, and then fits her content to that rhythm, it is logical that she does not favor preset forms, such as the sonnet. Instead, her patterns come from colloquial speech, from the black church (the gospel songs, spirituals, and sermons), from the King James translation of the Bible, and from writers such as Shakespeare, on the one hand, and Langston Hughes on the other. Angelou displays her range as a poet in producing works that include elevated language as well as dialect.

Language, Symbols, and Imagery
Sample Topics:
1. **"On Reaching Forty":** This poem sustains a figurative comparison throughout. To what does she compare turning forty? What are some of the elements of that comparison? Is it effective, do you think?

Compare and Contrast Essays
Sample Topics:
1. **The ceremonial poems:** Angelou wrote for Bill Clinton's inauguration ("On the Pulse of Morning"), for the fiftieth anniversary of the United Nations ("A Brave and Startling Truth") and for the Million Man March ("From a Black Woman to a Black Man"). How does she tailor each of the poems to the specific audience she is addressing?
2. **Poetry for young people versus poetry for adults:** Look at the twenty-five poems in Edwin Grave Wilson's *Poetry for Young People: Maya Angelou* (Sterling, 2007) and compare and/or contrast these poems to those in *The Complete Collected Poems,* written for adults. What makes the poetry for nine- to twelve-year-olds accessible to them? Pleasurable to them? What kind of themes or points does Angelou seek to convey to young people in these poems?

Bibliography and Online Resources for Maya Angelou's Poetry

Angelou, Maya. *Mother: A Cradle to Hold Me.* New York: Random House, 2006.

———. *The Complete Collected Poems of Maya Angelou.* New York: Random House, 1994.

Bloom, Harold. "Introduction." *Maya Angelou.* Bloom's Modern Critical Views. Ed. Harold Bloom. New York: Chelsea House Publishers, 2009. 1–2.

Blum, Walter. "Listening to Maya Angelou." In *Conversations with Maya Angelou.* Ed. Jeffrey M. Elliot. Jackson and London: University Press of Mississippi, 1989. 38–46.

Brooks, Gwendolyn. "We Real Cool." In *Black Voices: An Anthology of Afro-American Literature.* New York: Mentor/Penguin, 1968. 465.

Burr, Zofia. "Maya Angelou on the Inaugural Stage." In *Of Women, Poetry, and Power: Strategies of Address in Dickinson, Miles, Brooks, Lorde, and Angelou.* Urbana and Chicago: University of Illinois Press, 2002. 180–94.

Cookson, Sandra. "World Literature in Review: English." *World Literature Today.* Volume 69, Issue 4 (1995): 800. Page numbers here are to the EBSCOhost on-line version, 1–2.

Crane, Tricia. "Maya Angelou." In *Conversations with Maya Angelou.* Ed. Jeffrey M. Elliot. Jackson and London: University Press of Mississippi, 1989. 173–78.

DeGout, Yasmin Y. "The Poetry of Maya Angelou: Liberation Ideology and Technique." *Maya Angelou.* Bloom's Modern Critical Views. Ed. Harold Bloom. New York: Chelsea House Publishers, 2009. 121–32.

http://www.educationworld.com/a_lesson/01-1/lp2296.html (lesson plan on teaching inaugural poetry for high school, with links to the poems)

Elliot. Jeffrey. "Maya Angelou Raps." In *Conversations with Maya Angelou.* Ed. Jeffrey M. Elliot. Jackson and London: University Press of Mississippi, 1989. 86–96.

Forna, Aminatta. "Kicking Ass." In *Conversations with Maya Angelou.* Ed. Jeffrey M. Elliot. Jackson and London: University Press of Mississippi, 1989. 161–64.

Hagen, Lyman B. *Heart of a Woman, Mind of a Writer, and Soul of a Poet: A Critical Analysis of the Writings of Maya Angelou.* Lanham, Md.: University Press of America, 1997.

Hitt, Greg. "Maya Angelou." In *Conversations with Maya Angelou.* Ed. Jeffrey M. Elliot. Jackson and London: University Press of Mississippi, 1989. 205–13.

Holmes, Paul C. *Keys to Understanding: Receiving and Sending the Poem.* New York: Harper & Row, 1969.

Moyers, Bill. "A Conversation with Maya Angelou." In *Conversations with Maya Angelou.* Ed. Jeffrey M. Elliot. Jackson and London: University Press of Mississippi, 1989. 18–28.

Neubauer, Carole E. "Maya Angelou's Poetry Creates Hope." In *Readings on Maya Angelou*. Ed. Mary E. Williams. San Diego: Greenhaven Press, 1997. 136–44.

http://www.nytimes.com/2008/25/books/25poet.html (article by Dwight Garner called "The Intersection of Poetry and Politics" on Elizabeth Alexander's poetry before the inauguration and the previous inaugural poetry)

http://nytimes.com/2009/01/20/us/politics (text of Elizabeth Alexander's inaugural poem for President Barack Obama, January 20, 2009)

Rich, Marnia. "In Maya Angelou, a Caged Bird Sings." In *Conversations with Maya Angelou*. Ed. Jeffrey M. Elliot. Jackson and London: University Press of Mississippi, 1989. 125–30.

Sookia, Devinia. "Singing, Swinging, and Still Living Life to the Full." In *Conversations with Maya Angelou*. Ed. Jeffrey M. Elliot. Jackson and London: University Press of Mississippi, 1989. 188–93.

Tate, Claudia. "Maya Angelou." In *Conversations with Maya Angelou*. Ed. Jeffrey M. Elliot. Jackson and London: University Press of Mississippi, 1989. 146–56.

Thomas, Rachel. "Exuberance as Beauty: The Prose and Poetry of Maya Angelou." In *Maya Angelou*. Bloom's BioCritiques. Ed. Harold Bloom. New York: Chelsea House Publishers, 2002, 49–71.

Toppman, Lawrence. "Maya Angelou: The Serene Spirit of a Survivor." In *Conversations with Maya Angelou*. Ed. Jeffrey M. Elliot. Jackson and London: University Press of Mississippi, 1989. 140–45.

Traylor, Eleanor W. "Maya Angelou Writing Life, Inventing Literary Genre." In *Maya Angelou*. Bloom's Modern Critical Views. Ed. Harold Bloom. New York: Chelsea House Publishers, 2009. 91–105.

Weller, Sheila. "Work in Progress: Maya Angelou." In *Conversations with Maya Angelou*. Ed. Jeffrey M. Elliot. Jackson and London: University Press of Mississippi, 1989. 10–17.

ESSAYS

READING TO WRITE

MAYA ANGELOU has published three collections of short prose pieces which are accessible in vocabulary, structure, and length. To some readers, they are likely to be overly simple—*School Journal*, in reviewing the first one, called it young adult literature—but to others, the books can be eye opening and inspirational. Angelou is very much a generalist, not academically trained, and not specializing in any particular subject area or genre, but rather, basing her comments on her wide range of experience in the United States, Europe, and Africa. Here that comprehensive interest and experience is used to positive result. The first collection appeared in 1993. Dedicated to Oprah Winfrey "with immeasurable love" and including pieces that had appeared in *Ms. Magazine* and *Essence*, the collection is called *Wouldn't Take Nothing for My Journey Now*. The epigraph is from the biblical book Acts of the Apostles: "Wisdom was created before all things, and prudent understanding from Eternity." In one review of the book, Sandra D. Davis wrote that this collection "eloquently, gracefully and authoritatively waxes poetic, somber and sometimes silly" (quoted in Hagen 145). Clara Juncker and Edward Sanford call it "a theory of life travel and movement that communicates to readers across the globe the insights she herself has gained on/off the road," without leaving behind "the sense of community that informs her work and defines her self" (37).

The second book, much like the first, appeared in 1997 and is called *Even the Stars Look Lonesome. Letter to My Daughter* came out in 2008. For those who know that Angelou does not have a daughter but a son, she explains in the prefatory material that the book expresses "my thanks to some women who mothered me through dark and bright days," including her grandmother, Annie Henderson; her mother, Vivian Baxter; and James Baldwin's mother, Berdid Baldwin. She also thanks "one woman who allows me to be a daughter to her, even today, Dr. Dorothy Height" (who died in 2010) and "women not born to me but who allow me to mother them," including Oprah Winfrey and many others (Angelou *Letter . . .* n.p.). Then in the introduction to the book, she further explains: "I gave birth to one child, a son, but I have thousands of daughters. You are Black and White, Jewish and Muslim, Asian, Spanish-speaking, Native American and Aleut. You are fat and thin and pretty and plain, gay and straight, educated and unlettered, and I am speaking to you all. Here is my offering to you" (Angelou *Letter . . .* xii). A fourth book with essaylike material came out in 2004—*Hallelujah! The Welcome Table: A Lifetime of Memories with Recipes*.

Since, as Lyman Hagen says, "there is an autobiographical tilt" to these collections, the reader who is familiar with Angelou's six serial autobiographies will notice not only names reappearing but also similarity in themes, biases, and goals. Some things that for some reason were left out of the autobiographies also appear here. A prime example is in *Letter to My Daughter*, chapter 5, a piece titled "Accident, Coincident, or Answered Prayer" (29–34). In many ways, this is the most unusual piece in this book, both in its violence and in its appearance here and not elsewhere in the autobiographies. The piece tells a story that begins with Angelou sympathetically describing a kind lover with a "slow hand" but also with three fingers missing due to an automobile factory accident. All is going well until one evening when "Two Finger Mark" picks her up from work, takes her to a remote cliff, accuses her of cheating on him, and beats her until she passes out. She comes to in his room, a location unknown to her mother and the people with whom she works, though they are aware of the beating because Two Fingers has paraded the unconscious Angelou through the neighborhood as a sign of what happens to anyone messing with him. In his apartment, Two Fingers vacillates between threatening to kill himself or to kill her and promising to care for her. In the "coincidence" or answer-to-prayer part of the story, he decides she needs juice, so he goes to a nearby store, and a tobacco vendor nearby just happens to be robbed by some kids who throw their loot into Two Finger's car, which causes him to be taken in by the police. He calls a bail bondsman who in turn calls his friend, Vivian Baxter, Angelou's mother. The most dramatic part of the story, and clearly a large part of the point Angelou wants to make with the telling, comes when her mother with two burly friends storm into the locked room to rescue her—"'Break it down. Break the son of a bitch down. My baby's in there,'" Baxter says outside the door. When she sees Angelou's face "swollen twice its size and my teeth stuck into my lips," Baxter faints, the only time she does so in her life. The title of the chapter raises the question of whether this ultimate rescue is divinely ordained or happenstance. It is Vivian Baxter who first says that "somebody's prayers were answered," a conviction repeated briefly at the end of the chapter by Angelou: "I believe my prayers were answered."

A reader intending to write Angelou's essays will probably want to pick several with similar themes or styles—some essays, for example, include some of her poetry as well as the poetry of others. As always in doing a paper on a work of literature, it is good to read the material more than once and to take notes on the reading. With these essays, which are not arranged thematically, it would be good to select a one- or two-word theme or idea being conveyed by each and then look at the full lists and pull together those that are similar as a possible topic. Not everyone will come to the essays knowing the autobiographies, of course, but if you have some familiarity with any of them, especially the best known, *I Know Why the Caged Bird Sings*, it is worthwhile putting the works together to note differences and similarities.

TOPICS AND STRATEGIES
Themes
Sample Topics:

1. **Women, especially black women:** Beginning with Oprah Winfrey, to whom *Wouldn't Take Nothing For My Journey Now* is dedicated, and the first selection, "In All Ways a Woman" (5–7), the theme of the lives of women reoccurs throughout the essay books. "They Came to Stay" (*Even the Stars . . .* 41–44) is a strong tribute to the history of struggles of black women. "Is Anyone Ever Too Much?" (*Wouldn't . . .* 39–40) suggests terms like *super woman* can too easily lead women to try to become what they

are called. Do you agree? "Giving Birth" and "Mother's Long View" (*Letter to My Daughter* 23–25, 51–56) show especially the support given to Angelou during the trying time of the birth of her son and trying to raise him as a single mother. What are the particular enduring traits Angelou's mother shows here? What emerges from the use of this theme as to what Angelou believes to be the strengths of women? Of black women?

2. **Travel and home:** "Passports to Understanding" (*Wouldn't . . .* 11–12) argues not just for world travel but for the importance to Americans, particularly, of learning something of others' languages. Do you agree? "Morocco" (*Letter to My Daughter* 59–61) gives a concrete illustration of the understanding of "the other" that language learning might enhance. "Senegal" (*Letter to My Daughter* 91–92) is an example of the difficulties of cultural difference, more humorous than other essays, and at Angelou's expense. What are the lessons from these stories? "Home" (*Letter to My Daughter* 5–9) presents the other side of the equation, the need for a place to belong, to come home to. Does Angelou suggest that this is an internal place and state rather than an external, physical one? If you know something of her biography, does this make sense that she would use the word in a nonliteral sense?

3. **Vulgar and respectful language:** "What's So Funny" (*Wouldn't . . .* 43–44) is one of several essays in which Angelou rails against "vulgarity" of any kind—here she criticizes words such as *fat* used to disparage other people or oneself (even though she uses this term more than once to describe her second "husband," Vus Make, in her autobiographical volume called *The Heart of a Woman*). Do you agree with her saying in this essay that this kind of speech means one is unloved and unlovable? The issue also comes up in "Voices of Respect" (*Wouldn't . . .* 101–03), about the familiar yet formal means of address of slavery, based on African usage, calling people, for example, "Uncle Joe," "Aunt Mariah," "Sis," "Bubba." Do our terms for addressing others make a difference in the respect we hold for them? The short piece "Vulgarity" (*Letter to My Daughter* 41–44) deals especially with the popular language of entertainers. There are also several

essays in which she discusses positive words that have gone out of favor or usage, such as *charity* in "The Sweetness of Charity" (*Wouldn't . . .* 15–18) and *virtue* in "When Virtue Becomes Redundant" (*Wouldn't . . .* 69–70). Compare her discussion of charity here with her later essay called "Philanthropy" (*Letter to My Daughter* 12–14).

4. **Looks and style:** "Style" is in fact the title of an Angelou essay (*Wouldn't . . .* 27–29), with the author suggesting that it is as important as content, especially in relation to developing one's own style. In "Getups" (*Wouldn't . . .* 53–57), she zeroes in specifically on dress and the importance of looking good in order to feel good. Do you agree?

5. **Aging and sexuality/sensuality:** Typically for humans, thoughts about the elderly change as one grows older, including thoughts about sex. Angelou, too, tells what she thought of aging at age thirty-six and what she has learned at sixty and beyond. "Aging" (*Even the Stars . . .* 21–24) uses one of her own poems to convey the new wisdom. Despite all the aches and pains of growing older, what does she conclude one must do? Angelou argues vehemently for sensuality and sexuality throughout life, in "A Song to Sensuality" and "Age and Sexuality," for example (*Even the Stars . . .* 35–38, 79–85). Do the somewhat humorous stories she tells help her convey her points?

Character

Sample Topics:

1. **Grandmother Henderson, or Momma:** "New Directions" (*Wouldn't . . .* 21–24) is one of the nicest tributes Angelou has written to her paternal grandmother Henderson, who raised Angelou and her brother, Bailey, in Stamps, Arkansas. This piece is essentially repeated in *Hallelujah! The Welcome Table* (57–58), in the section called "Independence Forever." "Complaining" (*Wouldn't . . .* 85–87) also features Momma in order to make a very practical point, that whining is graceless and can also be dangerous. What do these pieces reveal and emphasize about Momma? Do you agree with Angelou's concluding point about whining? Do you have your own examples?

2. **Mother, Vivian Baxter:** "Further New Directions" (*Wouldn't* ... 79–81) is a tribute to Angelou's mother. Does the poem, "Mrs. V. B.," quoted at the end of the piece convey the same content? "Those Who Really Know Teach" and "The Rage Against Violence" (*Even the Stars* ... 137–39; 115–17) again show her mother in action, this time "educating" a young stranger in the grocery store and getting safely into and out of a dangerous building. How do the examples Angelou relates show the character of Vivian Baxter? "Mother and Freedom" (*Even the Stars* ... 47–49) shows us Vivian Baxter at the last stages of life. How does it sum up Angelou's learning from her?

3. **Aunt Tee:** "Living Well, Living Good" (*Wouldn't* ... 61–66) relates a story Aunt Tee told the author thirty years earlier, and "when a tale remains fresh in my mind," Angelou says, "it almost always contains a lesson which will benefit me" (*Wouldn't* ... 64–65). What is Aunt Tee's story? What is the "lesson" Angelou draws from it? Does the character of Aunt Tee disappear in the lesson, or do you learn something about her from this piece?

4. **Oprah Winfrey:** "Poetic Passage" (*Even the Stars* ... 59–62) is largely about Winfrey, even though Angelou uses her as an example of a certain kind of traveler through life. What is that kind of traveler and how does she/he contrast with other kinds? From what you know of or can learn of Winfrey, do you think Angelou gets close to her essence?

History and Context

Sample Topics:

1. **The enduring influence of Africa:** "Art in Africa" (*Even the Stars* ... 65–70) is a description of how women's expression through fabric and beads and leathers and feathers not only delights the senses but also helps people individually and collectively. What are some of those helpful ways? "Africa" (*Even the Stars* ... 13–17) describes a time when black middle class parents did not want Angelou to teach their children African songs and also tells of the discoveries Angelou herself made living on that continent for four years. What is the twentieth-century

progression of opinions on and interest in Africa among Americans? Black Americans?

2. **The impact of slave history:** Angelou comes back again and again to the impact of American slave history on her life and, by implication, on all lives, especially of black people. A piece such as "Danger in Denial" (*Even the Stars . . .* 111–13) suggests that black men and women deny their common history to their peril. "Rural Museums—Southern Romance" (*Even the Stars . . .* 89–95) describes a journey she made to Baton Rouge, Louisiana, to visit the Rural Life Museum, which she had learned contained slave cabins. What are some of the ways people in this narrative demonstrate their ignorance of their histories? How does the museum romanticize that history? Is this coverup typical of many histories of slavery? Has there been change and improvement in the past twenty to thirty years on how slavery is depicted in high school or middle school textbooks? If you are near a college or university campus with a teachers education program, the chances are good that you will be able to find some of the older and newer textbooks to compare and contrast.

Philosophy and Ideas

Sample Topics:

1. **Religion, Christianity, belief:** "In the Spirit" and "Power of the Word" (*Wouldn't . . .* 33–35, 73–76) are direct statements of Angelou's personal beliefs. What roles do Africa and African philosophy play? What roles do her grandmother and early church teaching play? Angelou's church and biblical allusions are sometimes obscure, but in "At Harvesttime" (*Wouldn't . . .* 91–92) she clearly uses the New Testament parable of the sower. Read the parable (Mark 4: 1–20; or Matthew 13: 1–23; or Luke 8: 1–15) and compare/contrast it to her use of it. Is this an effective way to make her point?

2. **The impact of fame:** "Godfrey Cambridge and Fame" (*Even the Stars . . .* 27–31) gives us Angelou's experience with the dangers of fame, ending with an African saying. What are the dangers, according to Angelou? How is the saying at the end fitting? Do you agree?

3. **"Art for the Sake of the Soul":** In the longest essay in the second book, *Even the Stars Look Lonesome* (121–33), Angelou
   states and illustrates the importance of black art, especially
   poetry, in bringing blacks to where they are today and in keeping
   people going. Look at the poems she quotes by Lucille Clifton,
   Langston Hughes, and Paul Laurence Dunbar and the words of
   the "Sorrow Songs." It would also be good to look at the essay
   by W.E.B. Du Bois, which she mentions, in which he dubs the
   spirituals "Sorrow Songs." That essay appears in the collection
   The Souls of Black Folk, from 1903. What is the point made by
   the concluding anecdote from this Angelou essay, about singing
   one of the sorrow songs for a Moroccan audience to thunderous
   applause? Do you find her description of the impact of art con-
   vincing? Can you think of other examples from your own life?

Form and Genre

A dictionary definition of *essay,* such as is found in *Merriam-Webster's
Collegiate,* reads: "an analytic or interpretive literary composition usually dealing with its subject from a limited or personal point of view."
Except for their brevity, what we have here called Angelou's essays
could be made to fit the definition. But the lack of arrangement or
plan—as Lyman Hagen says, "there is no obvious organizational structure, topically, chronologically, or geographically" (145)—makes it difficult for a reader accustomed to reading say, Ralph Waldo Emerson or
W.E.B. Du Bois and his *The Souls of Black Folk* to call these books of
essays. Hagen calls them "parables" and "personal vignettes" (145, 146)
and notes that "the broad swatch of topics rather brings to mind the
jottings from a writer's journal" (146). Some readers have called them
"meditations." Or they can "be read as theory, without the usual signals of abstract language, academic style, use of citations and so forth"
(Juncker and Sanford 39). Whatever we call them, however, we can say
that these books are quintessential Angelou, with their personal and
moral insights.

Sample Topic:

1. **Form:** Try to describe the form of Angelou's pieces and give that
   form a name. Are they close to parables, fables, anecdotes with

a moral? Who is the audience for these books? What does form tell you about Angelou as a person and as a writer?

Language, Symbols, and Imagery
Sample Topics:

1. **Imagery:** "Power of the Word" (*Wouldn't* ... 73–76) contains some interesting imagery, both literal and figurative, to describe a kind of conversion experience. Which images do you find most effective? Why? "A Song to Sensuality" (*Even the Stars* ... 35–38) also contains a lot of interesting imagery. Is this appropriate to the topic? Does she convey her point effectively?

2. **Repetition:** Repeating words or phrases to emphasize something important can be very effective in reaching a reader. Look at some of the repetition of "They Came to Stay" (*Even the Stars* ... 41–44): "Their faces.... Their hands.... Their wombs.... Their feet.... They are not apparitions; they are not superwomen; despite the enormity of their struggles they are not larger than life" (44). Is this an effective way to conclude this essay? Why or why not?

Bibliography and Online Resources for Maya Angelou's Essays
Angelou, Maya. *Even the Stars Look Lonesome.* New York: Bantam, 1997.

———. *Hallelujah! The Welcome Table: A Lifetime of Memories with Recipes.* New York: Random House, 2004.

———. *Letter to My Daughter.* New York: Random House, 2008.

———. *Wouldn't Take Nothing for My Journey Now.* New York: Random House, 1993.

Du Bois, W.E.B. "The Souls of Black Folk, Chapter 1, 'Of our Spiritual Strivings' and 14, 'The Sorrow Songs.'" In *Black Voices: An Anthology of Afro-American Literature.* Ed. Abraham Chapman. New York: Mentor/Penguin, 1968. 494–511.

Hagen, Lyman B. *Heart of a Woman, Mind of a Writer, and Soul of a Poet: A Critical Analysis of the Writings of Maya Angelou.* Lanham, Md.: University Press of America, 1997.

Juncker, Clara & Edward Sanford. "Only Necessary Baggage: Maya Angelou's Life Journeys." *Maya Angelou.* Bloom's Modern Critical Views. Ed. Harold Bloom. New York: Chelsea House Publishers, 2009. 37–47.

CHILDREN'S BOOKS, SCREENPLAYS, PLAYS, AND DOCUMENTARIES

READING TO WRITE

SOME WRITERS of essays on Maya Angelou's work might wish to examine the children's books she has written, or explore her film, stage, and acting career. As we have said previously, she is a variously skilled person, and her first mode of communication to the public was performance-based, particularly in dance. And she has from early on been concerned in her writing with how adults communicate with children and young people, so her work with children's literature is not surprising. The range of Angelou's work, the wonderful photographs following her career, and the many people who have been inspired by her and her work have made her a popular subject for young adult, or YA, biographies, of which there are many, including Patricia L. Kite's *Maya Angelou*, one of the better ones. This book puts emphasis on Angelou's successful battling of the challenges of poverty, race discrimination, and single motherhood and has good supplementary materials, including pictures of historical events, an extensive bibliography, an index, and many photos of Angelou. Some YA books provide good sources for understanding the visual impact she has had on people. Recordings and films of her reading her work and others' work give a person a good sense of the rich timbre of her voice even if one has not had the opportunity to see her live. That expressive, clearly enunciated voice has made her a sought-after narrator for documentaries even on subjects that are not part of her usual circle of concerns, such as a 2008 film on the way artists at the time of the Holocaust depicted their experiences *(As Seen Through. . .).*

Angelou's publications for children and young people include three poetry books. *Poetry for Young People,* from 2007, is made up of poems from Angelou's *Collected Poems,* with the addition of "A Brave and Startling Truth," written for the fiftieth anniversary of the United Nations. The editor of this collection, a colleague of Angelou's at Wake Forest University in Winston-Salem, North Carolina, notes that she is the first living poet to be honored with a book in the series of which this is a part. The book provides an illustrated life summary of the poet, brief notes at the beginning of each poem, and definitions of some of the words that might be difficult. The second book, *Life Doesn't Frighten Me,* is also a reprinting of a poem from the *Collected Poems,* illustrated with the childlike paintings of Jean-Michel Basquiat. The afterword to the book includes biographies of the two artists, a selected list of Angelou's other work, and a list of museums holding Basquiat's work. Third, *Amazing Peace,* is Angelou's poem for the White House Christmas tree–lighting ceremony in 2005 and is illustrated by the paintings of Steve Johnson and Lou Fancher. While the book looks like it is designed for children, the poem is much more for adults, emphasizing peace ("a harmony of spirit, a comfort of courtesies") and hope in a troubled world. Making sure she is inclusive of both the Christian nature of the holiday and of other religions, Angelou writes that "At this Holy Instant, we celebrate the Birth of Jesus Christ / Into the great religions of the world" and lists other faiths and nonbelievers, ending with three lines: "Peace, My Brother. / Peace, My Sister. / Peace, My Soul."

Angelou's prose works for children include two set in Africa, *My Painted House, My Friendly Chicken and Me* of 1994 and *Kofi and His Magic* of 1996, and both are illustrated with the photographs of Margaret Courtney-Clarke. *My Painted* is the story of an African eight-year-old girl of the Ndebele tribe and an exploration of the painting and beadwork of the women of that tribe. *Kofi* continues the cultural exploration with a seven-year old boy who learns to weave the multicolored and patterned kente cloth for which his West African village of

Bonwire is known. Magically (mentally), he travels elsewhere, including to the Atlantic Ocean and to a celebratory *durbar*, or thanksgiving, festival. (Angelou herself experienced a *durbar* celebration during her four years living in Ghana, West Africa, described in the fifth book of her autobiographical series, *All God's Children Need Traveling Shoes*.) Clearly, both children's books are intended to be educational and to make an African environment and childhood less foreign and forbidding than they might be to someone with no knowledge or experience of them. She has also published four children's books, grouped under the subtitle, "Maya's World," which have much the same intent for non-African locations by taking the reader to Lapland, Italy, France, and Hawaii. *Angelina of Italy* (2004) is an example of this quartet of books. It introduces some useful Italian words and tells a cute story of a girl who thinks the Leaning Tower of Pisa is a tower of her favorite food, pizza.

A writer who wishes to examine Angelou's works for children and young people has a wealth of material to use. Even where, as in the poetry collection, the material is culled from other books, it is interesting to consider why the author or the editor chose particular poems—what makes them suitable and of interest to the young? In looking at Angelou's prose works for young people, one needs also to examine the artwork and how it fits with or enhances the writing and the arrangements and font sizes of words on the page. Since some of the books are illustrated by painting and some by photography, comparing and contrasting the effectiveness of the two modes could lead to a strong essay. One might also want to look at descriptions of how to evaluate children's literature, including illustrations as well, such as in *Children's Literature: Developing Good Readers*, edited by Hannah Nuba and others.

When it comes to Angelou's work for stage and screen, including for television, her voice and eloquence lend themselves naturally to the narration of documentaries and television shows. The examples range widely, from a *Sesame Street* story about saving Christmas to an exploration of *Madagascar: A World Apart*. When looking at her work in film—writing, acting, directing—it is logical first to examine the script for the 1979 CBS television film of her highly successful autobiography,

I Know Why the Caged Bird Sings. Angelou insisted on being involved in the production and served as co-writer with Leonora Thuna. Since it is always difficult to separate the film version of a book from its original format if one has read the book first, a writer on this adaptation might want to emphasize either how successfully it conveys the essence of the book or how it departs from the text and stands alone as a film. Some of the questions you might ask are, What scenes are selected and why? What scenes or events are changed, and why, for example, Mrs. Flowers becomes Angelou's teacher rather than friend in the film and the graduation speech is given by Angelou rather than the young man in the book. Why does the film conclude with her graduation at age thirteen and leave out the subsequent trip to California? Do the actors depict the characters close to the way you imagine them?

Angelou's television and film acting credits are many. She appeared in a slight but impressive role as Kunta Kinte's African grandmother in the first episode of the blockbusting 1979 television miniseries *Roots,* based on the Alex Haley book. Young people who were not part of the viewing audience of this series might find it interesting to watch it in its entirety, keeping in mind the impact it had in the late 1970s. The thirtieth-anniversary DVD of *Roots* even includes a 2007 documentary, *Crossing Over: How* Roots *Captivated an Entire Nation*, and the 2002 documentary *Remembering* Roots: *One Year Later,* both of which would make excellent sources for a paper. Angelou plays parts in several other films accessible on DVD: she is Aunt June in John Singleton's 1993 *Poetic Justice,* with Janet Jackson and Tupac Shakur, and also wrote the poetry in the film; she is one of the older women who convey valuable life lessons to Winona Ryder in the 1995 *How to Make an American Quilt;* she is a conjure woman in the 2001 Hallmark Hall of Fame production of *The Runaway;* and she is an aunt in Tyler Perry's 2006 comedy *Madea's Family Reunion: The Movie,* in which she recites one of her poems, "In and Out of Time," at the wedding of two of the characters at the end of the film. The DVD of this film includes some extras, such as the director's commentary, that might be suitable as sources for an essay citing the film. Looking at the characteristics of Angelou's roles and acting over this wide time span of thirty years could make for a rewarding essay.

Finally, we have an example of an Angelou work as a director in *Down in the Delta,* which opened in theaters on Christmas Day 1998, after successful showings at film festivals, including in Toronto, where the director was given standing ovations before and after the showing (Ealy 1). The producer of the film, Reuben Cannon, had gone to Angelou's home in North Carolina with other producers and the script to convince her to direct it, and "she read the script and quickly accepted," saying, "In all of my work, I try to tell the human truth . . . , what makes us stumble and fumble and fall and somehow miraculously rise. . . . This is what drew me to *Down in Delta.* It is a story of these very kind of human truths, a story to remind us that, as human beings, we are more alike than different" ("Down . . ." *Ebony* 1). Filmed on a low budget in Ontario, it nevertheless has an all-star cast of Alfre Woodard, Wesley Snipes, Al Freeman Jr., and Esther Rolle in her last film. They "wanted to work with me," Angelou said, "so they came to work for peanut shells" (Lim 1). The story line follows a mother in trouble with drugs and unemployment in Chicago, sent with her two children by their mother/grandmother to their uncle and home in Mississippi. In a kind of reversal of the 1960s and previous decades, when segregation and violence in the South gave the North a liberating appeal, this film strongly suggests that to truly find oneself and be oneself, one needs an understanding of and participation in family roots, and that southern black family roots such as those represented by the uncle can serve as a site for recovery of self and purpose.

On her experience as a first-time director, Angelou commented that she would not want to attempt directing a film of her own work, but she felt that filmmaking and writing were similar: "I came to see the camera as my pen. I just let the 'pen' tell the story" (Lim 1). The *Ebony* reviewer of 1999 indicates that the cast praised Angelou as director "for her energy, sense of purpose and skill at motivating," blending "a historian's insight with a poet's vision." Angelou's friend Woodard (the two were also in *How to Make an American Quilt* together) described the way Angelou could lift the cast from getting bogged down in the mundane and the technical by holding up before them the historical significance of what they were doing (2). Angelou's ability to pull out the historical reverberations in the story definitely adds to the effect of the film. As reviewer David Bleiler, giving it three stars out of four, says: It is "a serious and sensible family drama that is filled with a sense of triumph and a profound connection to history" (175). Even the "sophisticates," as Angelou calls them—the critics "who tend to deride inspiration and simplicity" (Ealy 1)—found things to like more than dislike in *Down in the Delta.* Stephen Holden in the *New York Times,* for example, found the film "unabashedly inspirational" and "idyllic" with "the edges softened," yet concludes that, however much the film might depict an impossible dream, "the vision it offers is still a dream worth dreaming." He noted the movie has "the aura of a folk tale" (2), which, along with the goal of providing inspiration, is very much Angelou's bent in all her work.

TOPICS AND STRATEGIES
Themes
Sample Topics:
1. **The importance of relating to our history:** Angelou clearly believes that the personal story is an effective gateway to historical appreciation. How do the films on which she has worked deal with this theme?
2. **Families:** Closely related to the personal story and sense of history are families. What are some of the definitions of family in Angelou's children's books and films?

Character
Sample Topic:
1. **Child characters:** Take one or more of the children depicted in Angelou's prose books for that audience and attempt to hypothesize why Angelou has picked this particular person. What does she seek to convey with the selection? Do these children act and speak like real children would? Try reading some of the books to some actual children and then ask them about the characters—what they notice or remember or wonder about.

History and Context

Sample Topics:

1. ***Down in the Delta:*** Watch this movie directed by Angelou and see if you find things which seem to be "softened" or sugared over in the history presented. What things are presented in quite a bleak way? How does the film portray the importance of personal history? How does that personal history fit with group history or national history? Do you see evidence in the film of the ways in which Angelou inspired the cast by making them feel the importance of history?

2. ***Roots:*** The television series was a national and then international sensation. Watch the thirtieth anniversary DVD, particularly episode 1, in which Angelou appears, together with the background pieces on disc four on the legacy of *Roots* a year after and then more than thirty years after it was first broadcast. What were characteristic of black-white relations at the time of its first showing? Did the series change white appreciation of black history and culture? Did it change blacks' self-perception? Can you think of any other television story that has had a comparable impact on the country? If you know some of Angelou's written work, do you think working on that film changed her writing in any way? You might particularly look at her fifth autobiography in the series of six, *All God's Children Need Traveling Shoes*, describing her years living in the West African country of Ghana.

3. **The United Nations:** Angelou chose to include her poem written for the fiftieth anniversary of the United Nations in a book of poetry for young people. Look at the poem and try to determine why she would have thought this important. Do its language and vocabulary and allusions seem appropriate for the young? What does it say indirectly about the United Nations?

Philosophy and Ideas

Sample Topics:

1. **Children's literature:** What can you gather from Angelou's writing for children and young people that speaks to her

philosophy of childhood education? How does her philosophy compare with some of the standards in the field? Do her books seem to be aimed at black children or all children?

2. **Human difference:** Angelou repeatedly makes the point that human beings are more alike than they are different. What do you think she means by this? How does this belief come out in her work? Do you agree or disagree with her?

Language, Symbols, and Imagery
Sample Topics:

1. **Symbol of the candelabrum in *Down on the Delta:*** What does the candelabrum symbolize at the beginning of the film? What does it symbolize at the end? What is suggested by the fact that this inanimate object has a proper name, Nathan? Are there ways you can see Angelou as director putting special attention on the candelabrum? Does she direct the viewer's attention to it more at the end of the film than at the beginning?

2. **Language in the children's poetry:** Look at the poetry in one or more of Angelou's books for children and young people. Is the language appropriate for this audience? Do you find some examples, such as in "A Christmas Peace," where the language seems to be too advanced for the young reader? Read one or more of the poems to some young readers and solicit their reactions. (If the children are old enough, you can have them rate the poem on a scale of one to ten, with ten the very best and one the very worst.) What do you learn from their thoughts and statements? Are there particular images that seem to stick in the heads of more than one young person? If so, why, do you think?

Compare and Contrast Essays
Sample Topics:

1. ***I Know Why the Caged Bird Sings*—the book and telefilm:** Compare and contrast the way you see Marguerite in the book and the way you see her in the television film version. What details are changed or left out, and what is the implication of the alterations that were made?

2. **Angelou's roles and performances:** Compare Angelou's acting from her early films to the more recent ones. Does she repeatedly play the same kind of role? Is she attempting to convey a certain sensibility or message in her choice of roles and productions?

Bibliography for Maya Angelou's Children's Books, Screenplays, Plays, and Documentaries

Angelou, Maya. *Amazing Peace*. Illus. Steve Johnson and Lou Fancher. New York: Schartz & Wade Books, 2008.

———. (Narrator). *As Seen Through These Eyes*. Written and directed by Hilary Helstein. Menemsha Films, 2008.

———. (Director). *Down in the Delta*. Written by Myron Goble. Amen Rafilms and Chris/Rose Productions, 1998.

———. (co-screenwriter). *I Know Why the Caged Bird Sings*. Dir. Fielder Cook. Tomorrow Entertainment, Inc., 1978. 96 minutes.

———. *Kofi and His Magic*. Photographs by Margaret Courtney-Clarke. New York: Clarkson Potter/ Publishers. 1996.

———. *Life Doesn't Frighten Me At All*. Ed. Sara Jane Boyers. Illus. Jean-Michel Basquiat. New York: Stewart, Tabori & Chang, 1993.

———. (Narrator). *Madagascar: A World Apart*. PBS Home Video. 1998. 60 Minutes.

———. (Actress). *Madea's Family Reunion: The Movie*. Lionsgate and the Tyler Perry Company, 2006. 110 minutes.

———. *Maya's World: Angelina of Italy*. Illus. Lizzy Rockwell. New York: Random House, 2004.

———. *My Painted House, My Friendly Chicken and Me*. Photographs by Margaret Courtney-Clarke. New York: Clarkson Potter/Publishers. 1994.

———. *Poetry for Young People*. Ed. Edwin Graves Wilson. Illus. Jerime Lagarrigue. New York, London: Sterling, 2007.

———. (Actress). *The Runaway*. Dir. Arthur Alan Seidelman. Hallmark Hall of Fame, 2001. 98 Minutes.

Bleiler, David. *TLA Video and DVD Guide . . .* New York: Macmillan, 2005.

"'Down in the Delta.'" *Ebony*, February 1, 1999. Paging refers to EBSCOhost online printout, 1–4.

Ealy, Charles. "Maya Angelou's Film Foray." The Dallas *Morning News*. December 21, 1998.

Holden, Stephen. "Film Review: The Healing Power of a Delta Family's Roots." *New York Times.* December 25, 1998. Page numbers are to the EBSCOhost printout, 2 pages).

Kite, Patricia L. *Maya Angelou.* Minneapolis, Minn.: Lerner, 1999.

Lim, Grace. "Spotlight on . . . Maya Angelou." *People.* January 25, 1999, vol. 51, Issue 3.

Nuba, Hannah, Deborah Lovitky Sheiman, and Michael Searson. Eds. *Children's Literature: Developing Good Readers.* London, New York: Taylor and Francis. 1999.

http://www.starpulse.com/Notables/Angelou,_Maya (links to current news items, biography, film credits, other links)

INDEX